OFFICE POLITICS

OFFICE POLITICS

THE WOMAN'S GUIDE TO BEAT THE SYSTEM AND GAIN FINANCIAL SUCCESS

Book and Cover Design by *DYNAMITE*
Graphics by Joe Vecchio
Copy editing by Mary Thomas and Judy Hambric

Cataloging in Publication Data
Main entry under title:

Steele, R. Don
Office Politics: The Woman's Guide To Beat The System And Gain Financial Success

p. cm.
Includes index

ISBN 0-9620671-2-1 (paperback).—ISBN 0-9620671-1-3 (hard cover).

1. Success, personal
2. Success, financial

Printed by *Steel Balls Press*
Manufactured in the United States of America

First Printing: October 1994

10 9 8 7 6 5 4 3 2

To:

My mentor and lifelong soul brother,

Edward Meagher 1913-1991

Most of all, thanks for believing in me and trusting me.
Also, thanks for teaching me how to work smart
but to have fun all the while.
Lest we forget.

Damn Ed, I wish you could see me now!

PREFACE

Some reviewers of the manuscript strenuously objected to my refusal to use *he or she* when referring to a person of unknown gender, especially a boss. Others wanted gender-neutral words used in every possible instance. To anyone promoting clumsy writing or the destruction of English in any name, especially in the name of political correctness, I reply, "Nonsense!"

To the few who were put off by my casual writing style and refusal to use 50-cent words, "Sure, it's easy to read and understand, but it's not 'professional', people won't take it seriously," I cited Heinlein's advice to writers, "Eschew obfuscation." It went over their heads. Hopefully not yours.

REALITY CHECK NUMBER ONE

Many people believe the public relations campaign being waged by the media in cahoots with big business and big government. ***Their first fairytale:*** Women have made major gains in the workplace. They will continue to make progress until they share power equally. ***Their second fairytale:*** Big no longer works. Downsizing is the future. Small companies will be able to compete on a level playing field against corporate giants. Government will help this happen by reducing its own size and influence over the marketplace.

Check the statistics on women's progress put out by a group that has absolutely no motivation to skew numbers, NOW. Pay particular attention to the percentage of females in actual management, not Manager of Personnel or Manager of Public Relations. Next, examine the track record of government leaders who have promised to reduce the size of government and government spending since time immemorial.

Finally, take a look the Fortune 500 List for the past 50 years! Notice that the profits at the top of the corporate food chain keep going up. In short, the biggest companies always have the most money so they always have the advantage. It takes money to make money. If a small company becomes competitive and starts to take profits away, a big (rich) company simply buys it, end of fairytale.

If that doesn't convince you, as you read, let common sense tell you what's true. After you realize the truth, ask yourself why these fairytales are spun. Here's a hint. For a revolution to succeed, the status quo must first be upset. In the mid 1800s Europe was torn by revolution. Otto Von Bismarck developed a method to easily defuse revolutions. In the late 1900s, big business, big government and big media adopted Bismarck's strategy to assure women they've won. It's explained.

READ IT IN SEQUENCE — SET THE STAGE

Many women who reviewed the manuscript angrily objected to various chapters and topics. Most complaints disappeared when it was pointed out they had jumped ahead. Avoid this. Principles and facts that lead to understanding are presented before techniques and methods. Start at the beginning, please.

HOW* AND *WHAT* BEFORE *WHY

You can't take full advantage of what you are going to learn about the *what, how* and *when* of office politics unless you understand the *why* behind office politics. The same principles that govern the real world, govern the corporate world, so there are several frank explanations of why and how the real world actually works. After encountering them, you may lose heart and stop reading, as several manuscript reviewers did. Don't let that happen. You will be cautioned just before candid discussions begin — steel yourself.

In some chapters, tone may seem unduly cynical. It's not. Sometimes the tone is blunt, even severe. Why? Because men, beginning with Daddy, then boyfriends, then fiances, then husbands and ending with corporate bosses, never tell women the truth, the plain simple truth about us men. The truth about how we think, what drives us, why we behave as we do and what we want from women at work and everywhere else. The truth shall make you free.

Foreshadowing of what's to come:

Biology **is** *destiny.*
The big fish eat the little fish.
The big fish don't want the status quo disrupted.

Contents

What It's About 1
The Second Biggest Secret 7
Your Goals 11
Females Who Came Before 14
Creative Writing–Resumes 17
The Play's The Thing 25
Interviewing 34
Personnel 44
New On The Job 48
Whacked Out Co-Workers 55
Kept Down And Out 64
Capitalist Pig To Be 74
Dealing With What You Were Dealt 76
Time Is Short 80
Big Picture Research 83
Spying 87
Risk Taking Required 93
Friendship 98
Rivals And Enemies 104
The Other Woman 108
Alliances 117
Fighting 120
A Degree Of Difference 135
Run To Freedom 139
The Company Defined 141
Office Sex 144

Why It's All Screwed Up 158
Status Quo Forever 163
Corporate Decision Making 166
Defining The Terms 171
Helpful Hints 175
Avoid Layoffs 182
Unwritten Rules 187
Temporary Leave 191
Temps Get To Choose 194
Meeting Hints 197
Middle Managers 202
Understand The Boss 206
Manage The Boss 217
Rainy Day Woman 228
52 Random Truths 232
Get That Raise 241
Get Promoted 252
Understand Yourself 265
Hunters Not Gatherers 271
Mythical Glass Ceilings 276
Reality Check 280
Be Tough 285
Children? Now, Later, Never 293
Now What? 299
Must Books 302
In Summary 307
Other Books By R. Don Steele 322
Where To Turn For Help 323

ACKNOWLEDGEMENTS

To the key young women who shared their frustration, anger and pain caused by office politicians, my heartfelt thanks and gratitude for life: Janet Lee Riley, Barbara Jean Johnson, Lynn Kay Rhoton, Barbara Kristin Paddock, Kristina Marie Buono, Sue Marie Caroll-Tsunoda and Kimberly Ann Frazier.

Congratulations for having the courage, tenacity and perseverance to understand, confront and defeat the underhanded, conniving, manipulative women and men who attempted to destroy you.

Without your experiences, without your determination, without your questions, none of this would have been possible. I never would have stopped to consider the unique position of women, especially young women, in big business and never would have realized the extraordinary measures women must take to survive, then succeed in a man's world, the corporate world.

A special kind of acknowledgment goes to Syndee Ann White, my daughter. Thank you for being you! Had you been male, I never would have been shocked into realizing how our culture tries to brainwash females into being passive, polite domestics from the day they are born! By fighting them and forbidding them, I learned exactly what they try to do. Without that, I could never have become empathetic. Without empathy, I never could, or would, have written this book.

There are many people who helped substantially by granting what every writer needs — negative feedback and constructive suggestions: Cindy Anderson, Sandy Beckwith, Barry Boccheri, Mary K. Boyte, Pam Bye, Scott Carter, John E. Dempsey, Judy Hambric, Kris Mason, Debra Miller, Debbie Ng, Dick Ramos, Pam Scholl, Michele Snavely, Mary Thomas, Guy Zipp and Sue Zipp. Once again, thanks.

There are only two kinds of women
in the business world:
Those who have secretaries
and those who are secretaries.
UNKNOWN WISE PERSON

We are much beholden to Machiavelli who writes what men do and not what they ought to do.
1605 FRANCIS BACON

What It's About

For the past 30 years I've worked in major corporations. This book is about how the corporate world *really* works. It's everything, and much, much more, that I've explained to women who were my friends, lovers or wives. They were all bright, young college grads or college dropouts. Each asked for help in dealing with manipulative people at work. I explained how "The System" works.

But, before we start, you're probably asking yourself why, and how, does a man know what a woman needs to know, right? Take a moment. Flip back to the *Acknowledgements* page. See who I thanked, and why I thanked them so deeply.

Okay? That's how I know what women face and what they must do to survive in a man's world, the corporate world.

FOLLOW THE MONEY

The key point to understanding how "The System" works is simple, it's money. Major corporations are the *only* kinds of organizations that can pay $60k to women under 30. They are the *only* ones that do pay $150k to women of 37. They are the *only* places where a woman can make enough money so that *she* is the person who gets to decide how to spend the rest of *her* life.

WHAT YOU'RE GOING TO LEARN

Unlike men, women despise playing politics. To understand why office politics are necessary, and normal, first you'll learn how the world really works. As startling as this may seem, the world does not work the way you were led to believe by parents, preachers, professors and politicians.

The next thing you are going to find out is why men are always in charge. Then you'll discover some surprising things about how biology, plus the brainwashing our culture subjects females to, influences you and your behavior inside the corporation. Finally, you will learn that men really are animals. Once you understand this, you'll easily grasp the specifics of office politics, in short, how you can beat the system.

My goal is to have you (a) understand the reality of being female in the corporate world (b) accept the reality of being female in the corporate world. Once you understand *and* accept, you'll be able to use the techniques, strategy and tactics in this book to make enough money so that you can:

(1) Leave the corporate world and follow your bliss

(2) Stay in the corporate world and make $150k

(3) Stay in the corporate world and make $60k doing a job you enjoy while easily defeating office politicians who try to make your life miserable.

WHAT'S NOT COVERED

Nothing in this book has anything to do with improving women's lot. Everything in it has to do with helping an individual woman see clearly how the real world, thus the corporate world, actually works. That knowledge enables an individual, you, to make vital career moves. And, that knowledge gives you the power to make realistic choices when confronted with decisions that powerfully impact your private life as well as your career.

I'm not writing about how to get ahead working for the government or a non-profit company because only brown nosing and the old boy network can get you ahead there. My techniques and knowledge are useless. They're also useless when a company has its profits controlled by the government like public utilities or insurance companies.

The brand of office politics played in government, non-profits and controlled-profits is exactly the same as played in the United States Army — blatant obsequiousness, concerned only with extremely trivial pursuits. Since there are no stockholders to demand profitable operations, self-aggrandizement is the only possible payoff. Kissing up is the only way to move up.

Most jobs at non-profits are make-work, not make-money. There is no big money to be had unless you happen to know the President or someone on the Board. If you do know somebody, you don't need this book. He can hire you for $60k, now.

However, it is wise to take a brief side trip to a non-profit or controlled-profit company if you can get a substantial raise. The only purpose is so that you can return to one of the big companies and command an even larger salary!

Office politics in companies controlled by Asians are not covered. Their worldview, their culture and their belief that females are less than human pervades those corporations. My techniques are impotent.

Working at growing, small, profit-driven companies does not prepare one for office politics at any big corporation. In a small company everyone is visible and accountable, so appearances are useless. But, appearances are everything, in fact, the only thing, at a company where no one is accountable because the company is so filthy rich it can lose $8.1 billion as IBM did in 1993 or lose $23.3 billion as GM did in 1992!

Lastly, from departments to corporations, my techniques don't work in organizations staffed mainly by women.

WHO SHOULD READ THIS BOOK?

Anybody, male or female, from 18-58 can profit from it. I've aimed at a young woman of about 24.

You're ambitious, conscientious and unafraid of hard work. You have some college or a degree. You're experienced enough and bright enough to have an uneasy sense that intelligence, dedication, hard work and fair play are not all there is to success. You know this even though you were told otherwise by Mom and Dad, Girl Scout leaders and Sunday School teachers. You're right.

You're not a salesperson. They're different. They're special. They're born, not made. If you can sell, return this book.

At 24, you may believe business people wear nice clothes, travel in style, eat in fine restaurants, own prestigious cars and live a glamorous, exciting life. Articles and ads in *Cosmopolitan* and *Vanity Fair* are behind those ideas of yours. They are reinforced by TV commercials for American Airlines, Sheraton Hotels and Hertz.

You probably believe in and trust the company you work for. You most likely think the corporation will be honest, kind and fair with you, as I once did.

THIS BOOK IS REALISTIC

This book is not about how to do what you like to do, it's about how to get enough money so that you can do what you like to do. It's about how to achieve a long range goal, one step at a time. Learning how to get what you want out of life is what this book is all about. Learning to stop wanting to have your cake and eat it too is what this book is about.

Politically correct, gender neutral writing is for neuters. This book is for *real* women. (The *Preface* has a full explanation.)

To profit from this book, you must enjoy beating the system. If you're a Girl Scout who obeys all the rules or the sweet girl with a cute Garfield cat on her desk, quick, take this book back before you damage it so you can get a refund!

THE SECRET *THEY* WILL NEVER TELL YOU

Because they have been led to believe it, most women, young women in particular, think it takes a college education plus years of training and experience to make big money working for a corporation. Nope! A high school grad of average intelligence can do most jobs. Some tasks can be done by chimpanzees or trained dogs. In short, business is nothing more than common sense. No wonder they keep it a secret, right?

Everyone realizes this after a few companies and a few years. But, to preserve self-esteem and keep others from taking their jobs, people pretend the work they do is mega complicated, requiring years of experience and an MBA.

Bullshit! Paper pushing is paper pushing. That's all anyone does other than attend endless meetings and talk on the phone. Ninety percent of the job, your job, any job, is communicating clearly while getting along with people.

UNIVERSAL FUNDAMENTALS

The essence of most jobs is I-P-O. To computer geeks it means input, process, output. The essence of what every company does is nothing more than I-P-O. It buys raw material [input]. It does something to the raw material [process]. It sells the processed raw material [output]. Top Management's job is to sell the output for a price so high that there's a dividend for shareholders each fiscal quarter.

In every company you'll work for, the paper you push contains information. That information comes from someone who pushed the paper before you [input]. You do something to the information [process]. Then you push the paper to someone else [output].

Sure you have to understand what the [input] information means. Sure you have to know what to do with and to the information [process]. Sure you have to know where to send the information [output]. But that's what they *teach* you to do *after* they hire you.

There isn't any holder of an MBA or a single professor in the universe who can explain this to you. They don't get it.

COMPETITION IS REQUIRED

Fighting for what you want is necessary, normal and natural in the real world and in the corporate world. If something is scarce and desirable like money or a fun job, you must fight for it because everyone else wants it. The higher the stakes, the rougher and dirtier everyone fights. At work, office politics is how you fight.

OFFICE POLITICS REQUIRED

To drive your salary from $20k to $60k before you're 30, you have to get promoted quickly and often. But, every ambitious person wants the same promotions you want. And, since most jobs can be done by average high school grads, the promotion always goes to someone half as competent as you but twice as skilled in office politics.

That's not news, is it? Who got the best grades in college? Was it the girl who worked the hardest and did the best job? The girl who went to see the professor when he had office hours? How 'bout the girl who went to dinner with him?

Who else got good grades? Who else made cheerleader? Who else made class president or whatever?

Hey! Out here in the business world it's far worse. But it's out here where you can make the big bucks. Money, alone, makes it possible for *you* to be the person who determines *your* future. But, you're going to learn how to make big bucks without doing the equivalent of "going to dinner" with the professor.

Big companies are the *only* companies that pay females the big money you need so that you can determine your own future. That's the only reason to work for one.

YOUR FUTURE IS YOUR CHOICE

In ten years, you will have saved enough money and will be making enough money to have a bright, option-filled future. That's if you put into practice the ideas, strategy and techniques presented in the next few hundred pages.

Take what you want and pay for it, sayeth God.
SPANISH PROVERB

The wisdom of that quote means that each of us must choose our own future. And, no matter which choice you make, there's a price you must pay. Further, you, alone, must choose what you will do with the powerful knowledge, and sometimes disappointing truths, you are about to learn.

After you have money, you can choose to stay in the corporate world or you can choose something else, like starting your own business or starting a family or becoming a consultant or whatever you want. The point is, you will be independent. You will have choices. You will never be a wage slave.

And now, for *The Second Biggest Secret*.

Helpful hint: To avoid getting frustrated and angry, take a moment and read the *Preface* if you haven't.

All's fair in love, war and politics.
UNKNOWN WISE PERSON

The Second Biggest Secret

The key to making big money is advice given to me when I was young, fresh outta them thar hills of Appalachia. I followed that advice. By the time I was 34, I was able to live life on my terms, not the terms dictated to a wage slave by a monolithic corporation.

In 1962 I was 22. A family friend, Mancel Fore, was 55. His salary was $80k. Doesn't sound like much today? In those days, $80k would buy three large homes with swimming pools in upscale, suburban California. Today, that would take $800k. The guy knew how to make money! Here's what that wealthy executive told me:

Change jobs as often as possible the first five years of your career. Get at least a ten percent raise every time. When an interviewer asks why you left Job A or B or whatever, you say for a better paying position. Everybody understands that. Nobody considers that a bad reason. If you stay at a company you get five percent annual raises. In five years you'll be making one third more. Get ten percent and change as often as you can. In five years you'll triple what you're making now.

Once you drive your salary to the magic number, $20k, they think of you as special, different. Then they'll give you $5 or $7k to change. They believe that if Company X pays you $20k you're worth much more, if you're young. They *need an important job done. It's costing them not to fill it. They can't mess around. So, you say $30. They offer $25. Settle for $27. It gets easier. The more you make, the more you're worth, the more they give you to change companies.*

When Mancel told me that I was making $4k working in a factory. It was exhausting, dirty work. Five years later I was making $27k pushing paper. Five years after that I was 32, making $58k supporting executives. My wife and I lived in a hilltop home on two acres overlooking the infinite sea of lights of LA. To grasp how much $58k was in 1972, we sold the house a year later for $62k.

INDEPENDENCE EQUALS HAPPINESS

Turning 30 was traumatic. I had the mid-life crisis most men have at 40. A man's fortieth birthday is hard evidence that he's really going to die someday. Shocked, he stops. He looks around. He looks at himself. Sad and depressed, he wonders:

I did everything I was supposed to, why am I so miserable? Am I going to be miserable forever? Why am I doing this? When is it my turn to be happy?

During the next four years my wife of ten years and I divorced, I moved out of our house on the hill, sold my Cadillac sedan, moved in with my 18 year old secretary, quit my job.

Suddenly the dawn! I realized that doing what I enjoyed, with whom I enjoyed doing it, when I enjoyed doing it, was the true definition of success. Time, free time, was the most valuable thing in the universe. I reduced my standard of living so I could support myself working only part time. Life became a joyous adventure instead of a battle to succeed. Today, at 54 I enjoy the very same lifestyle, working five or six months out of the year. The rest of the time I work on my tan or write.

I was able to choose how I spent the rest of my life because I had money, enough money to get me started and sustain me when the rainy days came, as they always do. It's called "screw-you money." Independence becomes reality. Happiness follows.

Ten years from now, when you have screw-you money, you're the person who gets to decide how you spend the rest of your life.

Increasing your options is what this book is fundamentally about because you're the person who must decide which of life's infinite paths to take.

THE MAGIC NUMBER

Personnel Departments and Compensation Committees worship it. The magic number has its powerful mystique because only 20 percent of the population makes that much money. In reality, it is nothing more than a point on a scale, a threshold. Once you exceed the magic number, the next barrier is $200k. To earn that much you have to become part of Top Management. More about that in a few chapters.

In 1962 the magic number was $20k. Now it's $60k. The quickest way to get your salary up there is to change jobs as often as possible, getting raises of ten percent or better every time.

WHY OFFICE POLITICS?

The only function of office politics is to get what you want instead of what they offer:

1. Biggest raise possible.
2. Quickest promotion possible.
3. Assigned tasks you enjoy or with the best visibility.
4. Moved to the best office with the best equipment.
5. Transferred to the department with the best future.
6. Not laid off until you can find a good job elsewhere.

To achieve those aims you must:

1. Have your boss notice you.
2. Convince him you aren't after his job.
3. Arrive early, leave late.
4. Wear only the uniform, day in, year out.
5. Do your work efficiently, on time, without complaint.
6. Cooperate with everyone and help everyone so they all see you as a team player.
7. Give your boss credit for your ideas and suggestions.
8. Be polite and deferential to your boss and his boss.
9. Earn the fear and respect of your co-workers.

10. Identify and neutralize rivals and enemies quickly.
11. Develop powerful friends throughout the company.
12. Spy and gather data so you always have a big advantage over your boss and your enemies.
13. Have clearly defined short range goals with plans and schedules needed to attain them. Make certain these ultimately lead to your long range goal.
14. Never, ever, lose sight of your long range goal.

To profit from this book, you must know *what* you want, *when* you want it and *what price* you're willing to pay to get it. That's also known as *Your Goals*..

Gentle note to the reader: These are *Your Goals,* if and only if, you want to be independent ten years from now. Much of what's coming up may oblige you to re-examine your values and beliefs. You may discover that your primary goal is to be earning $150k before you are 35. Then again, after critically evaluating the brutal reality of corporate life, you may decide to move to Utah, open your own small business and become an expert downhill skier in your spare time. The point still is, it's your choice.

First say to yourself what you would be then do what you have to do.
90 AD EPICTETUS

Your Goals

If you don't know what you want, you can't go after it. If you don't go after it, you'll never get it. If you don't know where you want to go, you can't get anywhere. If you want to be financially comfortable by 34, you have to start when you are 24, or hit the lottery.

TWO POSSIBLE WOMEN IN THE SAME BODY

The divorce rate is 52 percent and rising. The average American marriage lasts only 9.1 years — death or divorce. The young woman who chooses a traditional life has a 50-50 chance of ending up a bitter divorcee at 28 years old, with two kids, no options, no job skills, no experience, no future.

At 34, she'll be a wage slave earning $27k, barely making ends meet. To the company, she is a nothing, a nobody, a grunt in Data Processing or Personnel. In four more years they'll give her a 10-year pin. That 34 year old woman has no options. But a 34 year old woman with ten years of experience, who has changed companies many times makes $60k. She can pick and choose what to do with the rest of her life.

Which 34-year old you become is up to you.

LONG JOURNEYS BEGIN WITH SINGLE GOALS

To get from where you are to where you want to be, you need short range goals. If you want to be the 34 year old woman with a choice, your first goal is to establish a life operations base.

That means a safe place to live, a dependable car and presentable clothing.

As this is being written (1994) that takes a minimum of $22k. Step one is to make that much money.

Goal two is driving your salary as high as possible before you are 34. At $22k, if you get the standard four percent raise every year, by 34 you won't even be making your age. Even worse, inflation is about four percent, so you won't have any more purchasing power in ten years than you do right now.

Your immediate goal is to make as much money as possible doing something you can tolerate. Your ultimate goal is to make enough money so that you can live comfortably while doing something you enjoy.

SETTING GOALS

Measurable, concrete goals are the only kind that can be attained. To be happier, slimmer, sleep better or exercise more are vague. Fifty situps every day is concrete and measurable.

I am a procrastinator. I can find millions of things to do instead of writing. A book doesn't get finished unless I force myself to meet a daily goal. That doesn't work unless there is a final deadline. My measurable, concrete goal is two pages a day. The pages don't have to be good or even mediocre. But there must be two pages in the out basket.

Set your goal at a realistic level. Develop a schedule that is attainable. Work toward your goal every day.

THE COMPANY'S VIEW OF YOUR GOALS

Management doesn't give a damn about you, your goals or your dreams. What you think, what you enjoy, what you want and how you feel is of absolutely no importance. To them, you are a peasant, whose lot in life is to work the corporation's fields until you die.

If you don't have a goal, a plan and a schedule, you'll be like the rest of the employee-cows at your company — getting milked dry, then sold for dog food (laid off before they have to pay you a pension).

HOW I GOT HERE

My goal was to be able to support myself working part time. That required a large savings account so I could survive when I wasn't working. I focused on accumulating money. I lowered my standard of living to slightly below comfortable. I bought nothing new for years. My last new car was in 1974.

Every job that came along, I took. After working without pause for four years, I had saved enough money to feel secure. I started taking only assignments that paid extremely well or assignments that were fun or assignments that were easy, with plenty of time off. To do this, I had to have transferable skills companies wanted on a part-time basis.

After three years of that, I was able to feel no sense of panic when I couldn't get work for months. My savings account was, and is, my security blanket. I keep adding to it so that eventually I can make my big break and move to paradise, Da Big Island in Hawaii.

These days, my goal is to support myself in paradise doing something I can tolerate, then by doing something I like, and finally, by doing something I enjoy part time.

YOU ALWAYS HAVE OPTIONS

There is no finish line in life. There's no place to get to. There is only living and loving and laughing as much as possible between now and the time they close the lid on your coffin. That takes money.

But, if making tons of money turns out not to be what you want, you can stop at any point along the path, get married, have babies, watch daytime television and eat ice cream. Or, you can move to Hollywood and try your hand at showbiz. The point is, you're responsible for the choices you make. I'm only here to tell you what the realistic odds are of making it in the corporate world.

Take a hard look at the *Females Who Came Before* you. I may seem cruel and harsh but my strongest belief about learning is that if the student knows *why,* it's far easier for her to learn the *what, how* and *when.*

Here's why *they* don't see you, or any other woman, the way you think *they* should.

Women, then, are only children of a larger growth: they have an entertaining tattle, and sometimes wit; but for solid, reasoning good-sense, I never knew in my life one that had it or who reasoned or acted consequentially for four and twenty hours together.

LETTER TO HIS SON 1748 LORD CHESTERFIELD

Females Who Came Before

Top Management believes what Lord Chesterfield told his son. They think you're no different than any other woman who has come and gone. You're plagued by their memory of your predecessors, Girls with a capital G.

JOBS OR CAREERS?

A career is something you plan to spend the next 10 to 60 years doing. A job pays the rent and makes car payments. Girls have jobs. They work until they can quit. Work is a place to meet men or a pastime until Prince Charming comes along and takes them away from all this.

They know it's only a matter of time before you announce, as did every predecessor: "Ken and I are getting married. We're moving to Montana." Or, "I'm pregnant. I'll be back four months after the baby's born." Or, "Like wow! I'm taking a year off, tour Europe. See Ya!"

That's why young women are kept in low-pay, minimum-skill, unimportant positions, jobs that convince even intelligent females that housewifery, motherhood and daytime television might be preferable.

The behavior of predecessor girls is also why you are judged differently, held to a tougher standard than young men. *They* watch you with greater suspicion and less tolerance for failure. They expect you to drop the ball, so they just wait for the inevitable. If you do something great they dismiss it as luck, merely delaying the eventual, known outcome.

If you do last long enough for them to start believing you're serious, they remember what happened when Wendy Johnson, 28, Senior Administrator went on the audit trip with Harry Dickerson, 51, VP Finance. Sure they remember Harry liked his booze. Sure they remember Harry fancied himself a stud. Most of all they remember Harry was pounding on Wendy's hotel door stark naked when the cops arrived. Everyone's certain it wouldn't have happened if Wendy hadn't gone. They aren't sure but they suspect Wendy led Harry on.

Wendy got transferred to Cucamonga. Harry got fired so the company could avoid a lawsuit. After a year of searching and begging, he shot himself when he couldn't get a job.

TURN THEIR HEADS AROUND

To convert disbelievers, they must realize that you're different. Make this message clear, "My career is a lifetime activity. I'm not working to buy clothes. I'm working because I like to work. I need to work. I enjoy my work."

First, your uniform must say all of that and say it the loudest. (Uniforms are described shortly.) Next you must say it with actions by working hard and by being prompt, courteous, reliable, efficient and conscientious. Finally, you must say variations of it to your boss, and his boss, in plain English every few months. Everyone needs to be constantly reassured. They all suspect your secret goal is to abandon the company so you can have children.

Forty five percent of the workforce is female.
Seventy five percent become pregnant while employed.
US DEPARTMENT OF LABOR 1993

They are most easily convinced if you are not a single, available woman. If you're available, men spend a tremendous amount of time competing among themselves for your attention. If you're a distraction, Management is pissed off and you're future there is over.

BECOME BETROTHED TO YOURSELF

As a young woman, it's worse. Other single females think you'll ruin their chance of capturing a husband. They band together and spend a tremendous amount of time plotting to get you fired. End this nonsense. Buy a diamond engagement ring at the pawn shop.

Don't wear your ring to the interview. Let fantasy reign. Your future boss may dream about being able to seduce you. He'll hire you instead of the other applicant, the one wearing an engagement ring.

PUT THE WORD OUT

A few weeks after you settle in, quietly announce your "engagement" to everyone by showing your ring to the department's gossip and simply say, "He finally asked." She'll want to know when you're getting married. Just say, "Next year, in the fall." Engagement rings keep wolves at bay and calm cows terrified of competition.

Make doubly certain your boss and his boss know you're here for the long haul. When Ms. Opportunity presents herself, mention in any conversation with anybody that you're not going to have children. Envious female co-workers will press you on this. Say, "That's just our decision. Children need a full-time mother. I'm dedicated to my career." Word gets back to your boss and his.

DON'T BE AVAILABLE AT ANY AGE

Later on in your late 20s, then in your 30s and 40s, if you're not married, visit the pawn shop and buy a wedding band. Wear it to the interview. Announce you're happily married, as you mention that you don't have any children and don't want any. (How corporations view women with children is coming up.)

Begin converting disbelievers months before you even meet them with *Creative Writing–Resumes*.

Show me an actress who has never lied on her resume and I'll show you a waitress.

HOLLYWOOD AUTHORITY SCOTT CARTER

Creative Writing–Resumes

At the first corporation I joined after getting out of the United States Army, my boss called me into his office a few months after I started work. He asked me to close the door.

This guy was about 35, nicely dressed, relaxed, confident, polite and on his way up. In an idle moment he had compared my resume with my application. He began gently by saying that Personnel always verified the information on applications, especially recent salaries and education. I nodded, "Uh, huh." Then he stated bluntly, "Everything's off the record."

He said I had been hired two levels below where I should have been based on my experience and education. It would take him a year to promote me to that level because of Personnel policy and rules. Then, as if trying not to hurt my feelings, he explained:

> *Everybody assumes resumes are inflated. So everyone who reads your resume automatically discounts it 10 to 40 percent. If you tell the truth you are offered 10 to 40 percent less than your actual experience merits. That's what happened to you.*

Inwardly I was outraged, indignant and offended. It didn't seem fair. It didn't make sense. To this day it seems foolish but that's how "The System" works. Sad but true.

YOUR FIRST CREATIVE RESUME

Get thyself to the library. Read as many different books on writing resumes as you can stand. Ten is minimum. Pick three different formats. Write your resume three different ways. Contact friends outside the company. Send all three versions. Ask them to comment, edit and to please send a copy of their resume when returning yours. Incorporate ideas you like.

No matter where you worked, the duties and responsibilities you describe must mention skills that are transferrable to a corporate paper pushing environment. Buzzwords for transferrable skills include: schedule, train, plan, hire, monitor costs, develop budgets, forecast, purchase, prepare reports.

Other facts newcomers must include (a) held a job (b) held a second more important job (c) held a third even more important job (d) worked with other employees and the public (e) did something other than lifting or serving.

INFLATING YOURSELF

If you were a Box Girl, call yourself Assistant Cashier and describe those duties as your own. You could have done them, right? If you were a waitress, your title was Lead Server. Duties: prepare work schedules, monitor employee attendance records, prepare register drawers, schedule job interviews, interview prospective employees, train cashiers and hostesses, arrange for equipment repairs.

If you were a Sales Clerk at Nordstrom, your resume title is Assistant Sales Manager. Duties: track sales vs forecasts, keep records on sales people's performance and bonus requirements, train new hires on the computer system, prepare inventory reports. Whatever is similar to corporate paperwork.

If you didn't do this stuff you certainly could have. That's the essence of inflating your resume. No big deal. Right?

RISK TAKING REQUIRED

Does this sound familiar?

To profit from this book, you must enjoy beating the system. If you're a wimp who obeys . . .

That was in the first chapter. But there is a whole chapter coming up with the same title as this paragraph to explain why and how you must take risks to beat the system. Inflating and slanting your resume is the first risk you have to take.

Creative Writing–Resumes should be taught in colleges. You'd have learned something useful, something worth thousands instead of answers to *Jeopardy* questions.

FRIENDS AS FORMER EMPLOYERS

At my suggestion, Lynn, a lifelong friend, used me as a past employer when she graduated from college. She had only worked summer jobs that had nothing to do with showbiz, her chosen industry.

She was bright, quite conscientious and a willing, dedicated worker, the only things needed to do just about any job, in any company, anywhere. Over a few Mai Tais we wrote a description of her duties at Steel Balls Press. "Responsible for contacting media outlets, arranging interviews for authors, making travel arrangements, maintaining production schedules, monitoring budgets, bla de similar to showbiz, blah de bla bla."

After interviewing with a company, she'd call and coach me on any differences required from the standard answers and glowing recommendations I gave Personnel geeks who checked on her.

By doing this, Lynn penetrated the toughest industry to get started in without knowing someone. Once inside, she met plenty of people on her wavelength who were able to coach her on moving up and changing companies.

Conspire with someone you trust. Have him do what I did for Lynn. Call him and role play. Try to trick him.

Once you're hired by a major corporation, you are a family member of the corporate universe. So, at your second corporation and beyond, Personnel never checks summer jobs. They always check the salary of your present job.

COLLEGE ACTIVITIES THAT IMPRESS

If you worked your way through college that's great. Say so right at the top of the sheet. Everyone is impressed, including me. If you worked part-time while attending college that's also impressive. Say that right at the top of the sheet.

The more full-time and part-time jobs you had, the better. List them all with inflated titles and duties. Corporate types are impressed if you've already learned some of the basics. Corporate types know that philosophy majors don't have the slightest idea what a Petty Cash Voucher looks like and English majors don't know how to prepare a T&E report.

Call yourself the Bookstore Assistant Manager if you were a buyer of used books for two weeks at the end of the semester. Describe the duties of the Assistant Manager. You could have done that job, right? Use this same technique for all jobs you held. Promote yourself. No one else will.

They see you as an independent, self-reliant person if you've traveled. If you've been to Europe, even if it was just two weeks, say you studied there six months. They can throw you on a plane next week to Washington DC and know you'll handle it.

Mention any team sport such as volleyball, soccer, softball, as one of your hobbies. Any team sport you actually played in high school or college is great. Corporations love team players no matter what the team played. Team players know how to get along.

Even if you didn't play, say you were Captain, Women's Field Hockey Team, MVP conference finals at Penn State. Sports awards impress corporate males.

Read a book on field hockey in case the interviewer wants to talk about it. I doubt it, because I'm a sports junkie and know absolutely nothing beyond it's played with a ball not a puck. I don't even know if there's a position called "forward."

Experience in running organizations is useful if business sees the organizations as good, such as Young Republicans or Capitalist Warmonger Club. Being on the Debate Team is good. If you were in student government, that's great. If not, say you were. There's no way they have the time or people to check.

COLLEGE ACTIVITIES THAT DON'T IMPRESS

The Peace Corps is viewed by business as a place where future socialists and environmentalists waste time and taxpayer dollars. If you were in the Peace Corps, say so but place the emphasis on going out into the real world and learning how to be tough. Describe it as a terrific learning experience that taught you how the world really works and how great America is. It is.

Don't mention Green Peace, Greens or whatever. You aren't left wing even if you are. Socialists and liberals aren't hired knowingly. If they get in, they never advance once discovered.

If you were into acting, don't mention it or play it way down. Theater people are suspected of being homosexuals, communists and drug users.

YOUR SECOND CREATIVE RESUME

During the early years, learn as many transferrable skills as possible on every job. Show progress on your resume. You started as a File Clerk and ended up as a Senior Resource Administrator.

Now that you're at General Cow, Inc., go to the company library or the Business Development department. Get some recent proposals. Resumes of key people are in them to show a customer the qualifications of General Cow's team. Study the style that's used. Later, when you're going to give your resume to someone in the company, follow General Cow's format.

Look up the same guy in ten different proposals. Notice ten slightly different versions of his resume. Each one is slanted to emphasize the experience most applicable to the job being proposed. Slant your resume in a like manner when you know which way to slant it. For example, toward your finance and accounting experience or toward your planning and scheduling experience. There's more on this coming up.

PLAGIARIZING — INTELLIGENCE GATHERING

After you've changed companies several times, your salary will be up there where you can get $5k just to change companies, if you have a kick-ass resume. Develop yours by using the best source of all, resumes of successful people.

Read the want ads every Sunday. Study the language used. Keep copies of ads similar to the job you want. Write your own ad. Rewrite it. Show it to friends. Work on it until it sounds like the real thing.

Describe the next job you want. Be concrete and specific. Extend the salary range so it's enticing, say $28-42k. Describe the company as a leader in your industry. Assure everyone of the strictest confidence. Be sure to state EOE, women encouraged to apply. Place your ad in the Sunday paper and in trade journals. Have applicants send a cover letter and salary history with their resume to a blind box you rent from the publication.

No book can include the specifics you learn from these resumes. You'll find out what credentials, experience and capabilities your competitors are offering, at least on paper. Certain jargon and buzzwords will appear in the best resumes. Use those words. The best format for your resume is the format of the best resumes. The style of writing in the best resumes is the style you adopt. The best cover letters are how yours must read.

> ASSISTANT TO PRESIDENT. Transport industry leader. Young and energetic a must. Able to work under stress and meet deadlines, self starter, use common sense and be able to get along with diverse personalities. Duties include speech writing, routine correspondence, staff briefings, coordinating daily activities. Salary $28-42k. Letter on career goals and qualifications with salary history. Resume detailing present duties and two previous positions. EOE. Women encouraged to apply. All replies held in strictest confidence. LA Times Box 807.

Use what you learn. Rewrite your resume. Send it to your friends again. Get feedback.

Of course you don't have to wait until you're ready to move up to $40k to use this technique. Use it for your first job if you can figure out what that job will be. You'll learn tremendous resume writing skills that cannot be bought at any price. This ad will cost you a couple of hundred bucks but it gives you ideas worth thousands when you land that new job.

COURAGEOUS, OUTRAGEOUS

Wait a few weeks. Call the top five candidates who sent their resumes. Present yourself as an assistant headhunter from a leading personnel firm calling to determine their interest in being recruited. If they ask how you got their name, say "You were anonymously recommended by someone at your company." (This happens all the time. When it happens to you, someone likes you or somebody wants you to leave.)

By talking with the best candidates, you get a feel for the competition. Ask them a few routine questions and some of the tough questions you expect to be asked when interviewed. Take notes. Say, "Uh, huh, I see," as required. Thank them profusely. Tell them you'll be calling back next week. Give them the legit number of the leading headhunting firm you're supposedly from. Tell them to call anytime.

Your confidence will skyrocket because you now know some answers to tough questions and you realize that you can do the job!

THE BOSS'S RESUME

Write a resume for your immediate boss. Describe his duties and responsibilities as clearly as you can. Next, find his job description. Revise your writeup of his duties. Look it over. Ask yourself, "Can I do what he does?" Nearly every time the answer is, "Hell yes!" What does that tell you about stretching your resume?

SLANTING TO FIT

This is nothing more than emphasizing your capabilities, skills and experience that most closely match the job you want. Emphasis is established by the order of presentation, most important first. Emphasis comes from the number of words devoted to description, the more words, the more important.

Emphasis comes from the format. For example, if the position is teaching or training, education should be at the top, followed by a heading, "Summary Of Training Experience," then a paragraph summarizing duties and titles. Follow that with a heading "Training Capabilities." Use an easy to read bullet-list of items such as "Work well with first time students."

Slanting your resume is what you must do to get the dream job you want. Dream jobs pay twice as much as you're making to do something you truly enjoy. Slanting is just as necessary to get a mediocre job for 10 percent more.

RIDICULOUS RESUME LAUNCHING

Sending out resumes to the universe and waiting for a reply is like waiting for Amelia Earhart to show up with Jimmy Hoffa. It makes you look weak and desperate. Devour Ringer's *Winning Through Intimidation.* His main point is that you must only negotiate from a position of strength. It's listed in *Must Books.* Respond to ads or requests only.

NO CHANCE OF GETTING BUSTED

Since 1985 many former employees have won multi-million dollar lawsuits against companies for damaging their chances to land a new job. Nowadays, companies absolutely do not permit anyone to give information beyond the dates you worked there, title and salary.

Remember, the person reading your resume is discounting it 10 to 40 percent. Everyone else applying for your dream job is blowing smoke on his resume.

How far do you inflate your resume? That's your call. Here's how I decide. I have to feel, that's feel in my gut, that I can look the interviewer right in the eye and say, "Yes, that multi-media presentation was a good one. We all had a great time at the Paris Air Show."

Your resume is the single most important piece of paper in the world. It gets you in the door, seated at the decision maker's table so you can sell yourself. Work on it with the creativity, diligence and perseverance it deserves. The cover letter is the second most important piece of paper in the world. Work on it with the same energy and tenacity.

GREAT MANDATORY BOOKS

The last chapter of this book is called *Must Books*. There are so many fraudulent "success" books published every year, that it's rare to find a good one, let alone a must one. Buy John Lucht's *Rites of Passage At $100,000+* and his *Executive Job-Changing Workbook*. What you learn will bring you tens of thousands of dollars during the next 10 years. He's an author who has done what he's telling you how to do, something that's as rare as it is wonderful.

Your appearance is the single most important means you have of convincing one and all that you are to be taken seriously. As strange as it seems, that's extremely easy. *They* actually believe *The Play's The Thing*.

Warning! This is the first *why* chapter. Yes, the tone is harsh. Yes, it's blunt. You must get what is being said. You must get it down in your guts. If you don't, everything else you are learning is absolutely useless. Corporate men assume that if you are not dressed for advancement, you are not suitable for advancement.

All the world's a stage
and all the men and women merely players.
SHAKESPEARE

The Play's The Thing

Those in charge (men) are only able to see corporate females as EITHER-OR: sexy or smart, competent or pretty, pushover or tough, strong or weak, female or human, too young or younger.

Since neither you, nor anyone else, can change this, make certain *men* see you as you must be seen to be taken seriously.

Every morning when you walk through that office door, "It's show time!" Every day, in every office, in every city of the land, the play is presented from 8 to 5. It's called, "Let's Pretend We're Important."

Push paper, attend meetings, talk on the phone and go to lunch, that's all anyone does. Seems like everyone's attire would be whatever's comfortable, right? Sneakers, sweat shirts and jeans. Why then do some people wear $2000 suits, $800 shoes, $200 shirts, and $100 ties? For the very same reason queens, generals and popes wear such non-functional, elaborate outfits — so the troops know who's in charge.

At the office, those in charge, and those who want to be in charge (make big money), wear the same type of non-functional, elaborate outfits as queens and popes.

YOUR COSTUME SPEAKS TO THE AUDIENCE

In any theatrical production, the costume you wear tells the audience what part you're playing and makes it easy for them to believe you. Your role is Company Woman: a competent, efficient, enthusiastic person who deserves a promotion.

First impressions are lasting impressions. After noticing that you are (a) female (b) young, the next thing the office audience sees is your costume. If that costume doesn't scream, "I am successful, all business, reliable and know exactly what I'm doing," nothing you ever say or do can make them take you seriously.

SEXY IS ONLY FOR SECRETARIES

You can never look sexy, even when you work weekends at the office or on casual dress day. The moment guys realize you're desirable, they no longer see *Donna Young from MIS.* They see, *The one with the USDA Prime Ass, works for DJ Wilson.* Promotion becomes impossible.

> *There are only two kinds of women in the business world: those who have secretaries and those who are secretaries.*
> UNKNOWN WISE PERSON

Don't use colorful or shiny lipstick. It's distracting. Instead of focusing on what you're saying, men focus on what oral sex might be like. Foundation and powder can be used if you suffered from acne or were born with rough facial skin. In general, the less makeup the better. Only use enough to prevent men from putting you in the she-male category.

The eyes are the windows of the soul and the third place men look when they check you out. As with makeup, only use enough eye liner, eye shadow, mascara and eyebrow pencil to have them see you're not trying-to-be-a-man.

Conceal all curves. If you have beautiful legs, wear long skirts every day. Keep your bosom out of sight, thus out of mind. Large breasts must be disguised at all costs. Men equate big boobs with small brains and no morals, thus a pushover. The end. Whatever your strong points are as an attractive, desirable female, downplay them until you are the CEO.

BUSINESS UNIFORMS

How seriously would you take a young man who says he wants to be Division Manager someday, but he wears skin tight, pegged, black pants, chrome belt, turquoise shirt open to the navel, with bleached-blond hair? Why?

Whoa! Take a minute. Think about why you don't take him seriously.

Will men take you seriously if you wear anything other than the business uniform?

Successful-in-business people wear the uniform. It is quiet, not loud; tailored, not form-fitting; classic not classy; timeless not trendy. Emulate the successful to be considered worthy of becoming one of them.

The uniform creates the impression that you, as a person, are sharp and crisp the entire day. It is something you can wear from LAX to JFK and back, without it making you look tired and wrinkled. But, this is a big BUT, don't out dress your superiors, imitate them. A $400 blazer is hard to camouflage, as are $200 shoes and $200 skirts. Don't make your boss or his boss jealous of your attire. Conservative, tasteful, moderately expensive everything. Nothing extravagantly expensive! Nothing that creates envy or makes anyone feel threatened. The edge you need is created by the detail of your uniform. Get your uniforms tailored, impeccably tailored.

Clothes are a tool you use to control
how others react to you and how they treat you.
Dress For Success JOHN MOLLOY

Your uniform says who you are and where you plan to be in five years. Girls going nowhere dress in stylish, sexy clothes. Their uniform says to men:

I'd be great if you could get me. Try so I can turn you down and feel superior. I only have this job to pay for my wedding and the Hawaiian honeymoon.

You don't have to try to attract attention, it will be given to you automatically. All eyes look in your direction in any gathering because you're different, not male. So, when they look in your direction, your uniform must say: quality, tasteful and understated.

DRESS FOR SUCCESS IN BUSINESS

Females dress in a way that announces to everyone what their career intentions are at a single glance. There are only two messages that can be broadcast by your attire (1) I'm here for the long haul. (2) I'm here for the paycheck.

Young women dress for success. Girls dress to attract males and to make other females jealous. Girls 18-65, with a rich husband, dress in expensive, fashionable clothes. Girls 18-65 without a husband or with one they'd like to cheat on, dress in trendy, attention getting clothes. Girls of all ages wear anything except the business uniform.

Look at any female in the military. Her skirt says, "I'm female." The rest of the uniform says, "I don't have any curves." Likewise, you must not have a noticeable waist or bustline.

Distracting males at the office gets you placed in the same category as trendy bride-to-be boneheads. A jacket, loosely tailored to prevent anyone from noticing your bustline and waistline, is mandatory, every day, everywhere. Blouses, buttoned to the neck at all times, make it easier for men to look you in the eye. Skirts long enough to hide shapely legs and loose enough to disguise your tush keep co-workers working, not wishing or gossiping. That's loose, not baggy.

From Psychology 101, remember Maslow's hierarchy of needs? Number one is air. Number two is water. Number three is food. Don't remind males what number four is. Don't remind the females either. They get competitive and catty.

The ideal look is female without being attractive. That's as hard to achieve as it is rare. Err on the side of severe as you develop this look, but not masculine or she-male. Dress like a serious, strong woman who knows where she's going and what she's doing. A woman officer in the US Marine Corps is the look you're after without appearing to be in the military.

JUST DO IT, DO IT RIGHT

When men don't comment on your appearance, you are doing it right. When a guy says, "You look nice today, very pretty." *Translation:* You look like a girl, a no competition fluff ball who might be a good lay. Other tipoffs from men that you're doing it wrong include "You look: cute, attractive, sweet." In short, any compliment. When you don't get a second glance walking down the hall, you're doing it right. When heads turn, you're doing it wrong.

JUNGLE WARFARE REQUIRES MOBILITY

In the corporate jungle, dress so you can take part in the rapid maneuvers the prominent natives often conduct about noon. Don't blow the opportunity when they spontaneously invite you to join them as they dash off to an early lunch. In the jungle, never carry a purse, it slows you down, causing the prominent natives in the group to notice you're different, not a man. Guys can make an instant getaway. Everything needed is in their pockets: wallet, keys and a comb. All you really need to make an instant getaway with them is paper money, keys, tiny comb and a lipstick. Keep everything else in your desk. Men have pockets. Get some.

QUIET PLEASE!

Clicking high heels announce, "Hey everybody, we're leaving early!" or, "Female coming. Turn around. See if I'm attractive." Get silencers on all your shoes.

Accessories that jangle announce to the whole jungle that the group is leaving early or coming back late. Not a good idea. Also, it forces prominent natives in the group to notice you're different, not a man.

Men don't jangle, clang, dangle or dingle when they walk or stand up in the presentation room. Everything about them is quiet and understated. A watch. A class ring. A wedding ring. A lapel pin. That's it.

Successful looking is expensive looking, not flashy. Limit jewelry to small earrings, a cameo broach, Seiko or such watch and the ever-present engagement ring. That's it. No ankle bracelets, no charm bracelets, no necklaces other than a single strand of small pearls if absolutely necessary.

KEEP UP WITH LOW SHOES AND LOOSE SKIRTS

Tight skirts require tiny, delicate steps like a tiny, delicate, subservient Japanese wife walking behind her husband. You must not appear to be walking two steps behind a man who is striding powerfully and purposefully. Loose fitting skirts are mandatory. You must walk at his speed without appearing to run. No rustling material. No sexy slits. Skirts are below the knee, the way a Marine wears her skirt.

You must be able to keep up with any man, anywhere. Heels, even low heels, slow you down as the both of you rush through the airport to catch the commuter flight to SFO. Heels slow you down when you both have to dash down the hall to catch JB before he leaves for LAX. Heels slow you down as you and your boss roar down the stairs to the Conference Room to rehearse the presentation at the last minute.

Choose a conservative shoe style. Don't cause even the slightest loss of flaccidity in the manager who has a secret shoe fetish. No straps, buckles or holes. Silencers, yes.

SHE-MALES NOT WANTED

Never wear anything that looks even remotely like a man's tie. That's his phallic symbol. You'll look like a she-male or dyke if you wear one. Wearing slacks instead of skirts gets you seen as trying to "wear the pants" in the corporate family.

Notice the haircuts of successful business men. Successful business women wear their hair in a similar style, slightly longer. Short hair, worn in a non-stylish manner is compulsory. If you insist on long hair, never wear it any way other than pulled back, bound in a severe bun, as a frigid librarian would. Never let your hair down literally or figuratively with anyone from the company.

NO NO'S AND YES YES'S

Being a real blonde is as fatal as not concealing large breasts. Men think blonde jokes are based on fact. Women resent blondes. Slowly, gently tint your hair light brown.

At the office, fix your makeup and lipstick in the women's room. Do likewise at lunch with people from the office. If you don't, men suddenly realize your aren't one of them.

Absolutely no perfume! That's for after hours with your boyfriend(s). It distracts men and makes them realize you are a female. No perfume! Ever. Not even scented soap!

To be taken seriously, wear the same gray, navy and dark blue that men wear. That costume says, "I am all business, a pro. I am strong and self-assured. I don't have to attract attention." Buy outfits that will never be out of fashion.

Discover how prominent female natives dress. Set up an observation post in the lobby of a major corporate center. Get there early. Spend hours studying the look of women who appear to make $100k. Develop their look.

EYEGLASSES EQUAL SEMI-EQUALITY

Women who wear glasses are taken more seriously. It makes no difference if you have 20-20 vision, get a pair. Nothing trendy! Something on the intellectual side, not too harsh. The idea is to be seen as bright, not an egg-head. Don't overdo it with black horn rims. Tortoise shell perhaps. Put them on a chain around your neck if the important men do. Get a pair that are slightly bigger than look good on you. Look serious. Don't look good. Women prospecting for a husband look good. See Dorothy Parker's wisdom about glasses in *Office Sex*.

TRENDY — THE KISS OF DEATH

Dress in the style of your Top Management. They set the fashion pace. Gently give a nod to fashion, about two years behind trend setters. Never be out in front or even near the front. Trendy people are seen as serious about fads, not about their careers.

JUDGED BY MORE THAN YOUR COSTUME

How do you form an opinion about people with whom you have no working contact? First, by their costume. Second, by the way they walk. Third, by the way they talk. Until you interact, you judge them the same way the Big Boys judge you. To everyone other than your immediate boss, only perception counts, not the reality of your ability and work output.

WALK THE WALK

Don't sway those hips. Don't wear clothes that make swishing, feminine sounds. Don't make clopping sounds. Don't make noise, period, especially high-heeled clicks that turn every man's head.

Until you open your mouth, the way you walk is the second most important way *they* judge you. Walk with purpose. Walk with quiet confidence. Walk with conviction. Walk like you know where you are going — head up, eyes forward, shoulders back. Don't stroll. Don't rush. People in a hurry are perceived as inefficient. People who stroll appear to be wasting time. People who stride purposefully are seen as productive. Make certain that's how *they* see you.

Walking differently than you do naturally can be learned. Acting classes help develop a confident, purposeful walk, but a camcorder is instantly helpful. Tape yourself walking in your business uniform. See how you appear to others. Simply modify your stride until you like what you see. Then, practice, practice, practice, from the house to the car, from the parking lot to the office, from your desk to the rest room. Soon your walk becomes purposeful, confident, successful. That's how *they'll* perceive you if, and only if, your business uniform says the same thing.

TALK THE TALK

It's not a sin to have problems. It is a sin to not know you have problems. Your grammar must be flawless. Diction likewise. Your vocabulary must match theirs. Take English and vocabulary tests at a Junior College. Find areas of weakness and begin correcting them immediately.

Even if you're dressed in exactly the right costume. Even if you walk purposefully. Even if you speak the Queen's English brilliantly you won't be taken seriously if your voice is cute, tiny or like a little girl's.

At work, tape yourself on the phone and during routine conversation. Do you sound like a confident, adult female? If not, get thyself to acting class, diction class, speech class. Should you be ashamed of how young or cute you sound, consider this. Most females of all ages sound that way. The only ones I met in the corporate world who sounded like adult females were the ones making the big bucks. That's not happenstance, now is it?

ON BEING TALL

If you're 5'7" or taller, never wear heels, even quiet ones. Select attire that does not emphasize your height at the office and at all other company functions. Why? Men dislike women who are taller than they are. Short men detest tall women. You make them feel even more inadequate. Never, never, underestimate the vengeance in a short man's psyche. These are the most insecure, domineering creeps on the planet. Many short guys end up in charge because, in the unreality of corporations, their angry aggressiveness gives them an edge.

Never stoop or hunch over in a futile attempt to pretend you aren't tall. This is seen by all as a sign of weakness and shame. Yet, you must never walk like you are proud to be tall. Simply be natural about your height. This is a bit tough but it can be accomplished the easiest with the help of a camcorder.

CAREFULLY CHEERFUL

If you bounce in with a bright smile, full of life and energy, co-workers are confused, then resentful, then suspicious, then anxious. For years they've been dreadfully miserable. They know that their future is more of the same. They have given up and accepted their lot in life. They are surrounded by people who are just as downcast. Your cheerfulness causes them to examine how miserable and empty their lives are. They hate you!

If you're bright and cheerful, Management thinks you are either naive or stupid. If you act and look serious, they think you understand the significance of the situation "we" face.

For now, simply accept that you must not let them see you're happy. In a few chapters, I'll explain why decision makers are so unhappy and your co-workers are so despondent.

A FINAL WORD ON DRESSING FOR SUCCESS

Buy and thoroughly read *The Woman's Dress For Success Book,* by John Molloy. He's got it down to a science.

If you're dressed like a corporate VP, it's hard for the interviewer to hire you as a Senior Editor. Underdressing is worse than overdressing but not by much. Dress for the part you want in the play.

Pay strict attention to how your future boss dresses during the interview. At the same time, examine everyone in his department you happen to see. You need immediate clues as to how the fish in this tank dress. Too conservative is just about impossible to achieve for the first few months.

Women who want to make $100k must dress like the *men* who do make $100k. If you don't dress for the part, you won't be considered for the part. The right costume doesn't guarantee you get to Mahogany Row, but the wrong costume guarantees you don't even get a promotion.

Wear the costume to the casting call. To be considered for the part, your costume must first speak to a geek from Personnel, then it must speak to your future boss when you're *Interviewing*.

Get a foot in the door.

Cry a lot when you have to say 'no.'

TOUCHSTONES FOR PEOPLE SELLING THEMSELVES

Interviewing

Most people don't give good interview because most people don't change jobs until it hurts too much to stay where they are. To them, interviewing is a humbling, humiliating process. With no practice, they come across as far less than they are, even if they're super at what they do.

Learning to get hired at the salary you want is nothing more than practice, practice, practice. After you finish this book, go to the library. Read a minimum of ten books on interviewing. Twenty would be better.

Next, go on as many interviews as you can arrange over the next four months. Two a week is great. Don't concentrate on getting a good offer, but do the best you can. You're merely desensitizing yourself to the interview process.

SUBCONSCIOUS LEARNING

After every interview, go to the nearest coffee shop and write down everything you did correctly and everything you did incorrectly. Later, review your notes. When you goofed, figure out what you wish you had done or said instead of what you did. Write that down beside the goof up.

This technique makes it easy for your subconscious to prevent future mistakes of the same kind. It now knows what you're supposed to do in that situation because you told it.

As you go to interview after interview, it becomes natural. After five interviews your anxiety level is cut in half. By the twentieth interview, the whole process seems normal. Eventually you'll be at ease, confident. Once you're there, concentrate on learning how to negotiate a higher salary.

GUIDELINES AND TIPS

Use the subconscious learning technique, above, for any situation you want to master.

As stressed over and over in *Avoid Layoffs,* nothing in this book will do you one damn bit of good if you're unemployed. Get good at interviewing while you have a job. If you go to an interview for a job you really want when you have a good job, you're negotiating from a position of strength. You'll radiate confidence.

Never, never complain about your present work, co-workers, boss or company. You get along famously with anybody and everybody. You're looking for a challenge where you can use more of your skills, use more of your brains or whatever phrases you can say believably.

Don't ask about benefits and pension plans. Ask about promotion opportunities and learning opportunities. Stress what you can do for them, not what they can do for you.

The interviewer's current employees have discovered they're going nowhere. They've become drones and zombies. Two things youth offers that few others have — enthusiasm and energy. Be a high-energy person.

Read every book on body language you can find. Be certain your posture says energetic, confident, relaxed, powerful, interested. Be assertive not aggressive. Show relaxed confidence, not arrogance. Look impressed when he's trying to impress you.

The Personnel geek who talks with you has read inane books on the strategy of interviewing. He likes to play the knowing, clever manipulator. It makes him feel important. Don't let this rattle you.

Be confident, or at least appear to be. Confident people are relaxed and slow. They don't rush. They take their time. They are never early, never late, but exactly on time.

The Personnel geek playing "important executive" likes to walk fast so you have to chase him to keep up as he takes you to meet your future boss. That gives him power. Don't chase! Let him rush. Walk a business-like pace. Let him charge ahead until he has to wait for you. That gives you the power.

SHAKE HANDS WITH EVERYONE

Begin by shaking hands with Personnel geeks and continue to shake hands with everyone you're introduced to. That's what experienced business people do. It gives you a leg up on what's going on emotionally with the other person.

The socially acceptable touching that takes place when shaking hands enables your emotions and subconscious to make lightning value judgements that are quite perceptive. After you shake with the guy who looks like he's ought to be the president, you realize he's nothing more than a frightened, confused little boy.

The woman who acts like a hard-ass is revealed as nothing more than a sweaty palmed actress when you shake her hand. Knowing what's going on with them gives you the edge.

If I can just press flesh with a man
I know how to control him, bring him over.
LYNDON BAINES JOHNSON

You must have a firm, not dainty, handshake. You must not just offer the tips of your fingers! Have your male friends coach you until you come across as a strong, firm person. Much more is coming up in *Kept Down And Out.*

BUZZWORDS FOR INTERVIEWS AND RESUMES

Ability to get along with every type of person. Tactful, loyal, trustworthy, intelligent, dedicated. Willing to make the extra effort. Ability to follow through on ideas. Thorough, attention to detail. Cost conscious. Common sense. Work well under stress and pressure. Conscientious. Integrity, enthusiastic, sense of humor. Work with little or no supervision, self starter. Diplomatic expediter.

HAVE A FULL COMMAND OF ENGLISH, SHUT UP

Do not speak until spoken to. Do not start small talk when walking to meet your future boss. Respond appropriately if the geek starts small talking. When asked a question by the geek or by your future boss, ponder, arrange your thoughts, speak up, then shut up.

Open ended questions are designed to have you reveal more about yourself than you want to. Rehearse your responses to standard and open ended questions from interviewing books. Have your answers down pat. They won't sound practiced to anyone except you. Act as if the interviewer actually asked an intelligent question. Pause, gather yourself. Deliver your lines with energy, eye contact and enthusiasm, then shut up.

THE JOB CHANGING QUESTION

I answered this question at least twenty times during my first six years. "Why have you changed jobs so often?"

> *To gain a variety of experience in my chosen field and expand my skills so I became (notice past tense) a much more valuable employee. Of course, each change was for substantially more than I had been making.*

There is a myth, perpetrated by writers of success books who interview Personnel geeks. It goes like this: people who change jobs often are looked down on. Nah! Only those who don't count look down. They're too frightened to change. It's envy, then anger, plain and simple.

Each of us can bullshit our own self. We get away with it until someone forces us to look. When you come along at 26, making $34k after five different jobs in two years, at first they're envious, then pissed off because you force them to realize what cowards they are. Caution!

Success book writers also advise: tell the truth, the whole truth and nothing but the truth. Ignore that Girl Scout crap! Those authors have never done what they're telling you how to do, interview for a job. They've only interviewed Personnel geeks who said it's important to tell the truth.

THE CAREER PLAN QUESTION

Personnel geek: "Where do you see yourself in five years?" Career plans feature job titles in a steady, logical progression. One does not leap from Administrative Assistant to Senior Systems Analyst in a year. Think about, dream about what you want. Write down the dream version, tempered with reality. Edit it. Summarize it. Memorize it. Deliver it with confidence in a matter-of-fact manner to Personnel geeks. More important, be ready anytime opportunity presents herself.

She, Ms. Opportunity, shows up during coffee break at a trade show. While everyone is standing around making small talk, Mr.

Big Shot from General Bull asks, "What are your career plans?" When preparation meets opportunity you won't mumble, "Yeah, uh, oh make lotsa money, uh, move to Idaho an' do stained glass, duh."

CAN WE BE SURE YOU'LL STAY?

Sell them on the idea you're not going to leave for *kirsch, kinder und kusch* (Hitler's idea of a woman's place, church, children and kitchen). Persuade them by the way you dress, talk, walk and sit. Speak of career paths and long range plans. *Forever Yours,* is the subliminal song you sing.

The best way to handle this question, and their concern, is to answer it before they ask it. Personnel geek: What about your long range goals?

> *I want a challenging, consuming career across time. I know I'll have to pay my dues. I accept that. But I want to grow with a company, have a solid future.*

Always work these thoughts into the interview: You don't have a baby or want children. Your career is a lifetime activity, a full-time lifetime activity. You're in this for the long haul. Your attitude says that, your uniform says that. You say that in plain English during the interview.

They want to believe it. They will believe it if you look the part and act the part. Appearance is everything. Reality is nothing. Recite the corporate rosary as if it had some magical power. It does, to true believers.

SCOUTING FOR PROMOTION POSSIBILITIES

Most companies promote by attrition. A dweeb has to die, quit or get fired for you to advance. Look around as you pass through future work areas. Notice if only geezers are managers. Can you spot any young managers? If there aren't any, forget about promotions. It's still okay to take the job if there's a substantial raise.

NO ENGAGEMENT RING FOR THE INTERVIEW

Let the mid-life middle manager fantasize about being able to date you. As a female in the male's world of corporations, you're playing with the deck stacked against you. Use every weapon you've got. They use every ploy and deception known. If they'd play fair, you'd play fair.

BOOK VALUE

Personnel finds out how much to offer you by checking a book. They look up: Female, 26, BA, two years experience, then offer 10 percent less than the book says.

Salaries in these books are the same in every company. Every company swears they took a survey of the industry. In reality, companies swap information so they don't have to pay what the free market demands. It's illegal but it saves them millions.

The book is only rendered useless when you are already making more than the book says you should be making. Do that by changing companies every possible chance you get.

PAID TO CHANGE

Job jumpers earn more because they have to be paid to leave the security of Mother Cow, Inc. and her milk-swollen breasts of comfort and convenience. No one likes change, everyone knows that, so they'll pay you more to change.

After three companies, you'll be making 40 percent more than contemporaries who stayed put. You'll know three times as much about how companies do things, how Personnel geeks operate, how to interview, how to get what you want, when you want, for the price you're willing to pay.

HOW CHEAP ARE YOU?

Don't discuss money until you have a definite, firm sign of interest, an offer. Hard to get works. When he asks how much:

> *Quite frankly, there are some assignments I wouldn't consider for several times what I'm making now. Possibly, there may be something I would be interested in for not too much more than I'm making now. It's really hard to answer until I know more about the specifics of the assignment.*

The "clever" personnel geek asks: Which is more important, the money or the work?

> *Both to a degree. If I'm not happy doing a job, no amount of money would be sufficient. If the money is right and I'm bored, the money doesn't matter.*

NEGOTIATING — ROUND ONE

When interviewing with your future boss, discretely notice his extension number on the desk phone. Note his mail station.

Write these down. Don't trust your memory. Your brain is too busy to be trusted.

As you start this ten year journey, you have to negotiate with a Personnel geek trying to look good by low-balling you. He also does it because that's the only power he has. Your salary will come from your department's budget. Personnel geeks have only ego involved. It's not Personnel's money.

After your first job, interviewing and negotiating salary is courtship. They want what you've got. Turn down the first offer. It makes you powerful. You don't hop into bed on the first date, do you? Don't hop into Company B on the first offer.

Getting hired is kinda like getting seduced. If you're easy or a pushover, the guy thinks you aren't worth much. If you play too hard to get, you don't get seduced. The ideal is finding something in between.

The way to get the best offer is to ask for twenty percent knowing you'd take ten. If you ask for ten they'll offer five. It's like that everywhere in life.

Even after the geek has read your cover letter that stated your present salary is $27k, he will "make an offer of $28k. *Translation:* see how little you'll take. After the firm offer, turn it down. They'll want a number. Give them a reason and a range.

> *I'm making $27. I'm looking for something between $33 and $36.*

The difference between $33k and $28k is insignificant to the corporation but it makes him feel important if he can screw you out of $5k.

HOW TO SAY 'NO'

Decline with sadness and regrets. My mentor taught me, "When you have to say 'no,' cry a lot before you say 'no.' Then they're not angry, they feel sorry for you!" It works. I cried many a time to Personnel geeks and future bosses. Not literal tears, just regret filled apologies, over and over.

Cry a lot. Appreciate the consideration . . . wish you could accept such an interesting and challenging position . . . would have loved working with Mr. Soandso and Ms. Wazhernam . . . Appreciate everyone's time and effort . . . deeply regret it but you have to decline. Why? "The salary's just not something I can live with."

The person who says "no" has all the power. This is an unchanging law of relationships, business, personal and romantic. Yes, romantic in particular.

After time passes, from one nanosecond to one month, they'll increase the offer. At first, they often feign being offended, calling you ungrateful or whatever. Apologize, but stand your ground. You have a job. You don't need them. They need you. They want you. All you have to do is say "no" and wait.

NEGOTIATING — ROUND TWO

Your future boss usually says during, or at the end of the interview, "I have no control over what they'll pay you." Absolute crap! All he has to say, "Hire her. Give her what she wants." But he's saving his budget so he can give a big raise to Debbie Doubledees, hoping she'll go out with him. The less he gives you, the more he gives her.

Here's the essence: The only thing that works is asking for more and settling for less.

APPLY PRESSURE

After you get back to your office, use the number you copied from your future boss's phone. Call and apologize for declining Personnel's offer. Again, use regret and sorrow. Say you're so sorry. Tell him you wish you could have "come aboard" and other inane amenities everyone says and expects to hear.

This makes you a player, someone who knows the game and the unwritten rules. If you can't call, write him immediately and say the same things. Do not tell Personnel you are doing this.

Your future boss said it's out of his hands but if he wants you he'll pressure Personnel. The more you make, the more pressure he applies. If you're in the low $20s he'll say something like, "Dick, this is Tom Lopez in Engineering. I wanted to hire Donna Young last week but our offer's too low. What can you do? Bring her on board as *Senior* Administrative Assistant?"

If you're in the $30s, he'll increase the pressure with something like, "Dick, this is Tom Lopez. Ralph Sharpe and I talked with Donna Young last week. We were impressed. Ralph wants her. Our offer was low. Bring her on board. We'd appreciate it. Thanks."

As soon as anyone applies pressure, the geek meets your offer within a thousand as a feeble attempt to save his own face. It's not the money. It's his ego. Nobody else cares about his loss of face. He's a clerk in a three-piece suit. They all knew that. Now he does.

If they want you, they must pay you more than you're making. In the interview, you radiated that you like your present job and you are good at it. You are not an economy model. You're deluxe. Quality. They know they have to make it worth your while to change jobs.

LAST MINUTE FACE SAVING

One of the last manipulative moves your future boss or the geek makes is, "We can't arrange the salary you want, but we can give you a salary review and a raise after 90 days instead of after 6 months."

This seldom results in a raise unless you assertively keep the issue on the table beginning about day 75. If you don't, things just drift and drift. You're stuck with the salary you accepted.

HARD-TO-GET IS PURSUED, THEN GETS MORE

When a man is trying to date you, the scenario is exactly the same. Nobody likes a pushover. Even if you hate every single second at Company B, don't jump at the offer from Company C. You're a busy, important woman at Company B. You'll consider it.

Fire me up with your resistance, put me in the mood.
'Til It Shines BOB SEEGAR

As Ringer commands, negotiate only from strength. You have a job. Other companies are interested in you. You'll choose between good offers, not the lesser of two evils. If you've read Harry Browne's *How I Found Freedom In An Unfree World,* you know that already. If not, read it. Life will change! It's listed in *Must Books*.

ALWAYS BE TOUGH

When a headhunter or a competitor calls, you're *not* job hunting, but you always listen to interesting offers. After a raise or promotion, you're simply informing headhunters of a change in your status. Send a new resume with a note, "Updated info in case something special arises."

Never pick up the check when the interview takes place over lunch. The same with headhunters. Don't offer to split the tab. You're being courted. Act like it. Don't be nice. Don't be sweet. Be businesslike. You have all the power.

INTERVIEW FOR SUCCESS — OVERALL ADVICE

Radiate you're deciding which of the many fabulous offers you'll accept. Radiate you're worth hiring and having. Radiate you're interested in contributing your immense abilities but only to a company that deserves you. Radiate that whichever company you choose, that company will be extremely lucky.

Chris Mullin, a short, slow, white boy in the NBA, practices his outside jump shot 300 times a day. When the real game is on the line, his shot is not something he gets anxious about or even has to think about. It's a reflex, automatic.

That's the way you want to be. When the shot is there, you'll make it — the right comment or ask just the right question, shift your posture just right to communicate you are confident, radiate you're the right person for this position while making them feel ashamed for offering only $42k.

When you're ready to break through the invisible barrier of the magic number, interviewers won't be a big concern. They'll be convinced by your calm, confident manner.

First impressions are lasting impressions. Get good at interviewing by interviewing. When you're relaxed and assertive you make a memorable first impression. Read those books on interviewing and go interviewing until it's as natural as a sunrise.

There are some other excellent interviewing and negotiating tips in *Temps Get To Choose*. But, when you're first starting out, you have to deal with *Personnel* geeks.

The second thing you must do as the new CEO is fire everyone in Personnel. Make supervisors who direct the work, hire the people who do the work.
Up The Organization ROBERT TOWNSEND

Personnel separates the wheat from the chaff then hires the chaff.
The Fast Track JOHN BUDD

Personnel

At the beginning of this ten year journey to independence, you must deal with Personnel. Later you'll be able to bypass them but for now you must master dealing with these geeks.

Budd's quote explains what they actually do, nothing constructive, productive or useful. Everyone in Personnel knows deep down he's a parasite. To pretend they aren't, they call themselves Human Resource Administrators.

Personnel's only useful purpose is to comply with the infinite bureaucratic red tape imposed by government to "ensure" employees are treated fairly. There is a ton of paper that must be faxed, be filed, be found, be copied, be forwarded, be fooled with. Personnel also administers benefits, which also requires tons of paper as well as experts in trivial aspects of the law. In short, Personnel people are bureaucratic clerks, nothing more.

Personnel's secondary responsibility is to hire underlings. They are not permitted to deal with any employee who makes big money as an expert or specialist. Valuable, important employees are the responsibility of the person who hires them. Personnel screws it up. Clerks are not diplomats or good negotiators.

Personnel people can only hurt you, they cannot help you. But you must get past these officious assholes.

Condescending. Impertinent. Meddling. That's what these self-important little people are. The only person in the universe they can lord it over is you, the applicant for a lower level job. The only way they can be above you is to not hire you! Ethnic tokens in these positions are extremely officious since they know they can't be fired, no matter what. It's their chance to strike a blow for the downtrodden and persecuted. Don't get mad, get past them.

PLAYERS IN THE GAME

The object of the game, from the Personnel geek's viewpoint, is to prevent you from talking to the person who can hire you. If he can't do that, he'll settle for paying you as little as possible while acting important. The possible cast includes:

Player 1. Young man in a three piece suit, pretending to all the world he's an "executive." He even wears the contrived wire-rimmed glasses and suspenders. This clown's formal and stiff. He doesn't realize he looks like a little boy playing businessman. Play along. Get past him.

Player 2. Fat divorcee of 46 who hates the sight of you. Her husband ran away with his slim, trim 22 year old secretary last year. You remind her that she's over-the-hill, going down the other side in flames. She'll be cold, rude and abrupt. She'd love to disqualify you and hire that lump who was sitting beside you in the waiting area. Be polite. Get past her.

Player 3. Adult male also dressed like a real executive. He wants to date you, may even ask inappropriate personal questions. Don't come on even a tiny bit with any male in Personnel. Any encouragement makes him think you'll take care of him if he takes care of you. Don't get flustered. Get past him.

A PERSONNEL STORY

This is a typical hiring scenario. The Manager of Administration has an opening. An intelligent, hard working, woman quit for a better job. He filled out the "rec" WTF-301R-93a, Requisition for New Employee, and sent it in to Personnel the day after she gave her two week notice. That was three weeks ago.

The paper has piled up in Administration with no one to push it. Other departments need that paper. Everyone's calling.

Manufacturing can't assemble shipping kits until they have written authorization. Yesterday, the Manager of Administration had someone who doesn't know what she's doing work overtime on the backup. Now it's totally screwed up.

Another week goes by. The VP of Manufacturing gets reamed in the staff meeting by the VP of Sales for not shipping. The VP of Manufacturing looks directly at the VP of Administration and roars he doesn't have the paperwork to ship. The VP of Administration promises to solve it.

After the staff meeting he calls the Manager of Administration into his office and screams, "Art chewed my ass in front of JB. What in hell's with the shipping authorizations?" The Manager whips out the "rec," points to the submittal date and tells him Personnel hasn't sent any applicants over for an interview. Struggling to save face he meekly adds, "I wrote a memo reminding them of our needs last week. I sent a copy to you," as if anyone "important" reads memos from underlings.

The VP of Administration calls the Manager of Personnel and threatens to have him sold into slavery if the position isn't filled immediately.

Everyone wants the first semi-presentable person who walks through the door hired. Everyone's pissed off, jumpy and skittish. They want the yelling to stop.

Nobody except Personnel cares if you've only been at your present job three months. Nobody except Personnel cares if you make $27k but are asking $33k. Sales wants the product shipped. Manufacturing wants Administration to send the authorization. Administration wants you to push the paper. To everybody except Personnel, $33k is insignificant.

UNDERSTANDING PERSONNEL'S POSITION

From the Manager of Personnel down to the Personnel Department Receptionist, not a one of them has ever had a real job in the real world. Even worse, they haven't even been out into the real world of their own company.

None of them has any idea what Administration does other than ". . . it's something about keeping track of stuff on computers." They don't have the foggiest notion of what type of person is best suited to push shipping authorization paperwork. They have no idea what type of experience is best suited for that work because they don't know what the person does. In short, Personnel geeks don't have a clue about what's going on inside the company or outside the company.

The geek in Personnel pretends there's no pressure on him. He postures like it is a skilled position when, in fact, a high school sophomore can easily do the job and have plenty of time left over to gossip, attend baby showers and gab on the phone.

The geek interviewing you makes $25k after four years, so he's beyond envious that you want $33k. But he cannot disqualify you because they want the position filled immediately. So, all he can do is pretend he's important.

Jerkoffs like this attempt to convince you they're important and powerful by making you wait and wait in the reception area. During the interview they look over your resume pretending they can tell if you're being truthful. In reality, these geeks can't tell a good worker from a sociopathic child molester.

WHY THEY PAY HEADHUNTERS SO MUCH

The company needs genuinely talented and competent people for some jobs. But, because of the company's own idiotic policies, they don't develop them within the company. Personnel doesn't recruit important people not just because they are bureaucratic bumblers, but because the incompetent Manager of Personnel wants to avoid criticism. He convinces Top Management it's a good idea to pay the outrageous fees headhunters charge because he doesn't want to be blamed if the new hire is another dunce.

THEY WILL CHECK ON YOU

When you first start out, you will be checked on. They check your degrees and your previous salaries. Bureaucrats know they won't be criticized if they pay you between ten and twenty percent more than your last job. Everyone wants to avoid criticism at all costs, as will be explained later.

After your second job they usually don't bother checking degrees, assuming their "sister" company in the family of major corporations checked. They always check your present salary. There are many more tips on dealing with Personnel upcoming in *Get That Raise*.

Once you've gotten the position you want for the money you want, office politics are crucial when you're *New On The Job*.

Take the tone of the company that you are in.
LETTER TO HIS SON 1747 LORD CHESTERFIELD

Whatever your hand finds to do,
do it with your might; for there is no work
or device or knowledge or wisdom in the grave
where you are going.
ECCLESIASTES 9:10

New On The Job

It's easy to get rid of you before the 90 day probation period is over, afterward, nearly impossible. During probation the primary goal is to create the belief in your boss's mind that he made the right choice by hiring you.

First impressions are lasting impressions. Your boss will introduce you around or will have his secretary or assistant do it. When you meet someone, man or woman, reach out your hand and shake. Look each person in the eye, in a friendly, relaxed manner say, "Nice to meet you, Marilyn." If you make small talk, use the person's name during the conversation and in saying "bye." That burns their name into your memory.

SHORTEST PENCIL VS LONGEST MEMORY

At your desk, draw a diagram of the area with everyone's desk shown. Write people's names where they sit. A location added to a name and a face helps you remember. Jot down anything revealed during the introduction or small talk, such as, "Donna Young, this is Joanna Lopez. She's our LAN expert."

Everyone, including you and me, appreciates being remembered by name. It makes us feel important. Everyone likes to feel important. Make everyone feel important.

Beside each person's name, jot down what your gut-level reaction was when you met him. Make a preliminary decision about that person based on your intuition and the emotions generated when you touched him while shaking hands. In particular, you need to know who hates you simply because you are you. Second priorities are detecting fundamentally dishonest, manipulative politicians. Any and all gut-level reactions are helpful. That's all you have to go by in the beginning.

If you can't remember someone's name, go to the person who introduced you around unless it was your boss. Don't bother him with this. If your boss introduced you around, go to his secretary. Discreetly point out the person you can't remember and say, "I've got everyone's name except I can't remember who that guy is." Write his name on your diagram.

LOW AND SLOW

Your most important task is to make certain nobody sees you as a threat to take his job. Keep a low profile for weeks. Keep your eyes open and your mouth shut. Fit in, blend in. Keep your thoughts and opinions to yourself about everything. Offend no one. Make no waves. Be polite and civil under all circumstances, especially when you are tested by other females.

You're being watched by every fish in this tank. Limit it to one personal call per day of no more than two minutes the first week. Only a few extremely short calls a day for the next month. Most companies have monitoring systems. A printout of every call you make, by cost and duration, goes to your supervisor weekly.

Keep a semi-neat desk and area. Too neat means you don't have enough to do. Too messy means you're a pig or a disorganized lump.

You must be above suspicion the entire 90 days. At lunch or coffee break, don't take even a minute longer than the allotted time. Don't leave early or come back late.

Do not gossip. Diplomatically withdraw when it starts, if possible. Otherwise, do not contribute.

When a man offers to open a door or some other such etiquette, don't decline with feminist looks or rhetoric. Smile and thank him. Assume it's a polite pass, nothing more. Don't encourage him in any way.

Observe the politics. Identify the players, the cows and the deadwood. Determine what the alliances and cliques are and who belongs to which. Figure out who the department squealer is, who the rebel is, who the flirt and playboy are. Notice who has the boss's ear, who's left out, who's the boss's favorite and who's his enemy.

Who in the department is the most frightened? Who is the most genuinely confident? Quickly identify those who hate you. There will be at least one, possibly three.

Identify nepotism. In particular, find out if any of the big boss's children are on the payroll. Make a special effort to avoid them until your probation is complete. These kids are extremely dangerous. Everyone resents them being here. Everyone resents anyone who associates with them, assuming the association is nothing more than sucking up.

Carefully make certain you do nothing to make peers feel insecure or threatened beyond the normal terror incompetents experience when they encounter a new face.

Decorate your area with company pictures or neutral pictures. Resist the urge to "'spress yo'sef."

Don't attract attention. Remember, 90 days is all you have to survive. Don't do so much work that you make others look bad. Do just enough to show your boss you can do the job. After probation you can begin to look like a rising star.

ABSOLUTE NO NO'S AND YES YES'S

These tips apply for the rest of your career, not just when you are new on the job. Although most seem obvious, some women don't realize these are mandatory.

Never bring or have flowers delivered to the office. When working weekends, always bring two dozen donuts to share with co-workers. Never carry a brown bag or lunch pail.

No matter where you are, never: file your nails, chew gum, smoke cigarettes, use a toothpick, wear an ankle bracelet or charm bracelet, let a tattoo be seen, drink beer, giggle, act cute, wear a cartoon character, carry a backpack, listen to a Walkman.

At your desk, never: drink out of anything other than a elegant personal cup or styrofoam cup (no soda cans); eat or snack; listen to the radio; gab on the phone; remove your shoes; let your hair down; sniff and snuff; blow your nose; nap or snooze; slouch; cry; scratch yourself; adjust your bra or panty hose; blot lipstick; fix makeup; brush your hair; look in a mirror, even the tiny one in the lipstick case; read a magazine, novel or newspaper.

On your desk, never have: designer water; affirmation calendar; more than one personal picture; anything cute; disk of candy for visitors; flowers or anything feminine; ultra-expensive desk items, such as pen and pencil holder; any clutter; novels, magazines or newspapers; your purse.

On your desk or work table always have: your discreet nameplate; sophisticated coffee thermos (ideal) or pot with styrofoam cups for visitors; one 5 by 7 personal picture in tasteful frame; and a refined day planner.

LIFE IN A FISHBOWL

The office is like a giant aquarium. There are few places where you can avoid being seen. Bosses watch workers. Workers watch each other and watch the clock.

If you've owned an aquarium you know how important maintaining the balance is. It's the same in the closed universe of the office. In an aquarium, every fish knows the limits of his territory. Each fish knows which other fish are dangerous and which ones he can chase away.

The fish are upset you got dropped into their tank. Each fish knew where he fit in the eco-system. Now, here you come and disrupt the delicate balance. You are an unknown, a change, a threat to every fish in the bowl.

Females are envious and want to rake your eyes out. Males are threatened. You might show one up by doing more, faster and better. You're "only a girl." He might lose his carefully constructed pseudo prestige in the tank.

TESTED IN THE TANK

The fish have to find out how dangerous you are. To find where you fit in the pecking order, they test you. This happens two or three weeks after you've arrived.

The Situation: you are asked by a co-worker to do his shit work. You don't know if he is higher ranking than you. Your response: "I'm not certain my duties include that. I'll check with MISTER Johnson. I'll ask him if it's okay to put this aside to sort your mailing labels."

Stand up and walk toward the boss's office. If the tester doesn't call you back, enter the boss's office. Ask the boss a question that doesn't make you look stupid. Go back. Look the tester right in the eyes and say, "Sorry. Gotta stay on this."

The Situation: After probation another fish will test you in a similar manner. Your response is different. This time you know the slimy creature is not your superior. "I work for MISTER Johnson, not you." Do NOT smile. Your tone of voice, body language and facial expression says, "Drop dead." Go immediately back to what you were doing.

The purpose of trying to unload shit work is twofold (a) establish he's above you (b) get out of doing unpleasant work. His goal is to put it into your mind that you must do what he says. Your response says, "I can't be intimidated by your childish crap."

THE END RUN TEST

Many men, and some women, will go around you, directly to your boss with problems in areas you're responsible for. Some will be testing to see if you'll fight. Others will be trying to push you out.

Those who need visibility from your boss to advance will do this again and again. They see you as an obstacle preventing them from doing their "important" job the most efficient way, directly with your boss.

Confront these twits instantly. Don't make a scene. Don't act like a girl who had her dolly stolen. As with every conflict, attempt to resolve it with diplomacy first. Assert yourself with, "Ron, I'm responsible for man-loading vu-graphs. Bring the changes to me."

He'll manipulate with, "Oh, uh, JB wanted Dick (your boss) to, uh, be up to speed on the latest changes, so he told me to take those three right to him, uh."

Your response, "I'm responsible for man-loading vu-graphs. Let me know if there are hot changes. I'll get the artwork started and let Dick know. That way *we* can be sure the whole package is ready for the presentation."

He might try, "Sorry, but you haven't been here long enough to know how JB is." Your response, "Just how is JB?" After a pause, he'll mumble "A tyrant . . . gets pissed off, fires people." Your immediate reply, "Sounds like you could get into big trouble if changes don't get included. Bring them to me (and I'll save your ass)."

If he does it again, write a memo to your boss with copies to End Runner's boss and End Runner himself. State what just happened. Describe the procedure. Explain why it is done that way. Explain what goes wrong if the procedure is not followed. State that End Runner has done this before and you have explained the procedure to him. Close with, "I'd appreciate your help in clarifying this situation for me."

Notice the vague, oblique wording of the closing. Just exactly what does that mean, anyway? In reality, it means that if your boss is the typical Tower Of Jello, he won't do anything. But End Runner doesn't know that. He's certain he's been busted. If your boss or End Runner's boss have even half a brain, they'll insist the procedure be followed to prevent JB from chewing their ass. Either way you stopped him and passed your first big test, but tests continue. New fish are tested until they prove dangerous.

Each fish who tests you is an exploiter. In the future, never trust or rely on any of them. They have revealed themselves as the cheats, manipulators, liars, deceivers and as eternal little people. Have little to do with little people.

SKIN THE CAT NINE DIFFERENT WAYS

Most young people believe, as all deadwood believe, there's only one right way to do something. Such as, only one way to compile the manhours vs foreign sales. Not so. Each company does the same things. Each does those same things differently.

Resist the temptation to say, "We didn't do it that way at General Cow." That gets the sheep-employees upset. They have a hard enough time just doing the job. They don't have the ability or the energy to think about the best way to do the job.

The key to becoming a valuable employee is to learn all the ways of doing the same thing. At your eighth company, after you've mastered diplomatic, save-their-face ways to present ideas, you'll look like a superstar for developing a "new" way that saves time and money. Even better, it makes your boss look like a genius for hiring you. But even better than that, he loves you because you share the spotlight with him.

STAY HUNGRY

At the second, third and fourth companies, only stay until you get a raise. Move on for ten or more percent at every opportunity. The longer you stay, the softer, lazier you become. We all tend to relax and coast once we get into a routine and have mastered the job.

Don't let it happen. Stay hungry. Keep that edge. Get out there and keep searching for a higher paying, better, more interesting job.

RELAXING IS WHAT YOU DO BETWEEN JOBS

When I started out, I hated having only two weeks of freedom a year. My co-workers lived for those two fleeting weeks. After spending months planning how to cram a year's worth of pleasure into 14 days, they came back exhausted, pissed off and deeper in debt.

I went directly from my first job to Company B. Another 50 weeks were staring me in the face before I'd be free! The next time I changed companies I pleaded that it would take me about two months to complete several projects that only I could do, plus I had to train my replacement. I suggested mid-August as a report date. They agreed, complimenting me on my admirable conscientiousness and loyalty.

I gave my two week notice immediately. The first three weeks of six carefree weeks of freedom were spent visiting California's tourist attractions, amusement parks and Las Vegas. The last three weeks I did nothing but hang out at the beach and read science fiction.

That's how I've changed jobs ever since. Later, when I was making more money, I was saving more money. It became eight weeks of freedom.

I recommend this freedom as the most powerful thing you can do to safeguard your mental health during the coming ten years. One's brain gets defrosted. One's perspective of what's actually important gets verified and reinforced. The unreality of corporate life becomes crystal clear. One's self-esteem gets forcefully disassociated from what they think and what they believe. In short, you regain a healthy perspective on the world.

That's a perspective you'll need since you must deal with *Whacked Out Co-Workers* every day until you free yourself for six more weeks.

The mass of men lead lives of quiet desperation.
HENRY DAVID THOREAU

Hell is other people.
JOHN PAUL SARTRE

Whacked Out Co-Workers

If you don't understand how lonely, frightened and neurotic your co-workers are, you'll never understand why things are so screwed up. If you don't understand why it's so screwed up, you can't develop ways to make it better and earn a promotion.

PRIVATE LIVES, EMPTY LIVES

In *Decision Making,* you learn about the private lives of Middle Management. Co-workers are even worse.

If you followed just about any of them home at night, you'd see how barren their lives are. You'd grasp why they fight so desperately to prevent change at work. You'd know why they value their little, insignificant jobs so highly. It's all they have.

Their wives are fat lumps who no longer care about themselves or anyone else. But, male co-workers don't have the courage to get divorced. After ten years of marriage, they have no meet-talk-date skills left, if they ever had them. Worse, they see themselves as failures, unable to attract another female, yet afraid to be alone.

Divorce is out of the question for the miserable wives. They have no job skills and three kids. They can't get a new husband, they're too fat. Like their husbands, after ten years they have no social skills. Their only escape is food and television.

RIGIDITY AND FRIGIDITY

Everything these couples believed in when they were young turned out to be false. They desperately don't want to know that. They desperately don't want to know they are miserable. They desperately dig their ruts deeper and deeper. They desperately do not want to break their routine. Any change may cause their carefully constructed false reality to collapse.

Subconsciously, each spouse feels trapped! Lurking just below the surface of awareness, intense feelings of betrayal, resentment, bitterness, disappointment, frustration, and hopelessness fester.

Day in and day out these rigid people make certain everything stays exactly the same. Any change might disrupt the carefully constructed self-deception and self-blinding. Emotions are pushed down, pushed away. If an emotion is felt, even a pleasant emotion, it might open the floodgates, then all those unpleasant emotions would come roaring to the surface! No change is wanted. No change is permitted. Eventually, one year is like every other once they've achieved the desired state of numbness. They've surrendered completely and await death for release from all this. Eric Berne, famous psychotherapist and author of *Games People Play,* calls this game, Waiting For Rigor Mortis.

GENERATION X IN ACTION

The children of these couples have problems. Now there's an understatement!

> *Ninety percent of families are dysfunctional*
> *and the other ten percent are in denial.*
> JOHN BRADSHAW

By the time these kids are teenagers, they realize they're a burden, not wanted, not respected. They react! Flunk school, run away, get pregnant, get arrested for drugs, and innumerable other ways to escape reality or strike back at these parents.

MINIMUM EXCUSABLE

Their father or mother, your co-worker is, shall we say, preoccupied at the office. Combine all of this with the fact that most of your co-workers realize there is no chance to succeed at work:

> *A man strives for promotion and reward and success up to a certain point, but, earlier or later almost all realize*

that whatever they do they are not going to get much further. Some will leave; a great many of the rest reach a switch-off point where they say to themselves, 'The difference between going on bursting my guts and taking it easy is about $1000 a year before tax. So, I'm not going to try.' They then change from aiming at the maximum possible to the minimum excusable.

***Management and Machiavelli* ANTHONY JAY**

THE OFFICE AS A LIFE

For most of them, going to work is an escape from a desperately futile situation at home. The job is all they have to put some contrived meaning into their lives, something to keep them from facing how miserable and disappointed they are.

Yes, their job is crucial to their existence. Yes, their job is all they have. Then why, you ask, don't they do their jobs conscientiously and efficiently?

For most, the office is just a paycheck and a place to get away from their spouse. For divorced women, it's a place to escape "the kids." Very few people care one way or other about the result of their efforts.

Most people, even those who do have a life outside of the office, don't like what they do, don't enjoy the task itself. They just do it to get it over with as quickly as possible. How well or how quickly or how accurately they perform their task is not important. Nobody has a sense of accomplishment, a sense of a job well done. Pushing paper is easy. There's a paycheck on Friday. It's the path of least resistance.

Liberty means responsibility. That is why most men dread it.

GEORGE BERNARD SHAW

Few, if any, of your co-workers want to be independent, self-reliant individuals. Being a member of the flock gives them a sense of safety in numbers. This, in combination with the loss of a sense of community in today's urban world, makes doing a good job quite low on their priority lists. The only companionship and socializing these lonely, empty people have is at General Cow. At work, they feel kinship, accepted and appreciated. Everyone has chosen exactly the same deadness.

COMPANY-AS-COMMUNITY

Today's apartment, condo, suburban tract home universe is unnatural. By nature, we humans like to get together. We have a felt need to talk and share experiences. Each of us wants to feel like we count, feel like we are members of the group. But there is no campfire to gather 'round, no village square, no small general store where our gregarious needs can be met.

The small towns of our ancestors were places where, to survive, everybody had to interact day in and day out, week in and week out, year in and year out. To survive today, we only have to interact with strangers at the supermarket, gas station, drug store, restaurant and such. These interactions meet no gregarious needs.

The office is like a small town. Everyone must interact with everyone else. Your co-workers enjoy this aspect of the office. It gives them a sense of belonging. They don't feel their loneliness.

The company-as-community provides them with bowling nights, ski clubs, softball teams, company picnics. They have a small town newspaper (house organ), birthday parties (cake at work and birthday cards), block parties (department lunches). They even have ceremonies to mark special days (retirement and going away lunches) and annual celebrations (Christmas dance).

As years pass, your co-workers develop a sense of security that comes from familiarity. They consider themselves residents of a small town. They think their "neighbors" care about them. They actually believe General Cow is Smallville, USA, where everyone helps each other.

The company-as-community fulfills your co-workers' social needs. They *need* the company, not vice versa.

UNDERSTANDING THEIR LACK OF SELF-ESTEEM

Everyday you watch yourself in action. Everyday you judge yourself by your own standards and your own values. You are the harshest judge in the world. You can't be bought off! Everyday you decide if you like, admire and respect yourself. Healthy self-esteem is the result of living up to one's own expectations while remaining true to one's own values. That's the definition of *integrity*.

Just about every co-worker feels deep down inside that he does not earn his pay. He believes in his heart that he's stealing from the company. Deep down he knows he's not worthy. He lives in terror that he'll be discovered.

Most resign themselves to the drudgery, feeling they deserve no better and believe they're incapable of doing better within the company or at a different company. They retire-in-place and enjoy the social life as they await rigor mortis.

Others, desperate for a sense of self-esteem, judge themselves by what others think. If their co-workers and bosses think they are good persons, they think of themselves that way. They spend nearly all their time seeking the approval of others.

HANDLING APPROVAL SEEKERS

If you're lucky, these types in your department seek approval by working hard and efficiently at their assigned tasks. If you're unlucky, these types seek approval by being a department snitch or a boring socializer who wastes everyone's time. Another unlucky version seeks approval by regaling one and all with stories of his accomplishments and brilliance outside of the company.

The self-esteem they gain is not real, but it is all they have! They're extremely dangerous to anybody who doesn't understand their motivation. Being so dependent on the company, they behave like heroin addicts about to lose their only source when anyone criticizes the company.

They're extremely protective of each other because they need each other. Never suggest to anyone that Barney Boring or Linda Loveme should be fired for wasting everyone's time. They'll band together and launch a five-front campaign to destroy you. Forewarned is forearmed.

To deal with braggarts, establish your disinterest at the earliest opportunity. Re-establish your disinterest every time they come around. Rudeness is all that works, "Sorry Dick, gotta get this done," as you stand up and sort through a pile of papers. Interestingly, they don't mind and move on to the next potential approval source.

Handling an approval seeker who works hard is nothing more than making certain you don't invade his area of responsibility. Do not interfere with his input, his process or say anything bad about his output. Your boss wants this guy left alone so he keeps producing.

Don't propose any ideas, no matter how obvious, that might disturb the approval seeker's work flow unless it helps him get even more approval. Before you take an idea to your boss, discuss it with the approval seeker. Present it so he sees that by producing more he'll gain even more approval if your ideas get put into place.

THE AUSCHWITZ SYNDROME AT WORK

The longer you're unhappy, the more normal it seems to be unhappy. Eventually, being unhappy becomes your natural state. You don't remember what it was like to be happy. You're not disappointed, not upset. You don't expect to be happy, so you don't even try. You don't force yourself to change.

This phenomenon was named for how the inmates of Nazi concentration camps behaved when American GIs liberated them. The poor wretches wouldn't leave the death camps. They had to be tended inside the barbed wire, among the filth and disease. They couldn't and wouldn't change. Misery was their normal state.

In marriage counseling, this phenomenon is credited with enabling people to remain in unhappy marriages for decades. It's obviously behind so many people staying in unhappy job situations for a lifetime.

The longer your co-workers have been unhappy, the easier it is for them to accept their unhappiness as normal. Don't open the gates of their private Auschwitz! It makes them confront reality, forces them take responsibility for their misery. They become extremely pissed off and plot revenge!

Warning! As soon as you realize you are unhappy, get rid of the problem: roommates, boyfriend, fiance, job, parents, friends. Do not tolerate being unhappy. You'll accept it as normal. GET OUT!

HOUSE ORGANS AND APPROVAL

The company newspaper is called the house organ because it only plays the company song. It's incapable of playing anything other than "Everything's Coming Up Roses for The Company and Our Team." It plays this song in the middle of massive layoffs brought about by the gross incompetence of Top

Management, now forced to sell because they pissed away billions in a lame attempt to prevent a takeover two years ago.

As stunningly stupid as this sounds, getting the equivalent of a kindergarten gold star keeps most cows standing quietly chewing their cuds, while they let themselves be sucked dry. A gold star prevents most cows from mooing, causing an uproar in the barn. Uproars happen when one or more of the cows moos out loud that the work they do is not necessary or moos that it can be done differently so money and time are saved, or worst of all moos that the chief cow doesn't have a clue.

Men will die for a piece of ribbon.

THE FIRST MILITARY LEADER TO BESTOW RIBBONS NAPOLEON

Employee-cows who save the company hundreds of thousands of dollars get a walnut plaque, their picture taken with a VP and a feature story in the organ about how they came up with the savings. Sometimes, but rarely, the company gives them ten percent of the savings for the first year, then nothing.

To buy long-term loyalty, the organ runs big pictures and long stories about the cows who've been in their milking stalls for 30 years, medium sized pictures and stories about cows there for 20 years. Everything gets smaller until there's only a list of names of 5 year cows. But all cows long for the day when their picture is in the organ.

Many cows are genuinely happy. They came from impoverished backgrounds and know what it's like to not have enough to eat, literally. They remember what it was like back in Tennessee or down in Compton, growing up dirt poor. Now, thanks to General Cow, all they have to do is get milked everyday and they can live in something other than a shanty, drive something other than a jalopy and eat something other than beans.

These are loyal cows. They're the equivalent of trustees in a prison. Never underestimate the loyalty of one of these cows. Never trust a trustee.

HAND TO MOUTH

To understand the unremitting fear your co-workers live with, realize that they are financially irresponsible. They'll lose their house and all their toys if they miss as few as eight paychecks!

They've trapped themselves in an endless cycle of hand-to-mouth feeding.

Co-workers seek escape from their forlorn, empty world by spending money they don't have for anything that might bring pleasure, no matter how short-lived — new car, 50-inch tv, boat, jet ski, camping trailer, motorcycle, anything to escape. They don't care how much it costs, only how much the monthly payments are.

They're stuck. They'll never be independent. They have to keep working for the company. Fat, boring lumps, with nothing to look forward to other than two weeks off once a year. Many even dread that, knowing they'll have to spend the entire time with their family.

What have your contemporaries done with their money? A cool truck? Stylish condo? Married with kids? They are trapped because they *need* the job to pay all the bills.

If you save your money as advised in *Capitalist Pig To Be,* when the next recession hits you'll be able to survive with your self-esteem intact.

LOVE *OR* RESPECT

Love or respect, emphasis on *or,* is what each and every single person in the office wants. Your mission is to quietly ask yourself, "Does this person want to be loved or respected?" When you decide, the edge in dealing with him is yours.

There is no middle ground. It's either love or respect. Not genital love. They want what mommy and daddy didn't give them. The ones who had loving, supportive parents or who've been through psychotherapy and resolved those issues, want to be respected.

RELINQUISH INTEGRITY FOR IMPLIED SECURITY

Even if their personal lives are not screwed up, most of your co-workers are essentially serfs, content to work the fields of General Cow in return for "guaranteed" security and comfort.

The company's deal is simple — give us your heart and soul and we'll make certain you never have to worry again. Trouble is, the company only implies, the company only intimates, the company only hints. The company does not put it in writing.

There are no employment contracts or parachutes of any color available to anyone who's not part of Top Management. When the company is sold, the serfs are included. The corporate raider who bought the package sells off all the profitable pieces and walks away. The retirees' health plan, pension plan, the trust plan, the thrift plan, the stock-option plan are worthless. The company's promises are worthless.

SO WHAT? SHE ASKS

Should you end up being in charge, think about this chapter for a long time. Understand what's important to these dregs. Understand why they behave as they do. Understand that you can't change anything unless you have the authority to hire and fire. Even that won't enable you to motivate anybody if unwritten rules forbid firing them.

THE MOST COMMON POLITICAL TRICK

If you can't trash deadwood, deadbeats and the brain dead, you're dead. Being responsible for a task without the authority to accomplish the task is career suicide. Suckering you into taking a job with out the authority to accomplish it is the most often used ploy in office politics. Don't fall for it!

Every single time you're about to be promoted, carefully determine if the authority-to comes with the responsibility-for. During discussions, say bluntly, "I want to be certain I have the authority to replace those who are not performing efficiently with people of my choice." After being assured, write a memo of understanding describing your responsibilities and authority. Send it to whomever will be your new boss and his boss.

If there's hesitation on anyone's part regarding your authority, be suspect of the motives behind the "promotion" and proceed accordingly. Sometimes your own boss is setting you up to fail! Unless your intuition tells you differently, decline the promotion with regrets about a sick mother, or any other lie you have to tell. Get a new job in a different department or company. There's no future here.

Now that you understand your co-workers, let's focus on the males. Most men don't deliberately want you to be *Kept Down And Out* at work, but they do exactly that anyway. Some men do want you kept down and out. Here's how they try. Use my ideas to beat them.

A man of sense only trifles with them,
plays with them, humors and flatters them
as he does with a sprightly and forward child
but he neither consults them about,
nor trusts them with serious matters.
LETTER TO HIS SON 1748 LORD CHESTERFIELD

Kept Down And Out

Many corporate men believe Lord Chesterfield's advice on women. To keep you on the bottom, they use many techniques, some quite subtle. To get on top, you must (a) understand why men do these things (b) know what to do when they try.

But before we get into the details of what men do, it's necessary to explain what drives big companies.

WHAT MAKES THEM TICK?

All major companies are essentially the same. They are lethargic, old milk cows. They absolutely are not strong, robust, growing enterprises. By "major," I mean corporations that are the largest, the top 3000, as tabulated by *Fortune* magazine, known for its annual Fortune 500 list.

Most young men, and most women of all ages, think the driving motive of these companies is to become bigger or better or more efficient or even more profitable. Nah! The single solitary goal is to survive. That means, take no chances.

The secret to making big money working for one of these milk cows is to understand that survival drives every decision. Not growth, not profit, not expansion. Survival is all everyone wants, from the CEO, down through Top Management, down through Middle Management, down through every employee over 35. Once again. Survive. Take no chances!

That goal shapes the management of all Fortune 3000s. Corporate values determine how the goal is achieved. What one values determines one's priorities, right?

The culture within a corporation is the same culture that's outside a corporation, a patriarchal culture with male values, male traditions, male principles. What are some? Hunting, killing, war, rape, pillage, plunder, military organization, fighting, spying, intrigue and politics. Yes, politics.

Okay! Now we're ready to learn some fundamental office politics.

NO HELP WANTED

A guy doesn't let you struggle and fail. He jumps in and does it for you. The person who gave you the assignment thought you were capable of doing it or capable of learning something by trying.

Sometimes when a man does it for you, he's making certain you stay ignorant so you aren't competitive for the promotion. Sometimes he's trying to win your favor so you'll go out with him. Sometimes he's helping a damsel in distress as most men were raised to do. No matter what his motives are, he continues to see you as incapable. Worse, you don't learn anything.

Decline help firmly, as diplomatically as possible. If he was innocently playing Sir Galahad, don't hurt his feelings or embarrass him. You might make an enemy. If he was trying to date you and he feels rejected, you might make an enemy. If he was eliminating you as competition, he tipped his hand. Now you know one of your rivals.

But, if a guy wants to show you *how* to do something, like estimating the manhours, great. Pay attention and behave like a pro. Make statements to ask questions.

STATEMENTS NOT QUESTIONS

Don't ask for help until you're positively, absolutely certain you can't figure it out, then go to the person who gave you the assignment. Ask for help by making a statement. "I've tried to do this but I can't figure it out. Who can I talk with to learn how?"

Don't be afraid to say you don't understand when you don't. A statement followed by a question is best. "Sorry, I didn't get that. Run through it again, please."

DIE BEFORE YOU CRY

When you don't do an assignment correctly, some men won't tell you. They are afraid you'll cry if criticized.

So, you turn it in. It's not right. He fixes it and sends it forward. He "helped" but you don't learn from your mistake. Even worse, when he moves on, his replacement assumes you know how to do that assignment and so do you. The new guy doesn't check your work, he just submits it.

Everybody above him gets yelled at. Shit flows downhill! However far up it went before it's spotted, is how much shit flows back down. Your boss is chewed on by his boss because he was reamed by his boss.

When you get blasted by the new guy for doing it wrong, you're hurt and angry because nobody ever told you it was wrong! If you cry, you're history! If you angrily blame it on the guy who never told you it was wrong, that's better. But the best response is to acknowledge facts:

> *I'm sorry it's wrong. I'll fix it. I thought I was doing it correctly. How should it be done?*

Getting that good at being assertive takes time and practice. It's all explained in *When I Say No, I Feel Guilty,* by Manuel Smith, listed in *Must Books*. Read it then take Assertiveness Training. It pays handsome rewards in promotions and raises! But even more rewarding is how being assertive makes your personal relationships easier and far more enjoyable.

In every man's past, at home, in college or at work, a female cried when criticized. Men are afraid you'll cry.

We men were raised to never hurt a female. If we make one cry, we feel small and ashamed. When a man makes a woman cry at work he feels terrible, but worse, he resents her because people think he's a monster for making her cry.

On top of all that, crying makes most men extremely anxious. That's why men, beginning with Daddy and your boyfriend, will do anything, promise anything, if you'll just stop crying. Sure, they feel bad for hurting you, but that's not the reason. If you keep crying, he's subconsciously afraid *he* might start! His own carefully suppressed years of pain and sorrow may come rushing uncontrollably to the surface.

Men don't have a clue as to why they get so anxious when a woman, or even a baby cries, unless they've been in therapy. I suggest you don't bother trying to explain it to any males in your life at work or at home. They are so out of touch with their feelings, they'll think you're crazy.

It doesn't make any difference why men get so uptight when others cry. At work, they get extremely uptight. In fact, they get so uptight that if you're the one who cries, they want to get rid of you so it doesn't happen again.

All you need to know is that some men won't criticize your work because they're afraid you'll cry. You don't get feedback, so you can't learn from your mistakes. Even worse, he sees you as incapable. You don't get any important assignments, only menial tasks that "even a girl can do." What's a girl to do? Ask for criticism in plain English:

> *I want to know when I don't get it right, so I can learn from my mistakes. Please let me know when I am not doing something the way you want it done.*

Say this after three or four weeks on a new job. Then when he says you screwed up, DO NOT get defensive. DO NOT explain why you did it that way. DO NOT blame anyone. Say,

> *I see how it should be. I'll get right on it. Thanks for letting me know.*

Once he realizes he can talk to you "like a man," he will. You'll learn much more because he, and other men, won't be afraid to tell you when you screw up. They'll see you as capable and worthy of doing more important tasks. You'll advance far more quickly.

SWEET UNTOUCHABLE YOU

Men don't extend their hand when you are introduced. That means subtly and subconsciously, you're in a separate category. As the Supreme Court found, separate but equal, ain't.

Some men don't offer their hand because they were taught it was inappropriate. Geeks and nerds are so attracted to you as a young, appealing female, they fear touching will cause them to become aroused in public. Other men don't shake your hand because they want to keep you separate.

Assert your equality in the business world from the absolute git-go, with each and every male, and female, you meet. Go first. Reach out your hand. Keep your palm perpendicular to the floor, not slightly up, not slightly down. Smile politely, not sweetly, grasp his hand completely and firmly, not with just your fingertips. Look him right in the eyes, "Nice to meet you, Bernie." Shake firmly and let go.

DO NOT have a feminine handshake! That's when you offer your fingertips, tilt your head, smile demurely and do a barely noticeable mini-curtsy. Puke.

If you don't know how to shake hands, get one of your male friends to show you. A strong, firm handshake is one of the best self-advertisements anyone, male or female, can develop.

Some manipulative men offer their hand with their palm facing slightly down. That's his way of getting on top. Don't turn your palm up to meet his! It makes you submissive. Extend your hand toward him but keep you palm perpendicular with the floor. Don't reach out all the way, stop short! Pause and hold it there. Make him reach for you. This establishes your equality.

However, when you meet and shake hands with The Big Boss, submit gracefully when he uses the domineering palm down maneuver. Most Big Bosses do. Challenging him even slightly prevents advancement, forever. (This is deferring, not kissing ass. There's more on this coming.)

SWEET TOUCHABLE YOU

Men keep you sweet and cute, thus down and out in a childlike place, by giving you pats on the head instead of pats on the back, literally or figuratively. You know, the way we adults pat little kids lovingly on the head when they've done a good job or when they've screwed up.

When a creep actually does pat you, do not be diplomatic. Recoil indignantly and say, "That offends me." GLARE. Say nothing more.

If you're lucky he'll apologize. Accept graciously. He'll leave awkwardly. A few days later, talk with him about the weather. You're saying, "No hard feelings on my part." Don't mention the confrontation. When a man actually pats you, it seldom ends like this.

Most often when you object and glare, he'll ask the mega-manipulative question, "What's the matter with you?" to make it your fault and your problem. Reply, "Don't pat me. I am not a dog or a child. It offends me." He'll attempt again with "Why?" or "What do you mean?"

He's trying to make you justify yourself, trying to make you, the child, explain to him, the adult, why you resent being treated like a dog. Don't explain! Let your anger and indignation show even more. Glare fiercely and repeat, "That offends me." Wait. He'll shrug, pretend he's hopelessly misunderstood and walk away. Or he'll keep trying to make you explain yourself. Only say, "That offends me."

He was way out of line. He knows he was a patronizing putz. His routine of asking for an explanation is a futile attempt to convince onlookers you're neurotic. Eventually he will shrug, pretend you're crazy and walk away. Everyone knows you were right. Now, everyone knows you are not to be touched, not to be trifled with, not to be taken lightly.

Figurative pats on the head are fatherly advice from a 52 year old or a 22 year old male. It's advice from El Patron, Señor Don Diego, patronizingly talking to one of his female peasants, not offering helpful advice, one friend to another. For example, Señor Diego says, "You did a great job on JB's question, but next time, you should be more respectful of VPs."

An assertive response to these pats is to stare at him with a look of astonished disbelief. If that doesn't trigger the same manipulative questioning routine as above, say "I can't believe you actually said that!" and wait. He says, "What's the matter with you?" You reply, "I resent being patronized." He pretends you're crazy and leaves.

Other figurative pats on the head include praising you for simple accomplishments that don't deserve comment, let alone praise. When they try this, use Smith's assertive technique and ask, "Exactly what is it that I did that seems so remarkable?"

EXCLUDING YOU FROM TRAVEL

They try to send a male in your place on a business trip to your customer's office without telling you. When you gently confront your boss, he mumbles ". . . policy not to have women accompany men." When you press, he mumbles ". . . prevents compromising situations." He's saying all of this (a) you can't take care of yourself (b) you are going to seduce the man so you get a promotion (c) the man will try to seduce you because you are not business-like enough to prevent that (d) you're not really important to the company or to the customer.

Companies do this because sexual harassment lawsuits are everywhere, and each has had a variant of the Wendy and Harry pandemonium recounted in *Females Who Came Before*.

What can be done? It depends on whether or not you want to stay at that company for years. It depends on how much power you have. It depends on how important the trip is to your advancement. It depends on the strength of your relationship with the customer.

Let's say it's necessary to your advancement at the company. If you have a strong relationship with your customer, call him. Explain, without blaming your boss or your company, that someone is coming in your place. Delicately mention an "outdated" policy regarding women on trips. With extreme diplomacy, ask him to request your presence without saying he talked with you. Suggest he call your boss and say something like, "We're going to have Donna to meet our new operators . . . bla, de bla." After your boss hangs up, you'll be invincible and respected.

If you can't depend on your customer, it's time to bluff. Go into your boss's office with a manner and a look on your face that says "Boss, you've been busted." Tell him your customer just called. Blurt out, "He wants to know who's coming with me and how long my presentation is." Imply you stalled him.

With a look on your face of "How do we get out of this?" bluntly ask, "What do I tell him?" He'll stammer and stall. Stand there. Make him feel the pressure. Look nervous. Unexpectedly say, "He doesn't even know Tim." (Tim is going in your place.)

He'll mumble about seeing if he can get permission, then dismiss you with his body language. Don't leave. Say, "I should get back to him today." Wait expectantly. He'll promise you an answer. Now you can leave.

If he doesn't get back to you in an hour, drop by his office. He'll say, "You're set to go. Get back to him." He'll cover his embarrassment with gruffness. Don't be smug. Don't smile. Just leave. Call your customer.

DIRTY WORDS ARE NO BIG DEAL

When men apologize for saying "shit" or "bastard" in your presence, they insult you. Apology implies you are a delicate, innocent, sweet, flower unable to cut it in the kick-ass world of big business where barracks language is the norm when "the girls" aren't around. Some are merely being polite as Dad taught, "Watch your language around ladies, son."

It makes no difference. Don't let them keep you separate, different from them. That labels you "less then adequate" for the business world.

Defeat them forever by saying in a mock tough voice, and a smile, "Watch your fuckin' mouth, buster!" If that's not your style, say, again with a smile, "I don't mind strong language." Get the point across. Don't let them keep you weaker than men by apologizing for language.

In general, men are disoriented by a female who uses a lot of profanity or they think she's an easy lay. After recovering from being disoriented or from being rejected, they begin the groundwork to get rid of her at the first opportunity. Reserve profanity for moments when you need to be emphatic. Save vulgarities for crucial situations when you want their undivided attention so you can make a key point.

HARD BALL, FILTHY LANGUAGE

A guy may try to keep you down and out by using extremely vulgar words. He wants you to blanch and get so befuddled you can't think.

This ploy is reserved for moments when the promotion is on the line. For example, to respond to a competitor's dirty trick, you and your arch enemy were tasked to develop separate strategies. There's a high-level closed door meeting. Mr. Arch Enemy has been waiting for the chance to crucify you on the can't-cut-it-because-she's-a-girl cross.

> (This is a long, complex explanation. Hang in there. The principles of handling yourself under pressure will pay handsome dividends in the years ahead.)

In the meeting, he insults the competition, "They're a bunch of cunts! afraid to face us like men . . . ." He continues using vulgarities as if he were in a locker room at half-time, making a crucial appeal to win one for the Gipper.

Everyone's watching to see if you can, or cannot cut it. If you show shock or are offended, he wins, even though most men in the room know it's only a power move.

Sit calmly. Look down at your notes. Write something, anything, in the margin. Make yourself breathe and relax. Gather yourself. DO NOT shift uneasily in your chair!

Force yourself to listen to what Mr. Arch Enemy is saying, the content of his strategy. Force yourself to hear exactly what he is proposing between the vulgarities. Do not focus on yourself. Do not focus on how you are coming across to the others in the room. Force your focus outward. Attack the environment with your eyes and with your ears. See! Hear!

Focus on reasons he gave for adopting his response. Aggressively think about whether or not it makes sense. Make yourself glance around the meeting table. Stubbornly use your eyes and intuition to see how each member is reacting to the ideas and emotions being presented by Mr. Arch Enemy. Jot notes on each member's reaction. Keep your focus outward.

Write down key words that spring to mind as you earnestly think about the risks and negative outcomes of his strategy. The key words are reminders for you to use in a few moments.

When he's finished his pitch, be among the first to respond. Ask him to recount the risks involved, ". . . *if* we were *all* to agree to *your approach.*"

Instantly he's on the defensive! Saying *your approach* prevents him from pretending this is a brainstorming session if his strategy gets shot down in flames. *If* puts doubt in each member's mind. *All* implies a unanimous decision is required. *All* also implies that you, the only woman here, are the equal of everyone at the table and it states clearly that he's being judged.

While your tactic diverts everyone's attention, you have time to regain your composure. As other members quiz him, gather yourself. Concentrate on the key points you want to make when you pitch your strategy. If the group grills him long enough, you'll have time to become relaxed and focused. Refer to the key words you wrote down. Zap him with a few pointed comments to end his session.

Without this tactic, you don't have time to get yourself together. If you're still upset, your presentation won't be nearly as pointed and powerful. Worse, you'll be vulnerable to Arch Enemy's rude interruptions. When he butts in with a leading question, you won't be able to calmly suggest holding questions until the end. If he's insistent, you won't be able to think on your feet. Should he manage to keep you flustered, you won't be able to defend your strategy from his attacks or answer the objections of others.

Pitch your ideas with energy and emotion. Be yourself. Absolutely do not use vulgar language!

No matter whose strategy gets selected, things will be different and better for you from that moment forward. You will have won the respect of every man in the room by passing an important test. They all know that you can cut it, even when vulgar language is spoken.

HAVE YOUR FRIENDS SWEAR AND CUSS

The only way you can hope to control your emotions at crunch time is to have dulled your sensitivity to vulgarities before crunch time. Hang out with guy friends not from work. Tell them about this book and what you are trying to learn. They'll have fun making you blush countless times.

This skill and this tactic are like everything else you're learning, expect to screw it up at a few different companies before you get it down. You're new to all this. Reading about it is one thing. Doing it front of a room full of men when the promotion is on the line, takes practice and learning from your mistakes, like everything else you've ever learned.

Why are you doing all of this? To make the most money possible! The only reason to make the most money is so that you can do what you want to do, when you want to do it, with whom you want to do it, sooner.

In short, you're a *Capitalist Pig To Be.*

Lack of money is the root of all evil.
GEORGE BERNARD SHAW

Money is the seed of money
and the first guinea is sometimes more
difficult to acquire than the second million.
1754 JEAN JACQUES ROUSSEAU

Capitalist Pig To Be

Capitalists, people with capital (money), lend it to you so you can buy things you don't need or can't afford. After you pay them back, plus interest, they have more money than ever, but you still don't have any. *The rich get richer and the poor get poorer* is not an empty saying.

The company you work for certainly doesn't want you to accumulate capital. Why? They know that when you do, you'll stop working for them and start supporting yourself doing something you actually enjoy, instead of being a wage slave. Then, horror of horrors, they'll have to go out, recruit, train, indoctrinate and brainwash a new wage slave. That takes time and time is money.

What does all this mean to a struggling young woman? Simple (a) Never borrow money unless you can make more money with it. For example, borrowing $25k to open a business that makes $50k the first year. ***Exception:*** Student loans backed by the government. Borrow every penny you can. Pay it back at $20 a month, forever. This is the only free lunch you'll ever get. (b) Save your money so eventually you can partake of the fruits of capitalism. This means do not spend money you can save. Do not buy anything with borrowed money, especially a car. If you do, you'll be a wage slave forever.

"So, what do you drive?" is not what Mr. Possible NuBoss asks during the routine small talk at the obligatory company awards lunch. He and every other successful-in-business person asks, "So, what do you do? Who do you work for?"

Dressing well is a thousand times more important to your success-in-business than owning an expensive, hip car. Of course, you can't drive a smoke-belching ghetto cruiser or a thrashed VW with flowers all over it. Anything that is not a total junk pile will do until you have enough money to do what you want to do, not what *they* want you to do.

Riches are a good handmaid but the worst mistress.
FRANCIS BACON

Money is not an end. Money merely increases your options. Money increases your independence and autonomy. Money is the power to say, "Screw you!" Money makes it possible to live your life where, how and with whom you want, nothing more, nothing less.

Female workers of the world, arise! You have nothing to lose but your chains!

Destroy your credit cards. Take charge of your life. Independence and freedom await. Become a saver not a consumer, a capitalist not a worker.

FROM *HOW* TO *WHY* AND BACK

The two previous pages departed from the *how* of office politics into the *why*. The next seven pages continue explaining *why*.

To understand the necessity of office politics, you must understand that biology and society deal from a different deck when they pass out cards to females. Let's take an unflinching look at *Dealing With What You Were Dealt*.

You gotta know when to hold 'em.
You gotta know when to fold 'em.
The Gambler KENNY ROGERS

Dealing With What You Were Dealt

Life deals each of us a hand of cards. In our society, we get to choose where to play our cards, selecting from a wide range of games called career choices. Some of the games: nurse, executive, priest, politician, soldier, farmer, housewife, waitress, manager, teacher, geisha girl, drug dealer, bureaucrat, cop, prostitute. Society makes up the rules for each game.

Living *The Good Life* is nothing more than getting the best out of the cards you were dealt. "Getting the best out of" means being the happiest you can be.

To live *The Good Life,* you must know what truly makes you the happiest. To do that, you must know honestly who you are. Not the *you* they made, not the *you* they reward when you do what they want you to do. But the *you,* the real you, the *you* as you really are deep down inside. Knowing what makes *that* person happy is central, fundamental, essential. Because, only after you honestly know what fulfills her, makes her feel alive, makes her enjoy the day, then, and only then, can you choose the right game, the one you win (are happy) just by playing.

An Aside On Self Deception: It is difficult for most people (you, me, everyone) to know what they really think, feel and believe in their heart of hearts. Why? We are so good at deceiving ourselves! We can convince ourselves of the most ridiculous things. Why? To preserve our self-esteem, what we think of ourselves. In short, we lie to ourselves so that we can admire ourselves, as foolish as that sounds. ***Caution!*** You may be deceiving yourself about what makes the real you happy.

WHAT MAKES YOU HAPPY?

Many young women who reviewed early drafts of this book asked, "How do I find out what makes me happy?"

Above all, develop self-awareness. Pay attention to your emotions and you'll know what makes you happy, sad, bored, lust-filled and angry. Notice when you're smiling. Notice when you're wiggling with delight. Notice when you're agonizingly waiting for time to pass. Notice what kind of entertainment you enjoy, from movies to smut novels. Think. Analyze. Evaluate. Mull over. Talk over. There's much more about this in *Understand Yourself.*

RULES OF THE GAME

The second most important thing you must know to live *The Good Life* is what the rules of the game actually are as opposed to what *they* say or imply the rules are. That's what this book is about — explaining the real rules honestly, now and then so bluntly you'll cringe. But it's better to know the brutal truth now than to waste precious years unable to win (be happy) because you're playing by the wrong rules.

Books will speak plain when counsellors blanch.
1607 FRANCIS BACON

As a female, you were dealt a hand of cards. You can *hold 'em,* play the game of life, or *fold 'em,* pretend to be the victim of a world you never made, become completely passive, helpless and depressed, then attempt suicide.

Let's take a realistic look at the cards you were dealt:

1. *FEMALE IN A MALE DOMINATED WORLD.*
2. *YOUNG WHEN YOUTH IS NEVER TAKEN SERIOUSLY BUT ALWAYS LUSTED AFTER.*
3. *POOR WHERE THE RICH GET RICHER AND THE POOR GET POORER.*
4. *BRAINWASHED FROM BIRTH TO BE HONEST, SWEET AND NON-COMPETITIVE.*
5. *POWERFUL FOR ONLY A FEW YEARS.*

These cards guarantee that you have a severe handicap if you choose to play in the game where the big money can be won, the Fortune 3000. Play without a handicap and no competition by choosing a different game, the one that makes *them* the happiest, wife-and-mother.

If that game isn't right for you, the "career choice" hassle can be avoided if you play in a game *they* reserve for females: teacher, nurse, dental assistant, secretary, clerk, waitress, bookkeeper, word processor, receptionist. Trouble is, this makes *them* happy, but *you* may never be happy.

THE HIGH STAKES GAME

Let's assume you want to play where you can make a ton of bucks. Here's how to minimize the damage your cards cause.

The first, *FEMALE IN A MALE DOMINATED WORLD,* will be neutralized after you learn how to handle the men and boys at work. There are solid methods and solutions coming up to prevent business males from dominating you. This card is easily defeated. ***Warning!*** In the business world, techniques that work on Daddy and your boyfriend won't work, in fact they'll backfire.

Card two, *NEVER TAKEN SERIOUSLY BUT LUSTED AFTER* is similar. Since you already have techniques to deal with those who lust after you, I explain how to modify your approach slightly so you can turn them down, and off, without destroying your chances for promotion. *Office Sex* explains how to bust the lust. To be taken seriously when young requires the creation of an image of maturity and seriousness as explained in *The Play's The Thing*.

Easily discard the third card, *POOR GET POORER,* by disciplining yourself to follow the advice in *Capitalist Pig To Be.*

In Fortune 3000s, the worst card is *BRAINWASHED FROM BIRTH TO BE HONEST, SWEET AND NON-COMPETITIVE.* The full description of that card continues . . . *when only cunning and deception, toughness and daring, together with a love of ferocious combat gets one into Top Management.*

A word of encouragement, you don't have to become a heartless, ball-busting bitch to become a success (make a ton of screw-you money) in the business world. And, you can maintain your personal integrity.

Eventually, you'll avoid catastrophic political errors caused by this card. But that requires *making* many catastrophic political errors, then learning from each and every one. After a colossal mistake, simply change companies, getting a ten-percent raise. Leave your mistakes behind!

Step one in this process is accepting the stark reality of being female in a Fortune 3000 company as explicitly described in the next 200 plus pages. Gradually your tendency, the one *they* instilled in you, to be sweet and trusting as well as expecting fair play from others, especially females, will diminish to a safe level.

The fifth card is the most dangerous, *POWERFUL FOR ONLY A FEW YEARS.* This single card has ravaged, is ravaging and will continue to ravage most women. Don't let it destroy your long-run happiness because you don't understand and consider, on a gut level, the long-run consequences of squandering your precious, powerful years (a) playing in the wrong game (b) playing in the right game without knowing what the rules really are (c) changing games after you've lost nearly all your power.

Danger! Two false beliefs most young women hold are (a) My life stretches endlessly into the future. (b) I can change my mind about career and family several times.

Reality! You can't change your mind even once. *Time Is Short* for young women. Let's look at the reality of being a woman in a world run by men. That world has a double standard for beauty and value. One for men, another for women.

As his wife becomes a prune
the man chooses a plum blossom.
CHINESE PROVERB

A woman's time of opportunity is short
and if she doesn't seize it
no one wants to marry her.
Lysistrata 411 BC ARISTOPHANES

Time Is Short

Growing up, we were all taught that life is simple and predictable if one works hard, pays one's debts, keeps one's promises and plays fair. As a young woman enters the corporate world, she brings with her these unquestioned beliefs from childhood.

She is certain the path to success is straightforward, with signs and milestones clearly marked. Being honest and hard-working, she joyfully, innocently throws herself headlong into performing assigned tasks.

At first, things appear to be rational and logical. Then, instead of clearly posted signs, she finds dead ends, ambiguous directions and intentionally misleading help. Everywhere she turns there's a bewildering verbal profusion of unnecessary but ever present analyses and incomprehensible hair splitting instead of accomplishing the task at hand.

Office politicians give lip service to her cultural values of hard work and personal integrity as they blatantly run roughshod over them. After confronting this reality several times, she reduces her faith to:

> *There are a few bad apples, but that doesn't mean everyone's rotten or the company's rotten. My break will come. Something will happen and "they" will notice me and reward me justly.*

With only a slight pause she drops back and redoubles her efforts. She relies on hard work, honesty, loyalty and fair play. To her surprise these attributes aren't rewarded. In fact, ass kissers and back stabbers not only survive, they prosper as she languishes.

Reluctantly she decides, it's "just this company." Two years later, after changing companies, she realizes it's the same at the new company. Trouble is, five years have passed, five of her most precious, powerful years. This exact scenario happened to a young woman I was madly in love with. *Understand The Boss* has the gruesome details.

YOUR FUTURE IS YOUR CHOICE

What do you want to be doing ten years from now? Arguing with your eight year old about putting the toys away or arguing with the Art Director about the layout? It's one or the other. You decide. You must choose, and soon.

> *A man is as old as he feels. A woman is as old as she looks.*
> 1857 MORTIMER COLLINS

If you marry and raise kids, then get out into the business world at 30, you'll only get an entry level job. *Entry level* is business code for shit work that pays diddly. If you work for a few years, then marry and raise kids, then re-enter the job market you'll be over 30. *Re-enter the job market* is feminist code for divorced with kids, no job skills.

Why? While you're away being mommy, the business world changes radically. What you knew how to do ten years ago isn't done that way any more. If it is, it pays the same as it did ten years ago.

SEEING THE TRUTH AND KNOWING THE TRUTH

There is no justice, fairness, honesty or fair play. There is only reality. Make certain you know the difference between reality and your hopeful wishes.

Reality! Your time *is* short. Accepting that is one of the hardest things you must do to succeed in the corporate world and in the real world.

What you do with your remaining short time is your choice.

Now, let's get back to office politics! You move up the ladder much faster than the men who try to keep you down when you grasp, and can intelligently discuss, the big picture. Know and understand more about your company, your industry, the Big Boys in your company and the Big Boys in your industry than anyone. Conduct *Big Picture Research.*

Simplify, simplify.
HENRY DAVID THOREAU 1850

Big Picture Research

As Thoreau's quote demands, to grasp the fundamentals, you must simplify, simplify. About 80 pages ago, I explained the biggest of big pictures about every company, I-P-O, input, process, output.

Find out everything you can about your company. You want to be able to understand what it does, what its concerns are in the short term and in the long term.

Once you understand the big picture, reduce your understanding to something nearly as simple as I-P-O. Then you'll be able to see what needs to be done to improve any situation quickly and easily. That will make you an extremely valuable employee, one to be promoted in a hurry and paid handsomely.

Begin by reading the last ten annual reports. Keep in mind that highly paid, professional writers dream up sugarcoated ways of saying "we really screwed up by selling the only profitable division." Don't be misled by their purposefully vague, downright fraudulent statements about the rosy future of General Cow.

Start with the oldest report. Notice how the company and its goals have changed year by year and who, or what, caused the changes. In the two most recent reports read, then re-read, the President's letter to the stockholders. In spite of the carefully selected words, decide what the most pressing short range problems are and how they propose to go about fixing them.

If a solution makes sense, gravitate toward that area of the company to get on a winning team. If the solution creates something new and makes sense, bust your buns to get in on it. A growing area is fertile ground for rapid advancement.

If any solution sounds like crap, do everything you can to stay as far away from it as possible. Don't be associated with a failed effort. ***Caution!*** A common move is to promote and transfer you to a losing organization or doomed project.

The company library is full of other important research material. Read the company's history according their paid historian. Although ridiculously slanted, it's a start. The company's myths, legends, slogans, and party line will be there.

When you reach higher levels later on, it's mandatory to mouth these platitudes. It shows one and all you're a player.

Read trade journals. Read about the history of your industry. Know how and why your company got here so you understand its present situation. Read the history books of your competitors.

FREE INFORMATION

Go to the public library. The most helpful people on the planet are research librarians. Politely ask for help finding as much about General Cow as possible. Copy everything that seems to contain facts and figures and descriptions about your company and your division. See if the Big Boys are in *Who's Who*. Take notes.

On the computer, search *Reader's Guide To Periodic Literature* for articles about General Cow. String together key words for a complex search such as: GENERAL COW STOCKHOLDERS LAWSUIT, GENERAL COW FEDERAL INVESTIGATION, GENERAL COW SEC, GENERAL COW IRS, GENERAL COW INSURANCE SCAM, GENERAL COW PAYS FINE, GENERAL COW OSHA VIOLATIONS.

Dream up more ways. It's a computer. It takes only seconds. Find whatever you can on the Big Boys in your division and in the corporation by searching for individual executives by name.

Next, look anywhere you can. The Los Angeles Times has a comprehensive index of their back issues. It's not yet on a computer, but once you have narrowed the topics, it's easy to get a copy of the articles you want. The major daily in your area has a similar system.

RIGHT UNDER YOUR NOSE

Most of your company's Big Boys have resumes in recent proposals. They have profiles in trade journals. In the company library, there are vanity versions of *Who's Who,* such as *Who's Who In Orange County.* The company buys these books if any executives are listed.

All that you're learning now prepares you for the payoff of office politics. When you get to the payoff chapter, *Get Promoted,* the research techniques are explained in detail. Do everything suggested.

WHY ARE YOU DOING ALL THIS?

There are Mormons at the top of major companies. There are Catholics, Jews, Seventh Day Adventists, even closet atheists. They have favorite clubs, charities, colleges and hobbies. Their wives are quite often alcoholics. Their children are frequently in trouble with the law about drugs. The list goes on and on.

When opportunity presents herself, don't make a *faux pas* by not knowing who's who and what's what. And, most important, be able to make small talk about topics a Big Boy doesn't consider drivel.

In the cafeteria or in the hall before meetings or waiting for elevators, you'll overhear conversations. If you understand the big picture, you can grasp the significance of what's said.

When you "just happen" to be sitting across from one of the Big Boys at the award banquet or Management Club dinner or at the Christmas Dance, the conversation you strike up can get you promoted three rungs in one stroke. As you talk, your knowledge of the corporation will strongly impress him. If you're current on the company's latest move to win the contract with the Airport Commission or their lack of progress in settling a labor dispute, he'll be amazed and interested in adding you to his staff.

UNDERSTANDING LEADS TO PROMOTIONS

Even if you don't get the chance to dazzle a Big Boy with your knowledge, you'll rise much faster if you grasp what the whole company does. As one of the few people who understands the big picture, that alone makes you stand out.

Even more important, much of what appears to be senseless gold plating suddenly makes sense if you understand that your company, Edison Electric, is forbidden by law to make more than a six percent profit because it is a utility. That means you won't put your foot in your mouth and ridicule expensive ideas presented by the Improvement Committee. Right? Be ready with some things of your own that need gold plating.

The most important reason of all to understand the Big Picture is so that you realize what your group, your section, your department, your division should be doing and why. Once you grasp the *why,* the *how* to improve becomes self-evident. Knowledge is power.

Right now, you're learning the *what, how* and *when* of office politics. Later on, *why* it's necessary is explained.

Spying is another method of gathering knowledge. The more knowledge you have, the more powerful you become.

All warfare is based on deception.

Every battle is won before it is fought.

The Art of War SUN TZU

COMMENTS ON THE DECISIVE NATURE OF INTELLIGENCE AND SPIES

Knowledge is power.

1597 FRANCIS BACON

Spying

Layoffs are coming because Art Alcoholic, VP Business Development, had four too many and blew the dog and pony show at Proctor and Gamble. Katy D. Kissass, Senior Purchasing Agent, will be fired for taking kickbacks. Studly Bigmouth in Manufacturing is fooling around with both Mary Maudlin Middleage and Deena Desperate Divorcee. One or both will quit as soon as either of them realizes it. Peter B. Little's AIDS test came back positive. He'll be on medical leave until death.

The more you know, the better your chances are of maneuvering into the right place at the right time to get the promotion. The more your know, the better you can position yourself to avoid the layoff until you can get another job.

Where do you gather information? Anywhere. What's useful? Anything. Really? Anything you can swap for other scuttlebutt, gossip or insider info about anybody, anywhere, anytime.

who's taking over Facilities
who's wife is running around
who's doing drugs
who's drinking too much
who's going to be in charge of Inventory
who's having an affair with whom
who's blackmailing whom
who's rising like a super star

who's stealing
who's taking bribes
who's getting promoted
who's pregnant
who's getting fired
who's sick and dying

The corporation is filled with rumors, conjecture, prognostications. The most valuable info is about changes, such as which department will be reorganized. Serious illness and death are clouds with silver linings for the woman who properly forecasts the events that will take place after the funeral. For the woman in the right place at the right time (ahead of time), change produces opportunities.

Other mega-important info regards "rumor of war": layoffs, takeovers and mergers, winner-take-all interdepartmental or interdivisional feuding and "temporary" division shutdowns. Knowing where the shit is going to hit the fan enables you to avoid getting splattered. Knowing where the rose garden will be enables you to come up smelling like a rose. Simple enough?

CHANGE IS MOST IMPORTANT

The grapevine, the underground communication network, in every organization is where useful information is exchanged. Public knowledge is useless. Distributed memos are useless. The newspaper is useless. What's "accidentally" overheard at the next table in the cafeteria is priceless.

The more you interact with people at levels above you, the more likely you are to uncover something to get the promotion or avoid the layoff. At your level, co-workers reveal more if they consider you harmless. Put on the naive act when someone shares scuttlebutt about the competitor beating your company on the Greek job. You say, with wonder in your eyes, "Oh! Will anyone get laid off?" then listen innocently.

You're interested in personnel and organizational changes, up, down or sideways. Change, to you, is opportunity. To most of them, it's a terrifying threat.

This is war of survival first, prevailing second. Information is necessary to gain an edge. Your co-workers see themselves as helpless pawns in a game of Corporate Chess. Most think of it as idle speculation, not particularly useful because they're so passive, but it makes them feel important to know something others don't.

Few people will tell you anything unless you have something to trade. In the beginning, go first. Let them think you are merely playing "Let's Trade Information" for amusement. Give the impression you like office gossip so they don't see you as a threat.

Keep giving them info and they'll give you info. It makes no difference with whom you trade.

Don't forget, there are rivals who want that promotion instead of you or smart, manipulative people who want to avoid the coming layoff. Both will throw you to the wolves. Fair trades with them make no sense because they won't give you anything useful or will give false info to deliberately mislead you. Give enemies useless gossip and misleading, semi-truthful information that may cause them to make a fatal misstep.

Develop info swapping relationships with people anytime they are not interested in the same promotion you want. You can ask your boss something your swapping partner can't without being obvious. He can do the same for you. Collaborators like this are invaluable. As they move up, they can bring you along, and will, because you've demonstrated across time that you're reliable and you understand the game.

Rumors and supposition are useful but this type of "intelligence" is just like information gathered by government spies. Before it is acted on, it must be verified with substantiating data from other sources. Don't go off prematurely.

ATTRITION CREATES OPPORTUNITY

In the late 60s, I worked at a division with 2000 employees. Cancer, bleeding ulcers, heart attacks took their toll. During a year, of the top 30 men in the division, at least one died or retired because of illness, others went on long term disability. One or two were promoted to corporate or left to head a major project.

Of the 70 men below them, at least two died or retired because of illness, several more went on disability. At least one left to attend Stanford's Graduate School of Business. He was being groomed for Top Management.

Among 150 middle managers, only two died or retired because of illness, five went on long term disability but at least one was fired for stealing in some manner. Three were transferred to the "field" for gross incompetence. Five went to a competitor. Two more took a leave of absence to complete MBAs.

Change is bound to occur. Spying is how you find out what will change, and when, so you can take advantage of the opportunities.

REORGANIZATION CREATES OPPORTUNITY

In a typical year, that 2000 person division underwent some sort of major restructuring at least once, sometimes twice. Empires came and went. Three departments were consolidated into one. A department was split into two sections. Procurement was made responsible for Office Services. Reproduction was made part of Facilities. Engineering was relieved of Pubs, which became part of Office Services.

In the late 70s, I worked for the main division of a 30,000 employee corporation. During three years, the entire corporation was reorganized four times! It first went from three divisions to three separate corporations owned by a holding company. When that didn't solve the problem, it became a single corporation with three groups. That didn't work either or they were running a tax scam on the IRS because it then became two corporations. One had two divisions. Finally it went back to its original configuration. The CEO's daughter owns the stationery printing concession was the joke-explanation.

WINDOW DRESSING REORGANIZATION

Companies reorganize to convince stockholders and Wall Street they are doing something about the problem. If the company is centralized, the Executive Committee studies the problem. Their report to the Board of Directors recommends decentralizing, saying that divisions can't respond quickly enough to changing conditions because they must get decisions approved by headquarters.

If the corporation is decentralized, the Executive Committee studies the problem. Their report to the Board of Directors recommends centralizing, saying that the divisions lack a common approach to business and there are too many duplicate organizations.

These reorganizations are as predictable as a sunrise, yet most employees don't realize they always happen, thus don't capitalize on the opportunity that change presents. You realize it, now. When you get out there, keep your eyes and ears open so you can predict where the opportunities will be.

SECRETARIES ARE BEST

Cultivate relationships with secretaries. They are secretly cheering for a woman to get the upper hand. If you don't act superior to them, they'll help you end up on top.

Many will "accidentally" let something slip when jabbering with you. One of them types the confidential interoffice memo about the internal audit of time cards, places it in a folder and nonchalantly goes to the copier and back. Sometimes she leaves the folder open "accidentally" while talking with you.

Knowing there's an audit coming means your records are exactly right. If you know Jimmy's been fudging, you might get his job after he gets caught because of an "anonymous" tip.

Why does Jimmy get the ax? *They* have to justify the time, expense, work disruption and demoralizing effects caused by the witch hunt-audit. If a witch isn't found and burned at the stake, the person who suggested the witch hunt looks like a fool.

LET THEM TALK WHILE YOU LEARN

Most sentences begin with "I." The person is telling you about himself, what he likes, who he knows, what he knows, in short, how important he is. The longer he talks the more you know about him and the less he knows about you. Advantage Ms. Young.

Listen for "I." That's your cue to shut up and tune in. Convey interest and acknowledge his importance nonverbally. Read those body language books!

You can direct the conversation with innocent questions, "Oh! Will anyone from our group get her job?" He can be diverted from prattle to useful topics when you insert, "Crystal said John Dempsey, in Environmental, is getting Scarcella's job after the funeral. What do you think?"

Don't pass on anything someone tells you in confidence. Earn his trust. Eventually, he'll reveal something priceless, if he trusts you.

OTHER SOURCES

Do not share what you learn unless you are trading information. Keep your mouth shut. Ask innocent sounding questions of co-workers. Don't appear to be gathering intelligence and building a file. You're just innocently curious.

As you move about talking with co-workers, read any and every memo you see from anyone about anything. Attend every meeting you're invited to. Listen. Make as many new contacts as possible at every possible opportunity.

Watch how your boss's secretary treats visitors and callers. The ones she ignores are useless. The ones she kisses up to are important. Watch the secretary of your boss's boss to be tipped off as to how important your boss is relative to other people who visit. Develop and cultivate something with her. She's an instant shortcut to promotion.

Study the organization chart. Dotted lines mean there is a power struggle, an unresolved struggle going on. That means someone eventually wins and someone loses. If your department is shown with a dotted line connecting it to some other group, it may get absorbed! Duplicated jobs will be excess! See *Alliances* and evaluate who's who in this struggle. Casually inquire about the conflict.

Wastebaskets are a gold mine. Snoop in your boss's, your enemy's, your rival's. Make certain you don't discard anything they can use against you. Throw that stuff in the shredder or take it home and toss it.

Review all info-gathering tips in other chapters and make a list of the potential sources and areas of interest. *Get Promoted* explains the extreme value of Five Year Plans, Job Descriptions and Policy Manuals.

Remember, everyone's single, solitary, fundamental, basic motive — survive. Help them survive and they will help you. Go first. Tell them something they can use. Show you know how the game is played. Tit for tat. That's how you get promoted. But to do that, *Risk Taking Required.*

Women are like tea, you never know how strong they are until you put them in hot water.
DUCHESS OF WINDSOR

Courage is the virtue that makes all other virtues possible.
The Psychology of Self Esteem NATHANIEL BRANDEN

Risk Taking Required

The way we, in Western Civilization, socialize our children causes women to see risk as entirely negative, the potential to fail. It causes men to see risk as positive, the potential to win.

Little girls, female teenagers, coeds, young women and adult women in our culture are not taught to take risks. In fact, they are rewarded for not taking risks.

From birth, when she acts afraid and helpless, Mommy does it for her, then Daddy does it, then Brother does it, then Jimmy, her boyfriend does it, then John, her fiance does it, then Jack, her second husband does it.

AIN'T NOBODY GONNA DO IT FOR YOU

To get promoted you have to take many small risks and several major ones every single year. "Take a risk" means doing things a sweet, nice, pleasant, quiet young lady normally doesn't do.

Here are a few fundamental risks you must take: speak up in meetings when it's to your advantage, volunteer for extra assignments, dare to dress all-business when contemporaries wear trendy fashions, confront a manipulative co-worker who's trying to make you look bad, take speech and acting classes, maintain eye contact during conversations, introduce yourself to strangers at business meetings, shake hands with everyone you meet.

FIRST RISKS AND FINAL RISKS

As you begin this ten-year adventure, the first risk you must take is inflating your resume. Ten years from now, the last risk will be starting your very own business with the savings you've accumulated. Or, gambling you can support yourself as a consultant. Then again, you may take the ultimate risk and try to beat the 52 percent failure rate of marriage. The point is, if you don't take risks you'll never get to where you want to be.

GROWING UP MALE VS GROWING UP FEMALE

A girl never learns to take chances like boys: stealing watermelons, shooting out street lights, breaking windows or hot wiring a car and joy riding.

Boys steal watermelons. Later they have the courage to steal a confidential memo on salaries that gives them a big edge on choosing the best career path at the company. Girls dress Barbie. Later they have fashion sense to ridicule the attire of the secretary who typed the confidential memo the "boys" stole.

Boys learned to yell and argue endlessly over whether the runner was safe or out. Girls learned to sit quietly so they were praised. Later, in a department meeting, the boys argue endlessly until one of them, not you, gets the window office.

LEARNING TO FAIL LESSENS THE STING

Striking out the first three times he's at the plate in a Little League game, then getting a hit the fourth time, teaches a young male he must ignore past failures and keep trying. If he cries about striking out, he's called a girl.

Losing is a part of the game and part of life. Boys learn that. Few of us were on winning Little League teams or Pop Warner football teams or JV basketball teams. Why? There can only be one winner. The other 15 teams in the league are losers. Boys on those teams found out that life does go on after losing. Girls never get the chance to learn this lesson. They're busy being domesticated, socialized and brainwashed to make babies and care for them.

Even worse, the only competition a girl is encouraged to enter is beauty contests: Prom Queen, Homecoming Queen, Cheerleader. This competition doesn't help. It only prepares her to compete for a rich husband.

FAILING IS NECESSARY FOR SUCCESS

Mistakes teach. Learn from each and every mistake you make. You didn't learn to ride a bicycle without failure, crashing. You didn't learn to skate without failure, falling. You won't learn to confront people without failure, losing it, screaming or crying.

If you literally or figuratively cry when someone criticizes your first man-hour vs revenue report, you're secretly called "unfit for promotion." To get promoted, you have to *take it like a man* and learn from criticism.

Carefully re-read my explanation of the absolute necessity to tell males, your boss in particular, that you want to know when you do it wrong so you can get it right. Obviously that requires taking a risk. It's called asking for negative feedback in assertiveness training jargon.

COURAGE AND CONFIDENCE BUILDING

If you're afraid to do something but do it anyway, you take a risk. If you're not afraid, it's not a risk.

If you take a risk and fail, it's hard not to see yourself as a failure. When you fail again and again, it's almost impossible to take new risks.

When you take a risk and you're successful, it's very hard not to see yourself as a success. When you're successful again and again, it's very hard not to become confident. To be respected and promoted, confidence is what you must radiate.

When trying to develop confidence, the Catch 22 is that success comes only when you're relaxed. Relaxation comes only from confidence. Confidence comes only from success.

The campaign to gain self assurance is done slowly. There's only one way to learn, by doing.

A good fight manager builds his young boxer's confidence slowly, never overmatching him, not giving him pushovers. He doesn't want his boy to take a whuppin' and lose his confidence. He doesn't want him to have false confidence, either.

Begin developing your confidence by taking risks that you'll probably be successful with. Small risks reduce the pressure. When there's less at stake you're relaxed and function better so you're successful. Catch 22 defeated.

Create the required, self sustaining loop of success-confidence-relaxation by being aware of your emotions. When you become aware of something or somebody that frightens you, think of ways to take small risks in that area, but risks with a high probability of success.

The greater your fear, the greater the risk is, to you. It doesn't make any difference whether other people are afraid to do it. It doesn't make any difference if everybody else can do it. If you're afraid, that's all that counts.

Fear, to be overcome, must be confronted.
The Disowned Self NATHANIEL BRANDEN

Build your confidence, don't crush it. Think about it. Plan it. Schedule it. Don't be in a hurry.

I simply tell you what's required, then explain how you begin developing it. You'll never be completely confident, since developing confidence is an ongoing, never-ending process. You only get better, never perfect.

THE RISK IS PROPORTIONAL TO THE GAIN

A relaxed, confident manner is mandatory to become part of Management, where the big bucks are. Relaxation comes from confidence which comes from repeated success. *Nothing succeeds like success* is an not empty platitude.

If you're going to be a bear, be a Grizzly.
APPALACHIAN ADVICE TO HIS DAUGHTER THE AUTHOR

In assertiveness training they teach you how to take risks so that you are successful from the beginning. You learn how to develop a posture that radiates confidence. You learn phrases and power words that give you confidence. Get into Assertiveness Training, today.

Typical things that cause females in our culture to be afraid are: being criticized, being praised, being yelled at, speaking in a group, authority figures. Make your own list. Make it as long as you can. Know all the areas where you can take small risks so that eventually you can take major risks. *The risk is proportional to the gain* is not empty advice.

Here's a hint given several other places. Work on being slow. Confident people are not in a hurry, not pushy, not nervous or excited. Moving slowly and talking slowly gives the appearance of confidence.

IT'S NOT A POPULARITY CONTEST

Not every person will like you, especially when you become a supervisor. This is a stumbling block for women because they've been brainwashed to believe that popularity is the key to self-worth. Boys were raised to find self-esteem in achievements. Popularity is nice, not crucial. Men feel comfortable doing what it takes to achieve. Women of all ages feel they must be liked as they work their way up the pay scale.

I'd rather be feared than respected.
LA RAIDERS, PRESIDENT OF THE GENERAL PARTNER AL DAVIS

It is impossible to be liked when you're in charge. The workers don't like you because the orders you issue are unpopular and stupid. It makes no difference that Top Management insists that the orders be issued. More important, it's impossible to be respected by your workers if you want them to like you. It's either being liked or being respected.

OTHER WOMEN HATE IT WHEN YOU TAKE RISKS

They can't accept or understand office politics. They can't accept or understand they'll be where they are forever unless they stop playing it safe. A risk taker like you forces them to confront these realities. It makes them ashamed at first, then angry. Be prepared.

Other women may offer *Friendship* but I strongly suggest you take your time. Don't trust anybody yet, women in particular.

Women, like princes, find few real friends.
Advice to a Lady 1750 LORD LYTTELTON

A friend is someone who knows everything about you but likes you anyway.
UNKNOWN WISE PERSON

Friendship

Lyttelton's quote is exactly right, especially in the corporate world. Read it again. Let it soak. Don't be trusting. Use your intuition.

THE TWO PERCENT SOLUTION

During the first six months, you'll meet about 100 people. You'll like two of them simply because of who and what they are. You'll want to slowly strangle two of them simply because of who and what they are. Polite indifference will be your feeling toward the others. Those 100 people will react the same toward you. Two will hate you, two will like you, the others will be politely indifferent.

Sometimes the two people that you like, like you. Far more often, the two that you hate, hate you.

I don't know why it's like this. I do know women have a helluva time accepting it because of the brainwashing they get while growing up about the supreme importance of being popular. At work, they waste time and energy trying to get the people who are indifferent and who hate them, to like them, then waste more time fretting when it doesn't happen.

What's important, is that you quickly identify the two percent who hate you. Trust your gut feelings. Adjust your behavior and tactics to compensate for their feelings, then go on about your business.

As for the two percent you like and the two percent who like you, identify them. In a few pages I'll explain.

GOOD WORKING RELATIONSHIPS

Dispassionate, objective relationships are all one can achieve at a corporation. Never, absolutely never, disclose anything personal, particularly to another woman. Never even mention your personal life to anyone.

Close personal relationships are for real human beings, not corporate creatures. Friends are for support and caring. Co-workers are for getting a raise and promotion or for finding out when the layoff is coming.

Don't become friends with young, naive employees who are full of the crusader spirit. Believing they can actually force the company to change something, they'll get you burned at the stake when it's time to make an example of what happens to revolutionaries. Likewise, don't associate with feminists. Top management wants to, and will, get rid of them at the first opportunity. Feminists cause problems. Don't be guilty by association.

REAL FRIENDS ARE FROM THE REAL WORLD

At your first few companies you can ignore most of these mandates. Become friends with people you like because you won't be there long. Later on, when you're learning a helluva a lot at a particular company, plan to spend a couple of years there. In that case, wait until a few months before you leave to begin socializing with people you really enjoy (the two percent) and with people you simply like. After moving on, stay in touch. You may end up being deep, close personal friends. But that's only one reason to develop friendships.

You must have, and keep, a circle of friends who have nothing to do with the company. Good friends prevent you from becoming too lonely. Being too lonely makes us (you, me, everyone) become careless about the kind of person we let get close to us at work and out in the real world.

Never attempt to get your social or sexual needs met by people at work. It means the end of big raises and big promotions. Even worse, you become dependent on the company, ripe for use and abuse by everyone. Why? Because you *need* them, not vice versa.

REAL FRIENDS AT THE COMPANY

After you've followed this advice for years, you can become friends, genuine friends with a person or two in a company where you plan to stay for several years. By then, you'll know how to handle yourself and the relationships.

These must be people you trust with your career. Because when you become friends, genuine friends, you are open and sharing, thus vulnerable.

The worst solitude is to be destitute of sincere friendship.
FRANCIS BACON

Even in Fortune 3000s you'll meet a *mensch* or two, real, honest, good human beings. When you do meet someone who radiates goodness, joy and life, you've proven yourself worthy to the gods. They're rewarding you for being a good person yourself. This glowing person, male or female, is precious indeed. He'll be part of your world for a lifetime, if you make it happen.

At your first few companies, when you meet a woman or a man in the two percent category move faster to make friends than described above because you will only be there a year or less. Now that I've said all that, listen with your intellect and with your heart to seemingly contradictory advice.

MEN — APPROACH WITH CAUTION

When that radiant someone is a male, go after him as a friend. But don't be friendly with *any* male until you have seen him in action over and over. You can be pleasant and civil but you cannot be friendly, sweet, charming or flirtatious. It sends the wrong signal, causing an erection and, at the same time, causing catty claws to be sharpened.

Once you're certain he is what he seems, just say what you want directly and honestly. With all males, myself included, be careful we don't misread your intentions as you approach us. If we think you're interested because of sex, and you aren't, that may be the end of a potential friendship. Why? Being rejected is sometimes so excruciatingly humiliating we'd rather never face you again. We men all have truly small egos no matter what kind of act we put on.

Every man, me included, wants you to say right up front, "This is not a pass." Immediately follow with, "I enjoy talking with you. . ." then before he can say anything, add that you'd like to be friends. Shut up and listen with your intuition and your brain to his reply.

After you become friends you can become lovers. But in all of my experiences, being lovers first then becoming friends after it's over is damn near impossible. After 54 years I have two female friends who were my lovers. It's so hard to do. One's motivation to be a lover is radically different from the motivation to be friends.

FRIENDS WITH MEN?

Some people think it's sad that it's so damn hard for men and women to be friends. I don't think it's sad. I don't think it's bad. I think that's just the way life is.

My responsibility is to tell you bluntly and honestly what's going through a man's mind and body when he tries to be your friend. Further, no matter what he says or thinks, he may be self-deceived and think he's not like me. If the guy's young, he is self-oblivious. Without experience, he has no way to know what he really thinks and feels.

After we males have air, water and food, the next priority is sex. We're the product of 50 million years of aggressive sexual behavior being rewarded.

Friendship? Yeah. We'd like to be friends too, but sex is at the top of our biological list. Remember that. Don't be hurt, don't be shocked, don't be naive. Sooner or later he'll make his move. Who knows? You may want him to. On a subconscious level, you may have been encouraging him. Okay? End of bluntness for awhile.

I can be friends with a woman I'm not attracted to sexually, of that I'm certain. I can be friends with a woman who is an ex-lover. But when I try to be friends with a woman I'm attracted to, we don't do well because my primary goal is to get her into bed. Things are always jumbled.

Everyone, that includes you and me, gets sex and love all mixed up. We get confused about who is who and who is what. We wonder: Is she my lover or my friend? Why doesn't she want to be my lover and my friend at the same time? Maybe she can be my friend and a casual sex partner? Is she a potential wife? Ad nauseam.

I don't have any answers for you. I have only tentative, preliminary answers for me. That's after being alive for more than 50 years, after two marriages, two divorces, four long term romantic relationships, six extremely intense sex-love affairs, and so on. I certainly don't know what you want, need or are able to handle. I'm only telling you what it's like for the male on the other end of your attention and interest.

In summary, close personal friends with a man? Doubtful. Close alliance with a man? Possibly. But don't attempt to be friends with a man from work until you're ready to bet your future at that company on it. He may misread your intentions. You may have a subconscious agenda. It may turn into an affair. When that's over it is painful and humiliating for both people. That's when anger, fired by the hurt, creates the desire for vengeance and the loss of rationality. Well, you can see where *that* leads.

FRIENDS WITH WOMEN?

Women who want the same promotions and raises you want are your enemies. Knowing there are only a few high salary positions for women, they see you as keeping them from climbing to the top of the ladder. Don't let one of them get close to you.

The common ploy is to befriend you. They reveal themselves by praising you too much, even a little is suspect! If they share precious inside information, asking nothing, expecting nothing, in return, be extremely suspicious. The move is designed to entrap you. *There ain't no such thing as a free lunch* is not an idle saying.

With women who don't view you as competition, it's just like with men. Don't approach her until you know she's for real. Often people are not what they seem, especially when you're young and inexperienced. Take your time. Pay attention to your feelings. If it feels like she's for real, she probably is. There is much, much more in *The Other Woman.*

WHAT ARE FRIENDS FOR?

In real politics and in office politics, it's called The Old Boy Network. You need friends in high places to get into high places. Once you get there, bring your friends along. Place them as high up as they can handle.

In every organization 20 percent of the staff accomplishes 80 percent of the work. Identify the 20 percent by noticing, they do what they say they will do, when they say they'll do it.

After you trust them, socialize with them and possibly become friends. ***Warning!*** Ruthless, manipulative back stabbers are in the 20 percent. That's where division managers come from. You can't trust everyone in the 20 percent. And, you won't like everyone in the 20 percent.

START YOUR OWN OLD BOY NETWORK

As you move from company to company, stay in touch with productive people from previous jobs. You'll eventually be in a position to hire workers. You'll want efficient, smart, loyal people who have proven themselves. Likewise, should any of them get into a high place, they'll hire you for the very same reasons.

What good are friends if you don't use them?
UNKNOWN WISE PERSON

In high places, things frequently go wrong for reasons beyond your control. A battle that you don't know about between rivals several levels above you is often behind things going wrong on your level. Associates, colleagues and allies take the opportunity to blame you as they step on your face to reach the next rung. But, friends understand and friends will back you.

Those friends-people are priceless. In my first ten years I only met four. Then, in the next twenty years, only two! These people are worth fighting for. They'll jump into the fray without hesitation when you are attacked by *Rivals And Enemies*.

A [woman] cannot be too careful in the choice of [her] enemies.
1891 OSCAR WILDE

We choose our enemies carefully.
1967 GENERAL MOSHE DAYAN
WHEN ASKED HOW ISRAEL WON IN ONLY SIX DAYS, OUTNUMBERED 20 TO 1

Rivals And Enemies

In the corporate jungle, enemies are everywhere, disguised and camouflaged like they'd be in the real jungle. An enemy is different than a rival. He wants to destroy you not just get the promotion.

Create an enemy by causing someone to feel extremely strong, unpleasant emotions: fear, shame, hurt, anger. Reject a guy trying to date you loudly, strongly and publicly when you could have been quieter and gentler.

Create and enemy inadvertently by saying, "Jeez, that new carpet in the cafeteria is UGH-LEE." Unbeknownst to you, he headed the decorating committee. That innocent comment caused him to feel shame, self-doubt and fear of being discovered as a tasteless geek.

Other ways: look better than she does, divert attention of men from her to you, embarrass him in the staff meeting by asking a revealing question. The point is, you turn rivals into enemies when you hurt them severely.

Enemies have time on their side. They watch you, take notes, keep logs, start rumors, plant seeds of doubt in everyone's head while you're busy trying to get promoted.

RIVALS

Ask yourself who gets the promotion if you don't. He's your chief rival. But, anyone who believes he deserves or has a chance for the promotion, is a rival. Rivals are on your level or slightly below. Uniforms show who the dangerous ones are.

After identifying a rival or an enemy, keep notes on his weak and strong points. Develop a strategy to exploit his weakness and avoid his strength. Sooner or later there will be a showdown.

Rivals don't become enemies unless you cause it to happen by showing them up in public. Once you beat a rival for the promotion, he becomes your enemy.

Rivals don't play fair but they're rational. Enemies play rough and dirty, but they're rational. If you beat an enemy for the promotion he becomes an arch enemy. The next time he'll be doubly driven, revenge and rage. Who knows how rational he will be? There's much more in *Fighting*.

HOW TO VIEW THE RIVAL OR ENEMY

In *Winning Through Intimidation,* Ringer explains bluntly how you must view those who are out to "steal your chips," beat you in simple English. In short, they don't have the same values you have. They don't have the same definitions of lie, cheat and steal that you have. So, if you expect them to play by your rules and adhere to your values and code of honor, you'll lose. This is a timeless truth. Don't forget it. *Must Books* lists Ringer's masterpiece.

BUILT-IN ENEMIES

If a rival is part of the two percent who hate you, he's automatically your enemy. If you humiliate, taunt, or in any purposeful way aggravate an enemy, he becomes an arch enemy.

Envy never takes a holiday.
FRANCIS BACON

You have several built-in enemies when you are young: older females and less attractive females of any age. Older females resent you. They're threatened simply by your presence. They lose much of their luster when you're in the room. Men pay less attention when you're around. They hate you for being young. Less attractive women hate you for the same reasons.

POTENTIAL ENEMIES

Mid-life crisis males have secret crushes on you and spend much of their time fantasizing about you and planning ways to meet you, talk with you, sweep you off your feet into the motel for a nooner where your youth restores their lost youth.

In *Office Sex* I explain why and how testosterone and estrogen cause so many problems. Right now it's enough to know that Middle Age Crazies are potential enemies. Their desires can be used to easily manipulate them. But, if you have to harshly reject one, he'll make you pay. Handle with care. They often have tremendous power over your future.

You must only be businesslike and borderline severe with them all. Anything even remotely friendly is interpreted as sexual interest, thus encouragement. Be all business. Be civil. Absolutely do not be friendly. *Office Sex has* details on how to nip everything in the bud.

Guys near your age may fall in love without you realizing it. You'll be sitting in the cafeteria with him and some other people. When they leave, from nowhere, he blurts out his love for you. If you laugh or stare in disbelief, you make an enemy for life. Struggle to maintain your composure. Look down at the table. Breathe. Get it together.

You know the routine. "I'm sorry, I don't want to hurt you, but I'm deeply in love and committed to my fiance." Apologize again, then quickly leave. Gosh!

ARCH ENEMIES

An Arch Enemy is someone who hates your guts to the point of wanting to completely destroy you. Just beating you for the promotion is not enough. He wants you publicly humiliated, fired and blacklisted.

I've had two arch enemies. Both times I had to spend so much time guarding my back and warding off frontal assaults that I no longer found any pleasure at work. A new job at a new company was my solution after I realized neither one would ever quit trying to get me.

Once upon a time I was the arch enemy. It is an all consuming hatred. It's compulsive and obsessive to the point of neurosis. I focused totally on destroying the traitorous prick for three months. I exhausted myself. I missed two deadlines in a row. My boss closed the door.

> *He deserves to be nailed, but, Jesus, he's John's Golden Boy. He'll never go down. Give it up! Go home. Get your shit together. I need you, we need you.*

Six months later I began to realize it was time to step off the corporate gravy train as described at the beginning of the book. Should you find yourself hating a corporate creature that much, it may be time to change trains.

Any enemy you defeat becomes an arch enemy. If you ignore my advice about office affairs, an arch enemy can be created from any lover you break with.

BISMARCK'S METHOD CREATED SOME ENEMIES

Sometimes you've never done anything to the enemy. You have never even met some of them but they want to destroy you. They don't care if you're humiliated, fired and blacklisted. They just want you gone.

Who are they? Every woman who's chosen to climb the ladder and stay at the company for the rest of her life.

Why? They know the government is adopting [1]Bismarck's method and forcing companies to promote females into high-level token, management positions. If they destroy you, there's one less candidate.

These women don't bother attacking until you've moved up the salary ladder where you might be considered for a magic number job, over $60k. These, the most dangerous of creatures, are *The Other Woman.*

[1] In the 1970s, big government, big business and big media joined forces to defuse Women's Liberation using tactics advocated by Otto Von Bismarck in the mid 1800s. Bismarck's method of defusing a revolution is explained later on.

There is no animal more invincible
than a woman, nor fire either,
nor any wildcat so ruthless.
Lysistrata 411 BC ARISTOPHANES

Hell hath no fury like a woman scorned.
SHAKESPEARE

The Other Woman

Dealing with men in the office is relatively simple. They're straightforward, uncomplicated, emotionally honest, not devious or malicious. By nature, men hunt as a team.

Dealing with women in the office is extremely complex and extremely dangerous. They are devious, two-faced, calculating, cold and catty. By nature, cats are solitary hunters.

WARRIORS WITH NO CONSCIENCE

In Marla Jo Fisher's 1989 LA READER article, *Caution: Women At Work*, Dr. Janet Wozniza, a psychologist who lectures on conflicts between professional women, said that while she was still in high school she realized that, ". . . when girls competed for guys, anything went. They could be conniving and underhanded and those moves were sanctioned and acceptable to all the other girls."

Explanation and Translation. It's not about being fair, forthright and just. Females are brainwashed to believe their ultimate worth depends on getting married and making babies.

A high school girl must have a boyfriend so he can become a husband. To her, getting the boy is life or death. When her life is on the line, of course anything goes. Every other girl realizes that and doesn't object.

Betty Lehan Harragan, author of *Games Mother Never Taught You,* said in the same article, "Without learning how to compete and that competition is necessary, young women fight in particularly petty, adolescent ways. And their victims are at a loss as to how to fight back fairly."

Explanation and Translation. By not participating in team sports, young women do not learn that competition is a necessary, normal part of life. By not participating, they never learn what good sportsmanship is, so they don't associate personal honor with fighting fair and square. Thus, when they attack or counterattack, rotten, underhanded, deceptive, double-crossing methods are standard. Their sense of honor depends solely on winning. They suffer no guilt for doing anything, no matter how atrocious. But worst of all, since they do not feel guilt or shame, their conscience does not restrain them from doing it again using even more despicable methods.

EVOLUTION, BIOLOGY AND THE SEXES

The two women quoted above, all feminist writers and success book authors don't have a clue as to why women are seen differently and treated differently from men in the workplace. The best they can do is blame it on a patriarchal society, then vaguely mumble about how women don't really see themselves as belonging there. These same writers loudly and arrogantly assert that there's no difference between men and women.

Attention Feminists! As shocking as this seems, the physical, psychological, emotional and hormonal differences between men and women cause women to behave differently than men. Women behave differently in the workplace, that's why they are treated differently in the workplace.

BIOLOGY AND HOW YOU SEE YOURSELF

On average, women are only 60 percent as strong and only 90 percent as big as men. Since the emergence of early hominids, females have not confronted males to demand anything because they can't enforce their demands with physical force. To get what they want, women have to manipulate and maneuver. (See note at end of chapter on manipulativeness.)

A woman's physically smaller structure results in an emotional and psychological sense-of-self that's fundamentally different from a man's sense-of-self. A woman's sense-of-self produces a radically different worldview than men have. In short, you don't see the same thing I see when we both look at people around the conference table.

For example, at a crucial meeting to determine whose strategy will be chosen for the ad campaign, yours or mine, there will be emotional discussions, implied threats, manipulation, attempts to shame, attempts to dominate and loud arguments.

As subconscious as it is, my sense-of-self tells me I can hold my own or win a physical confrontation (fistfight) with anybody at the conference table. My first impulse when confronted is to resort to violence. What's yours?

A woman is at an extreme disadvantage when surrounded by men. Her sense-of-self is that she cannot win a physical confrontation with anybody at the conference table. As subconscious as that feeling is, it inhibits her when she is confronted by a big, loud man who argues with her.

When confronting anybody, a man behaves as he does because of his sense-of-self, plus testosterone-induced aggressive behavior. He puffs himself up, narrows his eyes, flares his nostrils, clenches his fists, bares his teeth and growls. Men do this with each other all the time, starting when they are boys of five. It's normal and natural. They never stop.

Really now, men don't come to blows at the conference table or even outside in the hall. They just confront or react to confrontation with aggressive body language and an aggressive tone of voice.

This is one of the most important reasons for getting your tush into Assertiveness Training, instantly. Learning to handle confrontive, manipulative people is partly learning to handle men who use aggressive behavior to control females in the office and out there in the real world of romantic relationships.

BRAINWASHING AND SOCIALIZING

Girls are not taught to stand up for themselves. From birth, girls are taught that compromise is good:

When someone gets angry do whatever you have to do to calm everything down. Put yourself last. Take care of everyone else first.

On female basketball, soccer, softball, field hockey or whatever teams, pushing, shoving and confrontation are absolutely necessary to win. Competition teaches the necessity and value of confrontation. By not participating in team sports as girls, women do not understand how to confront, the need for, or value of, confrontation.

When confronted at the office, a woman does not know how to respond appropriately. When confrontation is what's needed to solve a problem at the office, a woman doesn't know how to confront someone appropriately.

It is extremely hard for women, and even harder for young women, to ignore decades of cultural conditioning when challenged at work by a loud, firm, emotional man or a loud, firm emotional woman. It takes practice and making mistakes, like everything else in this book and in this life.

That's another reason why you change companies often. Every time you screw up a confrontation, either by crying, withdrawing or with an over-kill attack, you'll have to change companies to continue your climb up the pay scale.

To make big bucks you have to stand up for yourself. You have to confront the people who are talking behind your back, starting rumors, sabotaging your work and other cowardly ways of fighting. Those people are almost always female. The next step is learning how to fight back and win. Get thyself into Assertiveness Training!

WHAT TO EXPECT

To us men, a woman attacks another woman without warning, without apparent cause, without mercy, with methods we'd never use. So, I really can't predict what your female enemy will do, when or where, or even why. All I can tell you for certain is that the attack will be covert: rumor spreading, subtle undermining with your boss, semi-cute putdowns in public and a million more.

An obvious, up-front confrontation by a woman at the office is extremely rare. But when it happens, she's trying to do the same thing as a male enemy — have management see that you can't hack it. If you cry, get angry or befuddled, she wins.

For [she] who fights and runs away may live to fight another day;
But [she] who is in battle slain, can never rise and fight again.
1760 OLIVER GOLDSMITH

Although it's rare, I can tell you that an up-front confrontation will only come from a woman who is wearing the uniform. Avoid situations where she can confront you until you've completed Assertiveness Training and practiced Smith's techniques over and over. You're not ready until then. Don't get into it with her. Don't let her start it.

HOW THE OTHER WOMAN SEES YOU

The enemies of The Other Woman are all women who want to get ahead. There is little room near the top because there are only a few positions up there for women.

Not knowing you're only here for the short haul, she believes that if it weren't for you, she'd have a lock on the promotion to Director of MIS with the $62k salary and perks. She knows she can do the job. She knows you can do the job. Most males don't want it. It's a dead end.

Although both of you are four years and three promotions away, you're the only competition she sees. The stakes are enormous. In this situation, it really is a zero-sum game. That is, if somebody wins *x,* then somebody has to lose *x*. She feels stress every time you're around.

THE MOST DANGEROUS OF ALL

All women wearing the same uniform as you want that opening near the top. The woman who smiles and acts like she's on your side is the most dangerous. She says her uniform is camouflage so "they" don't suspect she's really a "human being." Or, she says it keeps the wolves away, or it's expected in her position or some other excuse.

The red hourglass on a shiny black spider is the same as the Corporate Uniform on a woman, it's all you need to see.

Her treacherous plan begins with gaining your trust. Expecting nothing in return, she guides you through the first stages of the corporate labyrinth. "We women have to stick together." She'll share personal secrets with you to demonstrate she's really your friend, sincere and vulnerable. You reciprocate, confiding fears and desires. Listening for something useful, she probes tactfully for a weakness. She bides her time. After discovering your weakness, she'll develop a way to exploit it when the right time comes. *Translation:* when you least expect it. She will be able to destroy you completely and get that promotion.

Treachery and betrayal can only follow trust. She can't stab you in the back if you don't turn your back. She cannot strike your Achilles heel if she doesn't know where it is.

Do not let the female wearing the uniform close enough to probe for secrets or weaknesses. Be all business, civil, polite and cooperative about work matters, but never vulnerable.

PECKING ORDER DISRUPTED

Women fight for the attention of males even after they are engaged, even after they are happily married, even after they have blue hair. The 58 year-old secretaries, 22 year-old clerks, 27 year-old administrative assistants, 35 year-old contract administrators, 43 year-old staff assistants, each knows where she stands. You threaten the pecking order of male attentiveness. Females who feel you pushed them down a peck or two will hate you.

Most women over 35 resent young females. Youth is what men want. You have it. They no longer have it. You'll be resented no matter what you do.

At first they can't believe you don't want the men's attention. They think you're playing hard to get. If your "engagement ring" is prominent, it takes only a month for most to realize you aren't a threat after all. At that point, some will genuinely open up to you. Reciprocate cautiously and slowly.

YOUNG FEMALE COMPETITOR

Few young women are interested in competing with you for promotions. Most are competing for a husband.

Rivals come in two types (a) those in it for the long haul (b) those willing to give it a shot for a few years to see if they can hit a home run. If not, they'll bail out, marry Jimmy and make babies. A home run is a $40k salary in three years. No chance but they won't know that for two more years.

The long hauler is hungry, more focused, trains harder and takes it all seriously. A home run swinger has nothing to lose. She takes much bigger risks. Jimmy and living happily ever after is her fall-back position. She's relaxed. There's nothing at stake. That's her big edge.

OFFICE NEWCOMER COMPETITOR

Open and eager to begin her adult life, she's breaking loose from the nurse-teacher values of her parents, particularly Mommy's. Slim, trim, pretty, optimistic, full of energy, college grad and a Career Woman in the making. Not to worry, she's quick to run back home for a stroke or a safe place if it gets too rough. Not dangerous unless she's bright and owns a dog-eared copy of this book.

PSEUDO CAREER WOMAN COMPETITOR

This woman plays at a career. At thirtysomething, or even twentysomething, she's married to a guy who makes 20 times the salary she's going to get by betraying you.

Few people realize she'll stay in the corporate world for no more than five years. To her, this "career" is only diversion and entertainment until she retires to make babies or do charity work with other bored rich bitches. She dresses well, talks well, acts well and is a career woman for all appearances. It's all an act. Spot her quickly by noting the extremely expensive accessories and clothes. Armani, Gucci and Fendi tip her hand.

She's like the young one trying for a home run. Making long term enemies doesn't concern her. She plays rougher and knows more dirty tricks because she's learned from her rich hubby.

To you, the stakes are high. To her, the stakes are not even considered because of her husband's bucks. She has nothing to lose, so she's never rattled or nervous. It really doesn't make a bit of difference to her. The real thrill she seeks is to get promoted high enough so she can play Let's Pretend We're Important. Her fall-back position is the idle life and shopping.

DIVORCED HOUSEWIFE COMPETITOR

Never had a job. Frightened. Angry. Tired. Trying to get by. She has no idea who's on first, let alone what the hell is going on. She's 30 pounds overweight, has kid problems, ex-husband problems, money problems, no self-esteem, no confidence, afraid, worried and bitter. Dangerous if intelligent. Can't afford to back down because she needs the money and the job. Will lie, cheat and steal for the promotion.

SELF-MADE WOMAN COMPETITOR

You'll be despised by all females who feel you entered the company at a high position without paying your dues as they have done. A typical self-made woman came here directly from high school. Now she's number two in Data Processing.

She learned not to dress like a teeny bopper or seductress by trial and error. She learned how to get along with the old bats who make every young woman's first few years hell. She's busted her buns.

About 34, now divorced with two kids, she resents you. She resents your education, your clothes, your looks and most of all what she believes is your luck. You have not earned the right to be here as she has. She's indignant over a gross injustice. Extremely dangerous because she knows everybody and everything. She needs to stay at this company.

Defuse this one early. Tell her indirectly that you think she's great at her job, you appreciate the chance to learn from her, you're *lucky* to be here.

ALL FEMALES ARE SUSPECT AT THE BEGINNING

The saboteur cutthroat is camouflaged. Pay attention to your intuition. Make females earn your trust. Assume they're smiling cobras. Trust them no more than you'd trust a new man in your romantic life. They'll seduce you with friendliness, then whack you off at the knees. They'll use tears, helplessness, anger, rage, whining, anything to get close enough to slay you.

One or more of them will take you aside and appear to be helpfully explaining who the players are. Take the information with a grain of salt. You're seeing the world as she sees it. Even worse, she could be setting you up to fail by telling you exactly the wrong way to view the boss or the boss's secretary or whomever.

The cautious seldom err.
CONFUCIUS

Identify dangerous women early. Notice which ones spread rumors, which ones are catty and which ones are critical of other women. As always, study uniforms. Start files on apparent rivals or enemies. Jot down first impressions. Add information on weaknesses and strengths as time goes by.

To survive women and prosper in the man's world of the corporation, you must have friends and allies. Join *Alliances*.

On manipulativeness: Since women can't enforce their demands, they have to maneuver and manipulate. Today, females learn this early. It begins with, and is continually reinforced by, Mommy manipulating Daddy, sitcom wives manipulating sitcom husbands and soap opera females manipulating soap opera males. As a pre-teen she learns to manipulate her first male, Daddy. At the same time, she sees older girls manipulating their boyfriends. By the time she goes to college, manipulation is automatic. When she goes out into the real world of the workplace, it's hard for her to realize that she must use a different method of interaction. This is another reason women have a hard time climbing up the hierarchy. The antidote for manipulativeness training is Assertiveness Training. Get thyself into a class and read Smith's book.

When bad men combine, the good must associate else they will fall one by one, an unpitied sacrifice in a contemptible struggle.
1770 EDMUND BURKE

Alliances

Without alliances, you are powerless. Without power you are nothing.

As members of a group are isolated from all others by territorial animosity so they are welded together by territorial defense. The stranger must be hated, the fellow protected. For the foreigner there must exist no measure of tolerance or charity or peace; for the countryman one must feel at least rudimentary loyalty and devotion. The individual must protect the group; the group must protect the individual. ***The Territorial Imperative ROBERT AUDREY***

Any corporate group you are part of by choice or by assignment is bound by the territorial imperative. Veterans of every group have learned that another group, such as Administration or Data Processing, will usurp any territory left unguarded for an instant.

Territory can be literal, floor space or offices, or figurative, responsibility for some aspect of the company such as recruiting or facilities maintenance. It makes no difference what the territory is, some other group will try to take it. Mistrust and hostility abound.

MAJOR AND MINOR ALLIANCES

In prison, convicts form alliances along color lines. Blacks ally against Mexicans against whites. In there, just as out here in corporate prison, you must belong to an alliance. Loners don't survive, Rambo notwithstanding.

In corporate prison, alliances are along department lines or project lines, depending on how your particular prison is organized. Primary alliances are easy to identify. Look over the organization chart. Major groups compete for the limited money. Typically, Engineering is against Manufacturing. Procurement is against Administration and Finance. Personnel is against everyone.

In the major alliance there are smaller groups. Prison blacks divide into the gangs they came from, Crips against Bloods. Engineering divides into Civil Engineers against Mechanical Engineers.

In Mechanical Engineering, the division is along college lines or former employers or any category that's fraternal. In prison, it's the Trey Eight Crips vs the Hoover Homey Crips. In Civil Engineering, it could be Ivy League Grads against all others.

You can't figure it out until you're right there and one of the alliances recruits you or shuns you. When a gang fight breaks out it's easier to tell who's on whose side. You might even be able to figure out what the fight's about. Often it's just for the hell of it. These adult boys aren't much different from South Central gangsters shooting rivals on Saturday night to prove what bad asses they are.

SHORT TERM ALLIANCES

Forming alliances is not very useful in the short run. Don't bother allying yourself until you decide to stay at a company for more than a year. Then, alliances are mandatory for security and prosperity. Even when you don't join, you still have to know who's who and which alliance wants what so you don't tramp on the wrong toes.

PICK YOUR SPOT

Some groups you'll be part of: your department, Contract Administration; your section, Domestic Sales; your functional group, New Business.

Within Contract Administration, you'll have to choose between two alliances, the one supporting the Deputy Director, age 47, or the one backing the Chief Contracts Administrator, age 52. Your decision — when the 61 year-old Director dies or retires, will his Deputy get the job? You only have a few months to make up your mind which alliance to join if he retires at 62. But you have plenty of time if he's waiting for 65. Use techniques in *Spying* to find out.

Allying with a loser makes you a loser. If you pick the Deputy and he's passed over in favor of someone from outside, say Corporate Administration, it won't cause much damage. But if you side with the Deputy and the Chief Contracts Administrator wins, update your resume and warm up the getaway car. The new Director will hold it against you forever.

If you don't ally with either group, no matter which one wins, you're on the outside. Promotions and perks do not reach outsiders. Outsiders don't get protected from layoffs. Outsiders don't get inside information about a war being fought way up in the company. The outcome of that war determines if Contracts Administration is absorbed by Division Administration or stays independent. In short, decide who to back or you're an outsider, no place to be if you want to stay at that company.

TREACHERY FROM WITHIN

When Julius Caesar became Emperor, he was told he would be constantly protected by the Praetorian Guards. Demonstrating his prowess as a real politician, he astutely asked, "Who guards the guards?" Right! Betrayal can only come from someone close enough to discover your weaknesses. In the alliance you join, all members are potential traitors Follow my advice on caution and prudence given in *The Other Woman*.

CHANGING PARTNERS

You must stand ready to switch alliances at the drop of a heart attack. Don't be inextricably allied. Especially don't be publicly inextricably allied. Don't be public unless it is necessary to survive until you can change companies.

Weave a web of attachments you can break or redouble at a moment's notice. You're pulling the string on the puppet of alliance, not the puppet on the end of someone else's strings.

No matter if you stay or go, you have to be ready and willing to fight for what you want. *Fighting* is necessary to get what you want. Fighting is necessary to keep what you get. The corporation has no place for the fainthearted, at least no place above $25k.

To fight and conquer in all your battles
is not supreme excellence.
Supreme excellence consists of breaking
the enemy's resistance without fighting.
The Art Of War SUN TZU

If you want peace, the thing you've gut to du
Is jes' to show you're up to fightin' tu.
1848 JAMES RUSSELL LOWELL

Fighting

You didn't get what your male contemporaries got drilled into their heads and hearts — fight the good fight and win. Rules? Push against them as hard as you can. If you get caught, you get caught. Fighting and competing is life. That's the way it is.

Instead you got feminist propaganda about being the equal of males. Trouble is, males didn't, don't and won't get that propaganda.

Late adolescent boys hurl *pussy* at each other as the ultimate insult. Did you hurl *prick* to insult a girl who angered you? Nope! You called her a slut. Think about all the ramifications of that.

COMPETITION IS THE WAY OF LIFE

You're in the corporate jungle, naively expecting to be treated equally, justly and with respect. Wrong! It's a jungle, not a living room. You're another jungle animal vying for the limited resources of the jungle. There's only money and prestige, as if those aren't redundant.

There's competition for the most desirable of anything. In high school, it was for the handsome quarterback. At work, the contests are for the high paying jobs or the jobs with visibility or the jobs that are fun.

CONFLICT IS NATURAL AND NORMAL

Strife is a given. In life, things do not go smoothly. Understand and accept this or eternally grieve in a fairytale universe.

Tranquil is abnormal. Look at your own life, your own family, your own sorority, any group you belong to.

Life is bloody, nasty and short.
Leviathan 1651 THOMAS HOBBES

Someone wants something somebody else has. It is not bad. It is not unusual. It is normal. A fight happens when someone tries to take something that belongs to you and you resist. No resistance, no fight. Surrender to keep the peace or fight for what you want.

How do animals deal with conflict? Fight or flight. Most office dwellers are animals: sloths, toads, parrots, weasels, rats, mice, sheep and turkeys who flee. Aggression terrifies them. They don't know how to fight or they are cowards, so they flee. You can't. You must not only fight, but know when and with whom.

Most aggressive moves are designed to grab something without putting anything at risk. That is, greedy adversaries try to get more than they have without risking anything should you fight and win. They lose only a bit of face if you win. Although you win respect and instill fear in other aggressors, you only preserve what you had because he risked nothing.

Before entering the fray, make certain your opponent has something at stake, such as (a) the promotion (b) the corner office (c) the new color printer or whatever.

I repeat, don't get into it unless he's got something at risk. If he has nothing to lose, take no chances. You're only going to be there for another few months. However, once you're at a company where you plan to stay for a few years, winning every single fight, no matter how small, is mandatory. Even then, if nothing's at stake except face, don't engage him unless he's going to lose more than face to you.

A SHOW OF FORCE, POWER AND DANGER

Killing (defeating publicly) someone is brilliant office politics. After you've been there four or five months, choose an enemy you can easily defeat. Pick a fight. Then kill him.

For example, in the last staff meeting you suggested revenue could be improved if everyone in the department got more calls, adding that you thought many calls were being missed. A lightweight rival snickers and says, "Donna, how would we know if a caller doesn't reach us, intuition? Female intuition?"

In the next meeting, raise the issue and wait until the lightweight guffaws. Produce a computer printout showing how many calls were directed to your department versus how many were answered by your department. (You were able to accomplish this because you're on good terms with the Manager of Telecommunications.) Produce a summary showing the number of calls received by your department versus total revenue generated. (You were able to create this because you are on good terms with your department's bean counter.) Pass around a summary sheet. At the bottom, calculations show revenue increases a minimum of $3k each month if only a third of the obvious hangups were prevented. Pass out a memo from Personnel stating the cost of a temp receptionist is $1.2k, maximum.

Suggest that a temp be hired immediately. The supervisor approves. The lightweight rival sits in stunned silence.

Word spreads. The rest of your stay will be free from attack by lightweights and most middleweights, thus enjoyable. Don't get cocky. When the stakes make it worthwhile, anyone and everyone will attack. Some will be heavyweights.

FIGHTS ARE ALWAYS TO THE DEATH

Choose your enemies carefully. Only fight when winning helps you reach your long run goal. Otherwise, avoid fighting. Every fight has a winner and a loser. You can't lose if you don't fight.

Once swords are crossed, it's to the death. Avoid all duels with any workable compromise or by withdrawing. Never, never let potential opponents know you are so minded. Make them think you're ruthless and deranged. Convince them you castrate downed opponents, ram the testicles down their throats and laugh gleefully as they choke to death.

Should you get forced into a fight, kill your opponent with quick, deadly force. Don't let him gain the sympathy of the crowd. Show no mercy. Kill!

Once he's wounded (the supervisor gives him a dirty look as he objects to your idea), disembowel him immediately. (Sorry Jim, I know you have your own plans but this is best for everyone.) Don't let him enlist allies. (I can't imagine anyone being selfish enough to agree with you.)

Sudden death is the best for all to see. The reputation (rep) you earn prevents most future fights.

FIGHT TO GET THERE, FIGHT TO STAY THERE

If it's valuable, you must fight to get it *and* fight to keep it. The biggest shock and disappointment in my life was finding out how hard it was to stay on top. I was stunned, taking more hits than at any point on the way up. Shots were coming from everywhere now that the stakes were higher.

One man is much the same as another.
He is best, is he who is trained in the severest school.
ATHENIAN GENERAL THUCYDIDES

The people near the top are not the bumbling pot shot artists you meet on the way up. Nope! These guys have steel balls, big brains and ice in their veins. They are combat veterans. As one-time victims of all the tricks, ploys and ambushes, they are formidable adversaries.

Near the magic number, you are tested repeatedly until you show that you're deadly. Then they back off in an unspoken truce. However, the truce doesn't stop those from below. Every so often there comes along an unusually shrewd, ruthless, deadly opponent from below. One can never relax and enjoy, otherwise one won't stay on top.

YOU ARE EXPECTED TO FIGHT

Your boss expects you to fight with anyone trying to steal your department's floor space, equipment, people, parking space, whatever. Territorial squabbles go on all the time. When anybody encroaches on department turf, you are expected to fight. Don't run to your boss and sound the alarm. He won't fight because he's chicken shit.

Caution! Unless you can win something big for yourself, don't actually fight over department turf. The Tower Of Jello won't back you up if you piss off someone important and dangerous. Just make it look like and sound like a fight, period. Losing this fight does not damage your rep.

RIVALS AND COMPETITORS

Your rivals are males under 30 and women of any age with the same goals you have. The person who will get the promotion if you don't is the most dangerous.

Under-30 males actually believe they can make a difference, believe they can change things. They foolishly think maximizing profit is what the company is about. They don't know that maximizing survival is what the company, the division, the department, the section, is solely interested in. So, most younger males are predictable, thus easily defeated.

All that is required to win is to simply pitch your ideas so that everyone realizes survival is what your idea ensures, without you ever saying "survival." The young male will pitch his ideas in terms that blatantly say "maximize profit, requiring some sacrifice and some risks," often using those exact words! When you hear a rival's pitch that sounds like yours, look out!

A bright woman with five years or more under her corporate belt has found out the hard way that survival drives everything. She knows what to do and how to phrase her ideas. She identifies you as a competitor faster than you identify her. Remember, detect a competitor by noticing her uniform and image match yours.

Absenteeism: Women with children under six - 10.5 days
Men with children under six - 3.3 days
US DEPARTMENT OF LABOR 1992

Women married with children or divorced with children are not a threat for higher paying positions, over $40k. Top Management knows these women aren't serious about their long range careers. But that does not mean they are not dangerous, it only means that once you've decided to stay at a company for a few years you needn't spend a tremendous amount of time neutralizing them as long term threats.

Single or divorced women of any age, dressed like teenagers are no threat unless they are the main squeeze of a VP. If one is, she will destroy you should you inadvertently piss her off. That's why *Spying* is so important.

ONLY FEAR CAUSES SELF CONTROL

Peace is assured only when your rival's greed is controlled by his fear. He must be afraid to attack. To do that, you must increase his fear so that he controls himself. When you have no rep for being ruthless, it can't be done.

You must have a rep before your enemies control themselves. You get a rep when you earn it by killing a few challengers.

Until then, use an enemy's overconfidence about fighting with a "mere female" to your great advantage. He won't bother being fully prepared. You will.

SUDDEN, DEADLY FORCE

When it's necessary to do battle, never let it be known you are going to fight. Smile sweetly. Be demure. Then silently smash his skull, from behind. He must not hear your footsteps. He might tense up just as your war club lands, causing a glancing blow instead of a killing blow, giving him time to withdraw, gather his senses and kill you.

A "killing blow" is landed when you and Mr. Arch Enemy are in a meeting to review progress on reducing the department's reproduction expenses. At just the right moment, produce hard evidence that your idea has already been tested and shown to be extremely successful.

With no fanfare, you conducted an experiment using a mock form and log sheets two weeks ago. You had accounting extend the figures and write a memo describing the annual savings. Jeff in Graphics and Terri in Repro both owed you a favor. Fred, in Accounting, wants to date you. He bent the rules a bit.

HIS WEAPONS

Beyond the standard office politics tactic of setting you up to take the blame for a doomed project, he has innuendos about PMS, too emotional, being a lesbian, having an affair and being a home wrecker or any other character assassination.

You will be called a castrating bitch and a ball buster, but beyond name calling and lies he has nothing. You merely have to be ready when he resorts to his weapons. Being ready means that you overcome your hurt and disorientation quickly, then counterattack with the ferocity of a Viking Berserker.

Being ready requires that you identified him as dangerous long ago and began compiling information as described previously. You know what his weaknesses are and have developed a strategy to attack him there.

Being ready requires that you practice your response ahead of time. Talk with your friends from the outside. Tell them what the scenario(s) will be. Tell them what you plan to do. Then act it out. Reverse roles. Be the enemy and think about what his response might be. There's more coming shortly.

BLUFF, AVOIDANCE AND COMPROMISE

Some office animals have more than fight or flight responses to deal with aggression. Develop these responses.

Why do cats hiss, arch and screech so much? They want the opponent to be afraid to attack. Often you can avoid a fight with a show of strength, using only words and body language. Just the display scares away most aggressors. They figure, "I'll find a pushover somewhere else." Bluffing is a wonderful way of avoiding a fight, especially with aggressors you're easily capable of defeating. Remember, don't fight unless you absolutely must, since you never know for certain you will win.

Bluffing works until you get called, then you must use force. Don't bluff anyone with a rep for winning, he'll call you. Bluff him only if you're willing to fight. If you're not willing, flee, saving as much face as possible.

If he calls your bluff, then thrashes you, word spreads you're a bluffer. Everyone you fooled will be back. Even worse, those you could have bluffed in the future will call you. Then you'll be fighting all the time. Do not bluff unless you're willing to fight or if fleeing is too costly.

The goal of avoidance is to not lose anything. You win nothing but you preserve the status quo. Your attitude is, "If I fight I might lose. I'll just stay out of that jerk's way." Use avoidance when you're new and don't know who's dangerous. Or, when you're dealing with someone who has the protection of a powerful person "upstairs" who can do serious damage to you even if you kick the bejezus out of his flunky. Once again, this is why *Spying* is so crucial.

Negotiation can prevent a fight from starting or it can settle a conflict once started. Most aggressive types only negotiate after you fight them to a standstill or if you have a rep. Negotiation leaves both parties dissatisfied, but winning a little while losing a little is better than losing everything.

If avoidance is not possible and flight is not desirable for the long haul, a compromise has to happen. All these non-fight solutions are fully explained in *When I Say No, I Feel Guilty*. Read it.

FAMILY DISTURBANCE CALLS

Many cops get killed attempting to break up family disputes. As the Neurotic Offspring wail, Drunken Dad bashes Martyr Mom around every Friday night in a ritualized, demented family dance. When the cop tries to stop the dance, what do Drunken Dad, Martyr Mom and Neurotic Offspring do? They close ranks and attack the cop with all that anger they were diffusing on each other.

It's the same in corporations. A typical neurotic dance involves Engineering bashing Manufacturing who likes to bash Engineering. Never get caught playing cop attempting to stop this. Don't even try to be a traffic director. You can get fired by being an innocent bystander.

When you stumble into the fray, simply say, "Sorry, I can see how you'd think we screwed that up. I'll let Dick know right away. I can't do a damn thing about it from my level. Sorry." Then get out of there as fast as possible, gracefully or any other way.

The hate goes back farther than anyone can remember, like the Arabs and Jews, the Serbs and Croats. This too, is a religious war, fought for mystical reasons or just for the hell of it. It's never resolvable and extremely dangerous to the new kid on the block.

RUMORS — ROUGH STUFF

When the stakes get high enough (opening a new office in Hawaii, or the promotion pays $52k) you'll have to deal with false rumors. That's what an arch enemy does when he thinks you'll get the promotion instead of him. Or, you got the promotion, now he wants to make certain you never get another.

Mr. Arch Enemy spreads it around that you are an easy lay but really bad in bed because you have a drinking problem. His motives are (a) make you out as a drunken slut, thus unsuitable for further advancement (b) have fellow males think he's a lady killer. Rough, right?

The typical young woman denies the story on the spot. She angrily, or worse, tearfully, says to whomever relays the rumor to her, "That's ridiculous. I never even went out with him. He's a liar."

She doesn't understand a rumor of the sexual kind spreads faster and is embellished more grandly than any other rumor. She doesn't realize his audience will be the entire office while her audience is only one person, the person she denies it to. Worst of all, she doesn't realize her denial will not be spread.

If it's worth having, it's worth cheating for.
LA RAIDERS, PRESIDENT OF THE GENERAL PARTNER AL DAVIS

FIGHT OR DIE

When this happens, not responding is the worst thing. That makes everyone assume it's true. If you only deny it, you don't reach everyone who heard it. If you try to deny it all around the company, "Methinks the lady doth protest too much," is the result. In blunt terms, everyone assumes it's true unless you fully discredit this prick.

CONFRONTATION OR COUNTERATTACK

When his lie reaches you, return fire, overwhelming fire or he wins. Confrontation or counterattack by rumor are your only choices.

When someone tells you his rumor, it's impossible to be cool. Let the shock show on your face. Don't say anything except, "My God! That bastard." Get up and leave.

After you've gathered yourself, discuss the situation with your closest outside friends. Brainstorm about how to counterattack with a more vicious rumor. Weigh the advantages of counterattacking and confrontation. The choice depends on your abilities.

Confrontation is the absolute best, if you're able. It's cleaner. You end up being the Good Guy to everyone. Nobody will ever attempt this again. But the best reason is you earn a monster rep.

CALL HIM OUT

Confrontation requires that you are able to look confident and speak in a loud, firm voice. Further, you must have rehearsed what you'll say and do when he parries your thrust — denies starting the rumor and attempts to make you explain yourself or tries to make you prove he's guilty.

If he's a tough, quick-thinking political animal he may escalate the battle by embellishing his story in front of everyone. You must be ready for all possibilities.

The great advantage of confrontation is that you will be fully prepared for battle, rehearsed and practiced. He won't. The ultimate advantage is that you decide where and when to ambush him. He'll be surprised, disoriented and flustered, thus defeated quickly.

Choosing where and when to fight means you can stack the audience he must deal with. Your witnesses will be there without being obvious shills.

Attack! Come from the side while he is seated. Start talking in a loud voice before he turns around. As he turns, hover over him so that it's hard for him to stand up. Point your finger, say in an angry, strong voice that everyone hears,

> *Hey! Why are you telling lies about me? You say I'm a drunk. You say I'm easy. What in the HELL is wrong with you? I'd never go out with you.*

Hover over him. He'll try to stand so he's taller than you. Stay in his face. Make him slide his chair back in symbolic retreat, to stand. If he doesn't say anything, he's trying to gather his thoughts. Don't let him. Quickly, in a loud voice,

> *WELL? Why are you telling lies about me?*

He can only deny he started it or use questions to try and make you justify yourself:

> *What makes you think I started the rumor?* or *Why are you yelling?* or *Who said I started the rumor?*

Don't answer questions. No matter what he says demand an answer.

> *Why are you telling lies about me?*

He will deny starting the rumor,

> *I don't know who told you that. I never said that.*

You and your shills are ready. Point to them,

> *Jack told me. Eddie told me. Amy told me. Why are you telling lies about me?*

He tries to make you the bad guy for causing a scene.

> *We could have settled this quietly like professionals. Why didn't you talk with me?*

Don't answer questions. No matter what he says, demand.

Settle it! Why are you telling lies about me?

Another move is similar and so is your response.

I could have explained how this misunderstanding happened. We could have settled this quietly like professionals. Why didn't you talk with me?

Don't answer questions. No matter what he says, demand.

Explain! Why are you telling lies about me?

He can only apologize publicly or he can get up and walk out without saying anything. Or, he can get up and walk out with a feeble parting shot like,

You're crazy!

It makes no difference. When he flees you win! Embellished descriptions of the battle will roar around the company at the speed of light. Everyone will forget his lies. Nobody will start another rumor about you at that company, at least a rumor that can be traced.

But, let's replay that battle above. Let's say the guy who started the rumor is a tough, political animal who can think under pressure. He counterattacks.

Bullshit! You know you were drunk. You know you're easy. This act doesn't fool anybody!

He gets up, sneers and storms out before you can reply.

As Oscar Wilde's quote emphasized at the beginning of *Rivals And Enemies,* choose your enemies carefully. If you can't beat him by confronting him, you'll have to damage him with his weapon, rumor.

COUNTERATTACK BY RUMOR

After you gather yourself and have discussed the pros and cons of confrontation versus counterattack, go back to the person who related the rumor.

In private ask, "When did he tell you that?" After the reply, laugh smugly. Say, with stunned, laughable astonishment,

"Really? My God! He was scared. Couldn't get it up. Started crying. Begged me not to tell. Said he wasn't queer. Jeez? Do you think he's gay? Have you ever heard anything?"

All's fair in love, war and office politics. You didn't start the fight. If you don't fight back, you lose automatically. If you go through channels and file a complaint you will be marked as a troublemaker, worse your rep will be — unable to hold her own when the chips are down.

WIN WITH GRACE, LOSE WITH DIGNITY

As a woman, you have an added burden. You must win without looking like the aggressor or the bad guy. At the same time, you must make certain the fallen enemy does not look like the underdog. If you don't accomplish these two things, your victory will be hollow. Men hate, no, that's not strong enough. Men loathe, and will forever scorn, a woman who beat a man unless she is a generous and gracious victor. Why? Dammed if I know. That's just the way it is.

When you get beaten, and you will, never cry foul, never whine. Why? Because men are watching. Whining or crying foul makes you a two-time loser in their eyes. Men, and women, must be gracious losers, or at least appear to be.

If your opponent cheated in ways that most men consider genuinely unfair, his victory will be hollow and useless. His rep will be destroyed at that company and maybe forever. No man who witnessed his sin or heard about it will forgive or forget, ever.

Why? My God! He violated one of the most sacred unwritten rules of being a "real" man, he didn't fight fair and square. But that violation is minor when compared to his detestable betrayal of all men — to win, he had to cheat, against *just a girl!*

The conclusions every man, including me, draws — he's weak, cowardly, can never be trusted, can never be depended on. In short, he's finished.

Complicated? Yes. Necessary? Absolutely!

What are the alternatives? Become a cocktail waitress, meet a handsome, rich customer who'll marry you without a prenuptial agreement? Win the lottery?

STRATEGY AND TACTICS

Mutual Assured Destruction (MAD) is what kept us from toe-to-toe nuclear combat with the Rooskies during the cold war. When you can lose everything and so can your opponent, careful, thoughtful diplomacy is necessary at all times.

Be a statesman, not a warrior. Diplomacy and tact first. Threatening body language and tone of voice second. Warning shot third, put it in writing and show it to him. Broadside fourth, send the memo with copies to your boss and his boss. Rolling-thunder saturation bombing fifth, have a trial (meeting) making certain you have rigged the jury. Nuclear threat last, sexual harassment claim.

Sometimes a preemptive strike is necessary. The amount of power used depends on the situation and the importance of the battle at hand. A preemptive strike could be an off-the-record, private discussion with your boss regarding Mr. Arch Enemy's "passes" at you, or you heard he threatened to spread a rumor. Use the same hesitant, indirect style described below.

A preemptive strike is what happened to Egypt in the Six-Day War. Their entire air force was destroyed on the ground by a surprise attack from Israel while both sides were still posturing, shouting and blaming. The most famous preemptive strike was Japan's attack on Pearl Harbor while their diplomats were in Washington talking about how to prevent war.

Only the dead have seen an end to war.
PLATO

In office politics, preemptive strikes are useful when your arch enemy is stronger and better connected than you. It's easiest to destroy him when he least expects it. Take him out of the race for the promotion a month before he thinks the war will begin. You take him out by one-upping him in front of the person who will decide who gets the promotion. How you do this depends on your file of his weaknesses and strengths.

YOUR ULTIMATE WEAPON

Anita Hill incited the government to give all women, especially young, attractive women, the equivalent of a nuclear bomb — a claim of sexual harassment. You hold all the cards. The government is on your side, as is NOW and the courts.

Do not threaten. Do not brandish this weapon. Do not even imply sexual harassment until you're certain it is absolutely necessary.

ATOMIC BOMBS ARE THE LAST RESORT

A claim of sexual harassment is necessary when you have been beaten by an arch enemy. You're about to be fired because she, or even he, planted evidence, bribed witnesses and paid off investigators. (Your arch enemy is most likely to be female.)

Do not file a formal complaint. Do not put anything in writing. This is an off-the-record war. You are merely stalling. The war gives you time to find another job before they boot you out the door.

WAR ROOM ALERT — CONDITION RED

Climb down into the bomb bay and arm the weapon when you're called to the Big Boss's office and asked to close the door. Your boss is there. He tries to look serious but manages only sheepish. Big Boss and Tom Toady from Personnel attempt to pass themselves off as Supreme Court Justices with mock formality. Let them talk, pontificate and posture.

When they ask to explain your side of the story told by arch enemy, open the bomb bay doors:

> *What you don't know is that . . . I've tried hard not to, uh, bring this up* [pause for effect] . . . *but, Dan has been . . . uh, he tried to . . . I told him . . . uh, I was engaged. Well you know.* [pause for effect] . . . *That's why he's trying to get me fired!*

Just sit there. Look at your hands. Wait. They're stunned. They didn't think your ovaries were made out of titanium. They thought they could railroad you right on out without a fight. Just wait quietly.

They'll mumble, ". . . new information, have to know . . . more explicit, uh . . ."

Don't you say it. Force them to say it. "It," Dan tried to put the make on you.

They will grill you, saying you need witnesses and evidence. They will try to make you feel like you don't have any rights and have no chance of making the charge stick.

Your response is to look at them and say vague things: "not exactly . . . I knew what he wanted . . . dirty words . . . well, he made it . . . himself clear to me," and such.

They'll try to get you to withdraw what you've said. Say nothing. Get up, turn and walk out. Go to your desk. Take what you need and go home. Now, they don't dare fire you.

The next move is up to them, but you need a new job. Things are out of hand here. Don't worry. They can't tell any future employer anything except the dates you worked, your title and how much money you made. Call friends. Get the ball rolling.

Don't go to work for several days. Call in and say you're not feeling well. They'll have your sheepish boss call you at home and try to "talk sense" to you. This means they know they've lost. Hold out for justice as you see it. Keep up the search for a new job. Do everything advised in *Office Sex.*

Eventually they'll offer a half a loaf. Take it and get back to work. Stick around only until you have a new job.

DECLARED NUCLEAR WAR

A frontal assault is necessary when you have been sexually harassed by someone so powerful he, or even she, has not backed off and has said he, or even she, will fire you if you don't put out. In this case, you must file a formal complaint. You must stand your ground. Insist that everything is on the record. You must get legal advice from working women's groups listed in *Where To Get Help* at the end of the book. There's much more on nuclear war in *Office Sex.*

A Degree Of Difference exists in people, from the company's viewpoint. To get promoted fast enough, high enough, to make enough money to become independent, you must have a degree, any degree.

The only thing good about film school
is you meet people.
If they get into a studio they call you.
USC Cinema Alumni GEORGE LUCAS

Mother wanted me to get a good education
so she never sent me to school.
MARGARET MEAD

A Degree Of Difference

To gain entrance to the theater where the big money can be had, you need a ticket. A college degree is a magical admission ticket, nothing more. Even companies below the Fortune 7500 level endow degrees with a mysterious power that bears no relation to the ability of the degree holder.

Realistic people know a degree from today's universities establishes nothing more than the grad was tenacious enough to endure years of boredom, can read and may be able to write simple sentences. That makes no difference. An employee without a degree is a serf, unpromotable beyond a clearly specified salary grade in every corporation's Policy Manual.

Upon graduation your GPA is used by Personnel bureaucrats to justify the low salary you are paid. If you are Phi Beta Kappa, they say you don't have an MBA. But if you interned at the company before you graduated, the supervisor who hires you can prevent Personnel from low balling you. Otherwise, your first job will be low paying no matter what your GPA was.

In college, get a summer job with any company, anywhere, under any pretext. You'll have to work for peanuts at mindless tasks but you'll meet the right people, the ones with the power to hire you upon graduation without Personnel getting in the loop.

After your first job, the only thing companies care about is how much your present company pays you and that you have a degree, any degree from any college, anywhere.

THE COMPANY PAYS

Every company has a tuition program. Every company encourages employees to accumulate degrees. If you don't have a degree, get one paid for by the company. If you don't have an MBA, get one paid for by the company. If you have an MBA, get a JD. You know who pays, right?

When you've been at a company for only a few months, it's difficult to get into the Tuition Program. They don't want to pay until they're convinced you're going to stay forever. It doesn't say that anywhere in the Policy Manual because, like other important corporate rules, it is unwritten.

In short, everyone makes it hard to find out which hoops you have to jump through to qualify. The hoops are bureaucratic forms, signed by your boss, his boss and the Division Manager. The keeper of the forms is always Personnel but your boss is the biggest obstacle. He's afraid to sign the form and break the unwritten rule because he's terrified of criticism.

Have him reveal his fear level. Say to your boss, "You know your way around here. Who do I see about the Tuition Program?" Pay close attention to his body language, tone of voice, his choice of words and your intuition. Use what he reveals to plan your strategy.

If he manipulates or stalls with, "When do you plan to go to school," have a response ready, "Oh, in a few months. Who can help me get started?"

His focus is not on helping you. His focus is on avoiding criticism, or longer range, on not looking bad if you have an MBA and he doesn't. You may take his job! Once he reveals his level of fear, plan your next move.

If he's terrified, it is necessary to set him up so that his boss knows you are entering the Tuition Program. This is the same as some other techniques you are learning, a witness is required!

Affirmative Action or whatever code word is used for "quotas" by the time you read this, gives you, as a female, a big edge. Develop phrasing that includes the code words in conversations with your boss when his boss is present.

That memo from corporate about encouraging women and minorities to . . . is a key phrase that cause them both to willingly sign the forms. Another phrase that must be included is, *increase my value to the department.*

BS MEANS MONEY, MBA MO' MONEY

Strangely, companies value the MBA they pay for more highly than if you paid for it. I've never understood this.

A few months after classes start, don't ask permission, announce that you have to leave work early on Tuesday and Thursday next week for special sessions of the class. This establishes in the mind of your boss that your education is more important to the company than a few hours at the office. Later on, you can leave early many times with no questions asked.

When they pay you to take time off *and* pay for the degree that gets you a 25 percent raise from your next company, you have mastered the fundamentals of office politics!

FOR YOUR OWN GOOD

As a woman in a man's world, the cards are stacked against you making the big money. Thus you must have every edge possible. Get every degree, certificate, credential, diploma, license and permit possible but *only* if they pay for it. The more credentials you have the more they pay you. Volunteer for every company class.

I suggest paralegal training, CPR training, insurance, real estate, taxation, union negotiating, any damn class you hear about. Make it seem like it's for the good of the department and company that you learn whatever.

Selling yourself is the most important aspect of office politics. Learn how to get up in front of people and have them believe you, and believe in you. Even if you can't get them to pay for it, take Assertiveness Training, Acting and Speech classes. The paper you push can be pushed just as easily by a new woman. You want more, more money.

Learn the social graces and etiquette as practiced at the top of the corporation. Become a John Robert Powers grad. When opportunity knocks, you'll be glad to answer the door because you'll feel comfortable moving in high society circles, as well as making an impression on the people who can change history overnight, your salary history.

RISK TAKING IS REQUIRED

Become more confident about life in general. Get into, and stay, in good physical shape. Running is the best way. It's good for your self-esteem and that's good for your self confidence.

Beyond staying in good physical condition by running for the rest of your life, accomplishing something that appears hard and dangerous builds self confidence. It strengthens your attitude and manner in the office. Take part in Outward Bound. Sky dive. Scuba dive. High dive. Ride a dirt bike. Downhill ski. Water ski. Climb a rock. Shoot powerful handguns. Backpack into the Sierra. Master karate. *Run To Freedom.*

A sound body and a sound mind.
PLATO

Run To Freedom

Running is shouting, "I am! I will! I can!" to no one, to everyone, most of all to you.

Running is saying to yourself, "This is all for you, for you alone, for nobody else but you because I want to take care of you, because you are the best person I know."

Running lets you experience your ability, your tenacity, your indifference to pain, your power of concentration, your ability to focus on a goal and die to achieve it. Running makes you, become you. Running forces you to know how powerful, really powerful, you are.

You will passively resist becoming powerful. When it's still dark, listen as you convince yourself it's okay not to get up, to not stretch, to not attack the silent, indifferent universe. Listen as you talk yourself into staying passive. Listen as you talk yourself into waiting.

Female mammals who are not homo sapiens go after what they want. Nobody ever brainwashed them into being passive. The choice is yours — take life by the throat and make it give you what you want, or sit and wait for justice.

Running is aggressive, an act of will. It is the simplest way to begin the transformation from passive to active, from manipulative to assertive.

It costs no more than a pair of $40 shoes. You can run anywhere, anytime, with nothing but your own excuses to stop you.

Running fast. Running alone. Running nowhere, going everywhere. Run as if your life depended on it. It does.

Change yourself. Change your life. Run. Nothing less will.

When you are in top physical condition, you're relaxed, powerful and confident. That's when it's far, far easier to deal with the reality of what the company is. About a third of high-level corporate men understand this. Very few women, of any level, ever understand this.

The Company Defined prevents you from trusting it or marrying it as Top Management implies you must. It also puts the necessity for office politics into perspective.

Contradictions cannot exist.
Check your premises.
The Virtue Of Selfishness AYN RAND

The Company Defined

The corporation is ten times more heartless than your wildest nightmare imagination can dream up. The rule that applies within the corporate jungle does not apply anywhere else in your life, unless you're in the primordial jungle — eat or be eaten. There is no Supreme Court, no Constitution, no Bill of Rights. There is only you, your gray matter and your guts.

There is no company to sacrifice yourself to, or for. The company is a nothing more than a piece of paper in Delaware. That paper gives those who hold it the legal right to pretend the corporation is an individual before the courts, nothing more.

The corporation is not your parent. It is not god. It is not the tooth fairy. It is a bunch of people who work for the holders of that piece of paper.

WHERE THEY CAME FROM HELPS TO UNDERSTAND

The typical major corporation was founded 100 years ago by an individual with vision, courage, intelligence, decisiveness and perseverance. Those virtues died with him. They aren't for today's men in charge. In fact, they scoff at the Founder's virtues.

Under the Founder, the company grew so large, so wealthy, so powerful, so well connected that no matter how poorly it's run, it can't be seriously wounded for decades. Even when headed by a CEO who spends all his time in self aggrandizement and creative accounting, it takes years for stockholders to realize what every member of top management knows — the company is tottering on aging, diseased legs.

Today, most large companies are nothing more than lumbering juggernauts, powered by inertia. The business climate changes slowly enough for the man in charge, even if he's a lawyer, to figure out what has to be done to keep the company bumbling along. You're just along for that ride. The idea is to be extremely well paid as you ride.

BIRTH AND DEATH

The life cycle of a corporation is the same as yours — birth, growth, maturity, degeneration, death. During the past 50 years, major corporations have grown so big, further growth is impossible. All are in decline or approaching it. Death awaits.

Realizing this, Top Management concerns itself solely with milking every last possible perk and personal dollar out of the corporation. At the same time they conduct a shameless theatrical production to convince the Board of Directors and major stockholders they're tirelessly working to ensure the good, long-term, solid health of the company.

VIEW FROM THE TOP

To stockholders, the only thing that's important is their dividend check. What the CEO does to get the money for their check is of no concern. In turn, the CEO doesn't care how Executive VPs get the Division Managers to put enough money in the bank to cover the dividend checks.

From Division Manager on down the hierarchy, the rest of the employees are chattel to be thrown platitudes and crumbs. Work gets done in spite of management, not because of management. It gets done by those afraid not to do it. It also gets done by the few people in the corporation who are conscientious. Those people are usually young. They haven't become jaded, yet.

As an employee who owns no stock in the company you are absolutely insignificant to management. Even if you own 1000 shares, you're still only chattel in their eyes. To be somebody they even know of, you must own 100,000 shares. If you had that many shares, you certainly wouldn't be pushing paper for General Cow.

The company is a cold blooded business venture. As an employee, you are a grunt, a pawn, a foot soldier in the war of survival. The company will survive if it has to sacrifice all of you grunts, if it has to lie to all of you grunts, if it has to sell all you grunts to the highest bidder, the company will survive. If you're not at the company for the money, what in the hell are you there for?

It certainly isn't to meet men is it? *Office Sex* can ruin your career in a nanosecond. Caution!

Son, in a no-win situation, stall.
When you can't stall any longer, stall some more.
Wise Father 1968 A.W. ZIPP
DURING VIETNAM, EXPLAINING TO HIS SON HOW TO DEAL WITH BEING DRAFTED AND HIS FIANCE'S ULTIMATUM TO MARRY BEFORE LEAVING

Men seldom make passes at girls who wear glasses.
1923 DOROTHY PARKER

Office Sex

When males and females are put together in the same building, sooner or later they get together. Round pegs fit into round holes. It's as natural as a sunrise. It's inevitable.

Scientists, anthropologists and psychologists explain why people are obsessed with sex using jargon and psychobabble. Here's a translation. It's this simple — sex is the most important issue in all our lives because sex is where we came from, our genetic history. Sex is where we are going, our genetic future.

Sex is how our ancestors got here. We are replicas of them. While we are here, sex is how we replicate ourselves, how we get to the future.

Among primates, males compete. The victorious (most powerful) males choose which females they'll mate with. Which females the dominant males choose is of utmost importance for two decisive reasons. Selected females are ensured of replicating themselves. And, selected females have a strong, certain genetic future since the survival traits of a dominant male have become part of future replicas of themselves.

In short, we (you, me, everybody) are here because our ancestors loved sex. Your parents, your grandparents and your great-great-great-great grandparents indulged as often as possible, as did theirs, all the way back to early Cro Magnon. Even Cro Magnon's predecessors loved sex and indulged as often as possible, otherwise Cro Magnon wouldn't have gotten there, to put us here.

SEX BEFORE SECURITY IN THE OFFICE

Remember Maslow's hierarchy of needs from Psychology 101? Air is the most important. Water is second. Food is third. Fourth, before security, which is fifth, comes sex. Love is sixth. Self actualization is last.

Once the need for air is satisfied, one seeks water until that need is satisfied. Food then becomes the dominate need. If one has enough to eat, sex is the driving force, even at the office.

Everyone pretends we're not really like this, especially priests and parents. But when a male sees a desirable female at the office his fourth most important need dominates his perception of who and what she is. Your job is to (a) understand that (b) accept that (c) prevent that. Don't look, smell, walk or talk like a desirable female at the office.

A SHARK'S FIRST PASS

Anything you can dream up, rather, anything Jackie Collins and Danielle Steel have already dreamed up, can, and will, happen during the next ten years. You'll be propositioned by boys, young men, divorced men, married men, dirty old men, and even girls, young women, divorced women, married women and dirty old women.

It is inevitable. An office shark will make a pass sooner or later. When a real shark is about to attack, it bumps into the prey then darts away. If the prey fights, the shark merely swims on to the next potential meal.

At work, the shark's first pass is similar, some version of excusable, "Sorry. Don't get mad. I'm drunk."

Fight back instantly with no sweetness. "Get your hand off me! NOW!" Stand up and storm out. Any delay implies consent. Any politeness implies he's supposed to try harder.

AFTER HOURS ARE DANGEROUS TIMES

Serious (career-ending) passes happen after work at the bar or restaurant, and when working overtime or weekends. Once he makes a pass, he's trouble. No matter how gently you reject him, he feels rejected, angry and humiliated. He plots revenge. Prevent passes. Avoid overtime and working weekends.

SEX OUT OF THE OFFICE

When young women go to Palm Springs for the weekend, their rules of engagement with males become different. They're far more willing to engage when away from home.

Caution! When men, married or single, are away from home, their rule of engagement is — there are no rules.

Traveling on company business with a boss or peer is traveling in dangerous territory. No after dinner conversations. No sitting in the bar waiting to be seated. Meet him in the dining room, eat and leave. Even better, on the way to that city, mention you have friends there. Announce you'll be spending off hours with them. Call room service, then relax in the tub with the latest smut by Judith Krantz.

DON'T EVEN THINK ABOUT IT

You have your own values and beliefs. I can't tell you where to draw the line, only you know where the line is. Trouble is, you don't know exactly where it is until he's crossed it. *Solution:* Nip everything in the bud.

> *Son, don't dip your pen in the company ink well.*
> APPALACHIAN CAREER ADVICE

Being friendly is dangerous. Flirting is death. All business and no bullshit all the time is mandatory, especially at social events or on the road, to prevent passes. Guys with tiny egos that get dinged become revenge seeking ogres.

HANDS OFF! AND OTHER WARNINGS

Courtship is nonverbal. Courtship is subconscious. Courtship is natural and normal. Courtship destroys careers.

Never, absolutely never touch men except to shake hands. Don't even gently touch one on the forearm to politely interrupt or to get his attention. Don't dare even touch him on the shoulder to have him move over in the hallway. No touching!

Absolutely do not put anything in your mouth, such as your eye glasses, to aid thinking. Do not cross and uncross your legs when seated. Do not let a shoe drop off your heel and dangle on your toes when seated. Do not adjust your hair, clothing or accessories in a preening way.

Read every book on body language you can find. Avoid all courtship postures and gestures. This will take months of self-awareness and self monitoring. ***Warning!*** If you don't stop making nonverbal courtship gestures, men will always see a potential sexual partner rather than a co-worker who happens to be female. And that's no matter how severe your uniform is, no matter that you wear no makeup, no matter what else you do. Courtship is nonverbal and subconscious.

LOUNGE LIZARDS — SLICK TALKERS

Don't let any man address you as: Darling, Honey, Sweetheart, Sugar, Dear, Baby. These twits actually believe they're clever, sweet talkers who can get seduce you with crap like that. The first time, don't embarrass him. Without a smile, say:

> *I'd appreciate it if you'd call me Donna. I don't like to be called sweetheart.*

The second time, with iron eyes, say in a loud voice:

> *I am Donna. DO NOT call me sweetheart!*

WRONG SIGNALS GET EXCHANGED

Most men believe any female who is nice to them wants to get horizontal. A smile is an invitation. Laughing at his jokes is tantamount to licking your lips.

Younger guys and inexperienced guys always interpret friendliness as an invitation. An inexperienced guy can be a 27 year-old who's always been shy and now is forcing himself to interact. It can be the 34 year-old programmer who's loved only computers since 12, but is now realizing there's more to life than zeros and ones.

The most dangerous inexperienced guy is 37. He's been married since he was 22. At his age you think he understands friendliness. He doesn't and can't.

Once married, all of us, and I speak from painful personal experience, leave behind the chance to learn adult methods of courtship. The only skills one has, including this 37 year-old, are the skills left from when he was young, inexperienced and incompetent, as if those aren't redundant.

At 37, he's a completely different person than he was at 22 but he has only the social-sexual-dating skills of a 22 year-old. His wife is a completely different person than the one he married. She's fat, boring, whiny, unresponsive, uninterested.

When you smile at this poor guy, it means "let's jump in bed." That's what it meant the last time he was "on the market" 15 years ago. If he's aggressive, you'll have problems. At 37, he's far enough up the corporate ladder to cause trouble if you embarrass him while turning him down.

Coming on to a woman makes a man vulnerable, open to pain and humiliation. When you reject him, that's what he feels and that's what I feel, and that's what every man feels. Combine that with the fact that many of us males believe it is our duty to mate with every female possible before we die. If a female is seemingly inviting us, we go for it. When she says, "Sorry, just wanna be friends," that hurts.

If you get nothing else from my book get this — males interpret friendliness as an invitation. Don't be friendly. Be civil, polite and diplomatic. More important, be all business. It prevents anything from becoming a bud that must be nipped.

DICKIN' AROUND WITH NITROGLYCERINE

To let even one court you invites disaster. Everyone will notice. When he gets rejected, he'll feel humiliated in front of the whole office and have it in for you. Sometimes everyone feels sorry for him because they think you led him on by being friendly then shot him down. So, they despise you and plot revenge. Worse, he could sweep you away to the *Sea Of Love,* proving you are not stable or promotable.

Having an affair at work is extremely dangerous to your career. Sooner or later it has to end with feelings hurt, egos crushed and dreams smashed. Retribution and revenge ruin reputations and destroy years of dedicated work.

Affairs don't go undetected for long. You can't help but radiate. Others can't help but notice. You think you're so clever and careful. Others think you're so absurd and obvious.

Don't have an affair in the office until you're thirtysomething and know the harsh reality of the relationship merry-go-round. After you know what you're doing, you'll be able to choose a man who won't break your heart deliberately. He may break it accidentally but at least it wasn't because you chose the wrong one. That still won't prevent the explosive, destructive aftermath of a breakup causing havoc at the office.

MARRIED MEN — *COSMOPOLITAN* CRAP

In her book, *Having It All,* Helen Gurley Brown tells readers they can have everything she has by doing what she did. It's the worst book ever written for women by the most self-deceived female ever. The essence of 250 pages: "Be a mouseburger, keep at it and eventually you'll make it." She never clearly defines *mouseburger,* but essentially it's a good, non-assertive, loyal secretary.

Brown after Helen Gurley, is mega-millionaire David Brown of movie producing Zanuk and Brown, behind *Jaws* and other blockbusters. Gurley's a hillbilly from the Ozarks. She toiled for 20 years as a temp secretary. About age 40, she slept with a boss who fell for her. He bought her a magazine so she could play powerful, dynamic, smart, sexy business executive.

To aspiring young women, Brown advises sex with the boss. Her logic goes like this:

> You already have sex with men.
> All men are about the same.
> Therefore: sex with your boss is okay.

Gurley's talent is as limited as her logic. Here, in her own words, is the range of her talent:

> *. . . we, the royal we, decided to reprint our 'blockbuster' article in a tenth anniversary issue and started looking through ten years of back issues for the 'spectaculars.' We couldn't find any! Nothing was outstanding, no blockbusters. They all folded into each other like egg whites into a souffle.*

Gurley never acknowledged she repeats the same articles year in and year out. There's a different title and different author but the subject is the same. The "advice" is the same. The result is the same. The magazine sells. Why? She tells readers the Big Lie, the one every young woman desperately wants to hear, you can be *Having It All,* if you buy *Cosmopolitan.*

One of Gurley's articles that folds into every other when it runs year after year, *Married Men As Good Lovers.* Involved young women are vindicated. Young women who fantasize about it are titillated. The rest, stimulated.

What goes on in *Cosmopolitan* offices is not what goes on in the real business world. Gurley doesn't have a clue that in real business, a married man in an office affair is *getting some on the side, the sly devil.* The young woman is a slut, a home wrecker and someone who has clearly shown Management that she can never be trusted in a position of responsibility.

> ***Epilogue:*** Gurley wrote another book in '93. Now she says women should not spend so much energy and time attempting to attract men. She, like Friedan and Steinem hit the reality wall at Sixtysomething. They've all confessed they were wrong, not just in their own lives, but in the advice they sold as books from atop their Liberated Olympus. As hypocrites-to-the-end, they didn't announce they were wrong, they wrote books to confess, then sold them to the same women they had duped with books for the past 30 years. Disgusting!
>
> ***Comment:*** There's some justice, a little, coming up.

FAIRYTALE UNHAPPY ENDING

He tells you he has an arrangement with his wife about this. He says you make him see how meaningless his marriage is but he must keep his wife for appearances at the company. He strokes you about how good you are at the job and how you are going far in the company. He pretends to respect your opinion. But he pooh-poohs your ideas about the impropriety of married men, saying "It's the 90's! No one need ever know. Our on-the-job relationship will be strengthened, not damaged," and other fairytales.

The intrigue is exciting and erotic. Fooling everyone is exhilarating. He's safely ineligible. He's glamorous. But you are fooling no one. They refer to you as "Mike's strange stuff."

THEY AIN'T CLUTCH PLAYERS

Married men feel guilty and ashamed for breaking their vows. They're terrified of being discovered. Pressure builds when rumors and innuendos start to fly. Married men aren't pressure players, they're bumbling cowards. He'll lose his wife and his chances for promotion or, depending on the company, his wife and his job and have a hell of a time ever getting hired at this level in the industry again. So, he throws you to the wolves but he feels terribly guilty about using you for, oh, two, three weeks, possibly a month.

On top of all this, you're terrified of being used and discarded. Don't even think about a married lover until you're experienced enough to know what you're doing and understand there are always powerfully painful consequences.

At the first sign of interest from a married man say, "My fiance plays for the LA Raiders, linebacker. How old are your children?"

PUT THE BRAKES ON

If you don't fool around with married men now, how do you prevent yourself? How do you turn yourself off now? That is, how do you keep yourself from going after your friend's husband when he makes a pass? Whatever you do, duplicate it at work.

How do you prevent yourself from going after anyone for that matter. "Anyone" in this case is someone you consider a 5-S kinda guy, sexy, studly, strong, stiff satyr? Whatever you do, that's what you must do at the office. The essence of not getting used is to never let it get started.

THREAT ANALYSIS

Guys near your age see you as a sperm bank where they can make temporary deposits. They compete among themselves to make the first deposit. Unable to perceive you, or any female your age, differently than they did in college, they see an Omega My Thigh sister pretending to be all business. They merely have to penetrate that facade of yours and they can penetrate you.

They try college boy tricks, it's all they know. When you reject them, you risk little other than obviously false stories about what a bad lay you were. They don't have any power so you can be abrupt with all of them.

But, don't you dare be abrupt with one in front of a divorced woman with kids! When you shut a boy down in front of her, she sees you nonchalantly throwing away what she'd give anything for, the chance to go back and live her youth over again, the youth she lost by marrying at 22 and making babies. She'll hate you and get revenge somehow, some way.

Complicated? Yes. Necessary? Yes. Silly? Of course.

Salesmen are the hardest to convince. Having learned that if they don't take "no" for an answer, you'll eventually say "yes." With salesmen and other insistent hustlers, this is all that works: SLAP! "Get your fucking hand off of me!"

Recently divorced men are troubled, and trouble. I should know, I was one, twice. Don't listen to his sob stories. Don't comfort him. Briefly sympathize, then run like hell. They're too hurt, stunned and confused to be able to genuinely care for anyone or to even behave consistently.

Out-of-the-closet lesbians get amazingly pushy. Dykes can no longer be fired for being dykes. Knowing they can't, and knowing they won't be going up the corporate ladder, they have nothing to lose. Bulldyke-dozers!

Turn down any lunch or coffee invitation from a potential lesbian. Do not encourage her even slightly. If you suspect she's looking you over, defuse it quickly and clearly. Talk about your fiance, your wedding plans, your baby plans, how disgusting you think homosexuals are.

If men think you are sympathetic toward lesbians or homosexual men, your chances of promotion and advancement are shot. Nobody respects, or takes seriously, homosexuals of either gender in the business world, showbiz somewhat notwithstanding. *52 Random Truths* has more.

PUT OUT OR GET OUT — PASSES BY THE BOSS

During probation you're the most vulnerable. He can get rid of you easily, so he must never be given a chance to make a pass. The power to dismiss, with no reason necessary, during probation makes him bolder now than he'll ever be.

If you were unknowingly hired to service your boss, you're in a no-win situation. Flip back to the beginning of this chapter. Read the advice my friend's father gave him.

You must stall and stall and lie and blow smoke and delay and put off. If he's so pushy that you have to confront him, he'll fire you. You have no rights during probation. Personnel always looks the other way. They don't want anyone to know that they know he's a whacko. They'd have to do something about it!

Rarely it's a blunt put-out-or-get-out. It's more like:

Let's have a drink after work. I'll explain the promotion possibilities at General Cow. There's a spot in Data Pro-

cessing I heard about. Six months under me, you can snatch it up! Okay?

That's very nice MISTER Johnson. I'm meeting my fiance after work. He'd be delighted to join us.

After you neutralize that ploy, these disgusting users dream up a reason that you and he have to work overtime. He suggests a break for dinner. If you naively agree, he has a few to pump up his courage while plying you with a second drink before he propositions you.

Avoid overtime. If that's not possible, say you can only stay until six, then you have to pick up your sick mother. Avoid weekends. Apologize with a face near tears. You have to care for your sick mother. You love your job but you your duty comes first. He can't fire you for not working overtime but he'll fire you if he thinks you're avoiding him. There's another strong reason for acting lessons.

Pay attention to your feelings. If you feel like a piece of meat around him, you are. Immediately go after another job. In the meantime, don't give him any openings.

If you're in this situation, stall him with any lie you have to. It's crucial to make it to the 91st day without getting canned. All's fair in love, war and office politics. At my insistence, my second wife used these successfully on two occasions:

Maybe next month. Don'll be traveling. I won't have to rush home. Gotta run.

Notice you haven't said you would, only maybe. When next month comes around:

Don's trips were canceled. His parents are visiting. Sorry. Gotta run.

Make it through probation using any means possible. On the 91st day, straighten out a dyke boss or stiff arm a male boss.

PASSES BY THE BOSS AFTER PROBATION

Your boss has so much power over your future. If he ever works up the courage to make a pass, your time here is over. Follow all my advice about nipping everything in the bud. If his lust blooms anyway, be prepared for war.

As advised in *Fighting,* document everything. Write down, in your own words, what, when and where it happened. Write down what he said, what you said, who heard it. Draw diagrams. Any piece of paper lends tremendous psychological weight to your claims in any courtroom-like setting.

Tell non-company friends what he did and what he said. Write down their reactions. Talk with counselors for the women's organizations listed in *Where To Turn For Help* at the end of the book. See lawyers they recommend. Don't name names, not even the name of your company. You don't need evangelistic crusaders going off prematurely.

Get more hard evidence. Go to your doctor. Tell her you can't sleep and you're extremely anxious at work. Give her the short version of what happened. If she won't give you tranquilizers and sleeping pills, find one who will. Tell her the same thing. Pay the doctor and the pharmacy by check. You want evidence, hard evidence. Don't take those dangerous pills.

DO NOT QUIT! Get moving on being hired by another company while you're still employed. The next steps are described below, after the horror story.

SEX AT THE TOP

So many women have won multi-million dollar awards for sexual harassment since the mid-80s that companies no longer let it go on openly except at the highest levels. On mahogany row, powerful men do as they please, exactly as they've always done.

These men believe you know the unstated price for the chance to work at such a high level at such a young age. They believe you should be delighted to service them. They are indignant to the bone when you decline their sexual advances.

Get something on tape or in front of a reliable witness from outside the company. You need hard evidence to save yourself from these powerful guys. Get the evidence.

HORROR STORY

When my first wife was 24, we were both proud that she had moved up so rapidly at her company. In a year, she had gone from a secretary in Purchasing to Assistant to the President.

At the Christmas party in the executive suites, in front of everyone, under the mistletoe, her boss, President and CEO, kissed her politely, then shoved his tongue down her throat! She was shocked! She stood there stunned, unable to move. He sauntered away, pretending nothing had happened.

Twenty minutes later, loud enough for others to hear, he propositioned her with an offer to accompany him on his Miami trip. She recoiled in horror and ran into the women's room. He barged right in after her and angrily told her she was embarrassing him in front of "the whole damn company." He demanded to know why she was crying. He kept yelling as she ran out.

She never went back. It took her two years and three companies to get back to that high level. It took her three months just to get a job as a purchasing secretary. After ten good interviews didn't result in an offer, a friend at the old company told her, off the record, that when anyone inquired, they were told she was fired for theft! She had to omit that year, that pay level and that job title from her resumes and applications, forever. That was in 1966, way back before women's rights and sexual harassment laws.

YOU HAVE A FEW RIGHTS

Today, if it gets to that point, just your time at that company is over. Nobody would dare take a multi-million dollar chance to lie like that now. But at the first opportunity he'll fire you on a trumped up charge he can substantiate, should you sue.

If he's bold enough to make such a blatant move, he is so powerful he can say he didn't stick his tongue down your throat, didn't proposition you and he can make it stick. He knows he's able to pull it off with Personnel, his boss and with the Commission on Sexual Harassment or whichever bureaucrats come after him. The point is, you're finished there. Always nip it in the bud. Don't be friendly!

FIGHTING BACK WITH SEXUAL HARASSMENT

As explained in *Fighting,* if all else fails you can claim sexual harassment. Unless the guy is way up the corporate ladder, the company will cave in rather than take it to court. Even Personnel geeks know the company loses no matter who wins in court. If he's way up the ladder, you must have hard evidence and Gloria Allred as your lawyer. Otherwise, settle for half-a-loaf and move on, sadder but wiser.

Top management wants this squashed and squashed right now. Out of the newspapers is where they want it. Out of sight of stockholders and insurance companies is where they want it. Out of court is where they want it.

Insidious is the only word to describe how they'll pressure you. They'll say there are five guys willing to testify they've had you. Affidavits from men and women that describe you as a seductress, trying to sleep your way to the top will appear. Witnesses that you tried to get several managers to sleep with you will come forward. The company's defense will be explained to you — dumb old Fred, he just fell for the same seductive tricks you tried on the others.

HARD BALL, DIRTY TRICKS

Top Management sees you as the problem, not the dick who tried to screw you. They don't feel even slightly guilty about playing dirty and rough. You're a real threat to their future.

Marilyn Monroe found out too late how rough people at the top play! The scum who are your corporation's lawyers are cut from the same cloth as the lawyers who "proved" she wasn't murdered.

You don't want it getting close to that point, right? To keep it from getting close, keep it from getting started. If he finds you desirable, he'll make his move. Don't look desirable. Don't be friendly. Dress for success, not success with men.

REPETITION IS THE KEY TO LEARNING

Do not distract men from the paper they are supposed to be pushing. Look moderately severe, but not like a she-male. Look neutral, as neutral as possible.

From the first day, convince one and all you are unapproachable because of your engagement. Later on, avoid passes by avoiding situations where a move is possible — after work, overtime, weekends, travel.

DECLINING PASSES

You have two duties at Companies A through X. One duty you get paid for. Your other duty is declining propositions while remaining civil, if possible. Don't smile. Don't be polite. Be strong but not rude when turning down the first pass:

I'm engaged. Sorry.

Guys who are aggressive enough to make a pass while your engagement ring sparkles usually accept this without becoming an enemy. They were just testing you, like a shark does. They swim on.

Second passes must be dealt with harshly. If the shark comes back, he must be repelled convincingly. Turn him down with strength. Look him right in the eye. Show indignant anger:

DAMN YOU! I'm engaged.

After delivering these ultimatums in a firm, loud voice, so others can hear, walk away indignantly. If seated, get up and walk away indignantly. Don't vary the power in your response because the shark is a Big Boy of some kind. Witnesses intimidate Big Boys, too.

UNREALITY EQUALS DANGER

The less real the company is, the more real the sexual advances are. If you work for a non-profit company or a government agency like the Metropolitan Water District, making money is not their focus. Nobody is responsible since there is no way to measure performance without keeping score — the bottom line. Nobody can be fired. Nobody is accountable.

The more certain it is that the organization will be there tomorrow, the more certain it is that you'll be propositioned. Government, civil service and non-profits are for certain.

At not-for-profit companies, most bosses believe perks include perky young breasts and quickly promote young women who agree. Stay away from non-profits, except for a side trip to jam your salary another big notch higher. This book doesn't work there.

FINAL WARNING!

Much of this chapter seemed unreal to some women who reviewed the manuscript. They were as disbelieving as my wife was when that tongue was rammed down her throat!

As you wonder *Why It's All Screwed Up,* the corporation lumbers along making millions, somehow.

I don't rule Russia,
one million bureaucrats rule Russia.
PETER THE GREAT

If a man will begin with certainties
he will end in doubts
but if he will be content to begin with doubts
he shall end in certainties.
Advancement of Learning 1605 FRANCIS BACON

Why It's All Screwed Up

Sometimes a CEO starts believing his own PR and press releases. Thinking he actually knows what he's doing, he changes the 90 year-old formula for Coca Cola, or he builds a $3 billion F-20 fighter airplane nobody ordered, or he insists main frames are the foundation of the computer business into the next century, or he authorizes $80 million budgets for films like *Howard The Duck, The Last Action Hero* and *Ishtar*.

Self-deluded CEOs surrounded by yes-men are not why most major companies are screwed up. The primary reason is that everyone who reports to the CEO tells him what he wants to hear. Even worse, everyone from the Boiler Room to the Board Room tells his own boss what he wants to hear. Nobody ever really knows what the hell is going on "down below."

WHY IT DOESN'T CHANGE

When I made it to the top floor, I was so naive. One day, after witnessing an obvious-to-anyone, excessively blatant pissing away of company money, I said to my friend, Paul, the corporate lawyer, "If Harvey knew what these assholes were doing, he'd ride down this hall with a battle ax like Richard The Lion Heart and behead every one of them." Whereupon he said, "Yeah, if he knew, but he doesn't know, too busy lugging the millions we make for him to the bank."

I thought about that. I worked on the secret Revenue Forecast portion of the Five Year Plan. I prepared the secret graphics for quarterly reviews. Harvey was pouring millions into his coffers every week, just from our division's contracts.

The money I was whining about, $280k pissed away last month by our self-aggrandizing salesmen, was literally a drop in the coffers. It was so far to the right of the decimal point on charts used to brief Harvey, he'd never notice it.

ONLY WHEN IT HURTS BAD ENOUGH

The guy on top only realizes it's going to hell in a handcart when the big bucks stop rolling in. When it slows down, Harvey, the CEO has Harry, the Division Manager and his Division VP of Finance fly up to corporate headquarters. They reassure him, ". . . have to fine tune a few things, revenue'll be right back where it was." The CEO smiles. They smile.

Back at the division, Harry and the VP start an investigation to find out why revenue is slipping. Observant office politicians realize trouble's brewing. Rumors fly. Fear paralyzes the incompetent. The moderately competent batten down the hatches and hope to ride it out. The cunningly competent begin back stabbing and maneuvering to end up several rungs higher after the chaos subsides.

News from "down below," the boiler room, begins to work its way around the company. It's bad. We're running out of coal, boiler's cooling down. Soon there'll be no steam. Corporate raiders have been sighted on the horizon. The smartest and most competent people jump ship and enlist with competitors.

The probe is impotent. From the bottom to the top, everybody tells his own boss sugarcoated, half truths. Near the end of the quarter, the Division Manager secretly invites his VP of Finance and VP of Operations to a meeting at the private Jonathan Club, downtown.

They conspire to fudge the figures and work out a plan of *plausible deniability* should they get caught. That gives them at least another quarter before the truth comes out. That's three months to find a scapegoat or take early retirement or join a competitor or prepare golden parachutes or something, any-damn-thing other than tell the CEO the truth — they don't have a clue as to what's wrong.

A spy tips off the CEO something's up. To his most trusted Executive VP, Harvey says, "Grab the Falcon. Get down there and find out what the fuck's going on. Take DeMartillo from Finance and Travis from Legal. Put the fear of God into them, especially Harry."

THE INQUISITION BEGINS

Arriving unannounced the next morning, they barge into Harry's big corner office and chase everyone out. Word spreads. Harry's on the carpet. Three hours later, they move into the Executive Conference Room and continue the inquisition.

Each executive on the top floor is called in. He gets fried, parboiled and grilled. At day's end the inquisitors don't know any more than they did in the morning. But nobody knows that. Everyone's scared. Someone might have squealed.

Harry is summoned to the conference room. In vulgar English he is told that not one damn executive knows what's going on "down below" and that's already been reported to Harvey. He's ordered, "Get revenue up before next quarter. No mumbo fuckin' jumbo accounting tricks or Harvey's gonna put your balls on display."

Harry assures the inquisitors he'll get to the bottom of this. Heads will roll, he promises.

That night he gets to the bottom of it in a meeting with his top executives. In the morning, he fires every single guy his executives blamed. To take their places, Harry promotes all the ass kissers recommended by the executives. He personally congratulates the ass kissers, then orders them to straighten out the mess.

CHARGE OF THE LIGHTWEIGHT BRIGADE

Notice that the cause of the problem is still unknown. Ass kissers have been ordered to solve a problem that has no known cause.

The more ambitious ass kissers charge around holding investigative meetings with fear-paralyzed middle managers. They issue ridiculous, conflicting orders. After a month of this, all good workers have left the company. The only workers left are so incompetent they can't get new jobs. Now they're being supervised by ass kissers. Of course, neither the ass kissers nor the incompetents realize this has happened.

At quarter's end, Harry is kicked upstairs. The CEO picks a VP and makes him Division Manager. Eventually the division gets closed or sold. Ass kissers supervising incompetents cannot produce a profit.

HOW DOES THIS HAPPEN?

Why don't the people below tell the people above the truth? Well, sometimes those on top kill the messenger who brings the bad news, but that's only a minor cause.

The major reason is that those at the very top, by their method of oblique communication, have made it crystal clear that to survive you must be as indirect as possible but make it seem as if you are being straightforward. See Unwritten Rule VII. Also see the story of my futile attempt to change this style of communicating in *Manage The Boss*.

Every comment, memo and order has three or more possible interpretations. Vagueness is the key to flexibility. Even written orders are open to misunderstanding. One always misunderstands to his own advantage. The person issuing the order deliberately confounds the wording so he can later deny or claim responsibility, depending on the outcome.

"Damn it, Steele. This is too clear! Weasel word it," my boss used to say.

NO COMMUNICATION UP THE CHAIN OR DOWN

The other cause for everything getting, and staying, so screwed up is adopted from the military. A higher ranking guy doesn't tell the guy just below him everything. That keeps the lower ranking guy at a disadvantage. It's the mirror image of telling your boss what he wants to hear.

> *What we have here is a failure to communicate.*
> Strother Martin playing THE WARDEN
> As he whacks Cool Hand Luke from behind with a blackjack

The CEO doesn't tell his Executive VPs everything. The Executive VPs don't tell their Division Managers everything and of course the Division Managers don't tell their VPs everything, and so on all, the way down to the poor grunts who have to do the actual work. Everybody is kept in the dark and keeps everybody else in the dark. Straightforward, honest, clear, unadorned communications do not exist. It's that simple.

GRASPING AT STRAWS OF EXPLANATION

Another explanation about why women don't do well in corporations has been making the rounds. Failure is blamed on the different styles of communicating men and women have. Women talk about feelings, men talk about facts. Men think while listening, women listen attentively.

Nonsense! When men and women look at *x*, they don't see the same thing. They are incapable of seeing the same thing because their brains are [1]wired differently. Further, when a woman looks at *x*, her sense-of-self, created by her physical and hormonal nature, causes her to see *x* differently. Biology prevents exact communication between men and women.

CRYSTAL CLEAR COMMUNICATION

You and I know that within the corporation, or anywhere else for that matter, if everyone knew where we are, knew where we're trying to go, and knew what the plan was, we would all be able to get there quicker and cheaper. But now that you know the goal is not quicker or cheaper, it's survival, some of this insanity may start to make some sense, kinda, maybe?

WHAT SHOULD YOU DO WITH THIS TRUTH?

The purpose of this chapter is to make certain you don't doubt yourself and your ability to see what you see and know what you know. Once you begin to realize how totally screwed up your company is, you'll know you are not misperceiving reality. It really is that screwed up. So, you must accept that which you cannot change and change that which you can, because it's *Status Quo Forever*.

Warning! A frank explanation of *how* and *why* the world really works is on the next two pages. These truths shocked some manuscript reviewers. But once again, it is necessary for you to understand the *why* if you want to succeed at office politics. And, don't forget, you are the person who must choose what you do with this knowledge.

[1] Brain wiring differences are explained and documented after other innate characteristics of men and women are presented.

Nothing is ever done in this world until men are prepared to kill one another if it is not done.
GEORGE BERNARD SHAW

Status Quo Forever

Military intervention, sex education, illegal immigration, health care "reform," it makes no difference what "issue" is being argued. In reality, there's only change the status quo or keep the status quo. The question of changing the status quo is never even raised if those who want to keep the status quo have enough power (money). Changing the status quo becomes an issue only if those who want to change it have enough power (money) to put, then keep, the idea in the public spotlight.

Deep Throat gave Watergate's Bernstein and Woodward the single most important clue when he advised them, "Follow the money." If you want to understand any issue today, or forever, follow the money.

There are no real issues, only who's going to make money if the status quo gets changed? or who keeps making money if the status quo remains?

FOLLOW THE MONEY

Ask yourself who makes money when the government requires illegal aliens be "educated equally?" The National Education Association and the millions of pubic education bureaucrats.

Who makes money if the government requires illegal aliens with TB and AIDS be treated instead of deported? Public health doctors, nurses, hospitals and the millions of bureaucrats in "public" health. Drug companies. How about all the social worker-poverty pimps in the land.

Who makes money as millions of illegal aliens pour across our borders? Giant corporations who sell things they buy, like Pampers, gasoline, Pepsi, Budweiser, Chevrolets, electricity, gas, food, clothing? The more people there are buying, the more those kinds of companies make. Think about it. Who makes money?

Follow the money. Who wants illiterate, non-English speaking, diseased, third-world peasants to come here, have babies here, go on welfare here, form drug dealing gangs here? It's not you and me.

FOLLOW THE MONEY AT WORK

To understand who's keeping or changing the status quo in your company, follow the money. Who keeps his job or growth options if the status quo stays? Who loses his if the status quo changes? Too many people have too much to lose if anything changes. It's that way at your office and it's that way worldwide. That's why it's so hard to change anything.

ILL WINDS BLOW SOMEBODY PROFIT

People only go to a dentist when it hurts bad enough. People only go to a shrink when it hurts bad enough. People only change jobs when it hurts bad enough. People only get fired when their boss hurts enough to fire them.

Profit from this phenomenon. If a situation at the office is causing pain, that's when people are open to new ideas. It's politically brilliant to let the wound fester until there is major trouble, then present your proposal. Even a Tower of Jello is happy to listen to a woman's ideas if he hurts bad enough. He's delighted to institute your plan if you make it clear he'll share the spotlight and credit.

Caution! In your own life, personal and business, don't wait until it hurts so bad that the pain forces you to change. Pain distorts your vision, preventing accurate choices. Change boyfriends, jobs, friends, stop visiting relatives, lose weight, whatever, before it hurts too much.

FOLLOW THE MONEY BEFORE PROPOSING

As explained in the upcoming payoff chapters, *Get That Raise* and *Get Promoted,* before you suggest "improvements," carefully consider who profits and who loses because of your proposal. Think about how to present ideas so the most powerful people are on your side. In short, figure out how to convince the boss and his boss and even his boss, they'll profit from the "improvement," by gaining a bigger budget, more floor space, more importance, more visibility, whatever.

It is an immutable law of hierarchies that change only occurs from the top down. If the guy on top does not want the change, it will not change. From your position, decide where the top is. Convince him.

Begin with modest proposals that are easily approved and instituted. Build a track record before springing your proposal to open an office in Hawaii, with yourself in charge of the advance team.

NAKED EMPERORS MUST KEEP WALKING

Remember the fairytale? The emperor buys a new suit from swindlers who make it from "invisible" cloth. He decides to parade down the street so everyone can admire his judgement. His subjects pretend to adore the new suit. Then, a little boy shouts, "The emperor wears no clothes!"

Well, the emperor can't acknowledge he's a fool, even after he realizes he's naked. He must keep up the pretense. He must keep walking. He has no choice.

Fortune 3000 CEOs operate the same way. Even when he knows he screwed up, even when he knows he doesn't understand what's wrong, even when he doesn't know what to do, he can't admit it! He'd be fired. Like the naked emperor, he must keep pretending and keep walking.

When the corporate equivalent of the little boy (a whistleblower) shouts the truth, everyone pretends he didn't hear anything, including government investigators. That's another reason it's status quo forever. Enough of the *whys,* let's get back to the *how-when-what* of office politics.

AS ALWAYS, IT'S UP TO YOU

What do you want to do with your life? Independence in ten years? Comfortable job with no stress? Married with children? That's a choice you must make some day, some way. The information you are now gathering will help you be rational when you consider the long range consequences of various options. The process of *Corporate Decision Making* is something entirely different.

Don't confuse me with facts, my mind is made up.
METRO GOLDWYN MAYER SAM GOLDWYN

Indecision is the key to flexibility.
CORPORATE OFFICER'S CREED

Corporate Decision Making

At the top of the largest hierarchy of all, the US Government, serious, controversial decisions are made only by Blue Ribbon Commissions. Every politician knows he must avoid blame, thus must avoid responsibility. Politicians band together and appoint a panel to make disputable, unpopular decisions. At election time, each politician can, and does, proclaim his innocence.

The Warren Commission, the ultimate Blue Ribbon Commission, decided Lee Harvey Oswald, acting alone, killed JFK. Being a committee, they could ignore the fact that no expert marksman has ever been able to duplicate his shots. Being a committee, they could ignore the fact that no ballistics expert could explain the path of "magic" bullet that went through JFK and wounded Governor Connally, leaving fragments in his wrist, yet was found undamaged. Yet every politician was able to say, "The Warren Commission decided that, not me."

PRAGMATIC, PRACTICAL DECISIONS

None of top management's decisions have anything to do with what makes sense, what makes the most money, or what ensures the prosperity and survival of the company into the middle of the next century.

Stockholders want a return on their money. If it's too small, heads roll. Top management is concerned only with their own heads. Survival depends on the next quarter's dividend. Therefore, the most effective short-run pragmatists, as if there were long-run pragmatists, rise to the top of a corporation.

Decisions are not arrived at by considering principles. Decisions are pragmatic, that which works. In the case of top management, "works" means: What do we have to do so that we can pay the stockholders a dividend next quarter? or, What do we have to do so the stockholders don't fire us when we don't pay a dividend next quarter?

Like their counterparts in Washington DC, top management knows that serious, controversial decisions must be made only by committees for the same reasons Congress formed The Warren Commission. Top management does not want the Board of Directors or the stockholders to be able to single out anyone for blame, so they form The Downsizing (Layoff) Committee or the Distribution Enhancement (Move Out Of The Ghetto Without ACLU-NAACP Lawsuits) Committee or the Asset Improvement (Sell Profitable Divisions to Survive) Committee.

A TOWER OF JELLO, YOUR BOSS

Below top management, everyone is terrified to make decisions. Change is what actually frightens them. A decision means something might change.

The incompetent are afraid of change at any and all times. They fear being discovered, humiliated and fired. Every incompetent fears that change may cause his hiding place to be uncovered or his camouflage may not work and reveal the fraud beneath. Everything incompetents do is motivated by that fear. It dominates their thinking, runs their lives.

If your boss is an incompetent, that's normal. Understand that so you can control and manipulate him.

Your boss does understand and feel greed, slightly. He knows what ambition is, at least intellectually. He sees it in others but sees it as something dangerous to him. He doesn't have a clue why the Big Boys do anything. He is incapable of grasping what motivates them.

He certainly doesn't understand loyalty, ability, intelligence or conscientiousness except how to suck off them like the parasite he is. Fear is the dominant emotion he has left. It's the only way his boss can motivate him. Your boss believes everyone else is like he is, including the people under him and his peers.

Long ago, before he was afraid all the time, he was frustrated most of the time. No matter what he tried, he was never successful or happy, at work or at home. As the years passed, frustration turned to futility.

About age 35, he slowly became aware he was miserable unto death. Now and then, when he forgot to distract himself, he'd become aware that he despised his wife, that his children had no respect for him, that he had nothing to look forward to, nothing. He began to focus on the company, not on doing his job, but as a place to escape from misery and loneliness.

'Tis a miserable state
to have few things to desire and many things to fear.
FRANCIS BACON

When he turned 40, he resigned himself to not having a life at home. The only life he had was his job. At least people who worked under him pretended to respect him.

By the time you arrive on the scene, he has endowed his position at the company with a significance far beyond any realistic evaluation or your comprehension. To him, his job, his title, his place in the company are life itself. That's all there is in his universe. His self-esteem, what little he has left, is derived solely from his title, Manager of Information Delivery Systems.

His job is his life. Now, at age 48, it's the only life he can ever have. This is all there is, or can ever be. He knows that. He knows it deep down in his bones. He also knows he's incompetent. He knows that deep down in his bones. That's why he's so afraid. That's why he'll lie, cheat, steal, back stab, betray and sabotage anyone who threatens his position, even in the slightest way.

CRITICISM IS THE ULTIMATE THREAT

A reprimand from higher-ups is the worst thing that can happen. Terrified they'll realize he's a fraud, he conducts his life to, above all else, avoid criticism. He reveals himself as driven by this fear when he explodes over what, to you, is a minor mistake in the memo. When he acts like it's life or death, to him, it is.

If you have an ambitious boss, be thankful. Your stay will be interesting and exciting. But most bosses are not ambitious, they are suspicious. Fear rules their lives, everything they do is defensive, not offensive. They don't act. They react.

If your boss is typical, he never takes action, he reacts to action taken by others. The initiative, thus the advantage, is always in the hands of others.

A rabbit has only his camouflage and his ability to hold still to protect him. The rabbit knows that if the wolf doesn't notice him, he'll live another day. Middle managers believe that by doing absolutely nothing, no higher ups will notice them. If no higher ups notice them, they can't be criticized. If they aren't criticized, they won't be discovered as incompetent. They stay alive one more day.

DECISION MAKING BY MIDDLE MANAGEMENT

Now that you understand your Tower of Jello and how he got this way, understand what happened to those great ideas you gave to him. Follow his "logic" as he decides whether or not to approve your idea:

1. If I approve it, and it works, they'll wonder how a girl could think of it and I couldn't, then I'll look bad.
2. If I approve it and it doesn't work, they'll think I'm stupid for approving it, then I'll look bad.
3. If I approve it and it works great, they'll pay attention to her. They might think she should be doing my job, then I'll get transferred or demoted.
4. If I approve it, it might work so good that next year I could only justify 23 people. I'll lose three offices, the floor space and that much budget.
5. If I approve it, bucks come from this quarter's budget. I won't be able to give Debbie Doubledees a big raise.
6. If I approve it, there's nothing for me to gain and everything to lose. Things are fine now. I'll tell her Jim won't approve it. I'll imply he thinks she's stupid. She won't have the courage to ask him. Why take chances?
7. She's so naive she didn't put it in writing with a copy to Jim. After I get rid of her, I can pretend it was my idea. I'll put it in a memo to Jim, with a copy to Ralph so Jim can't steal it. I'll puff it up so I can get two offices added when it's approved.

8. I'll look really good unless I embarrass Jim. I'll have to weasel-word the memo so it sounds like he helped. I'll take him out for drinks, plant a few seeds, stroke his ego. The putz will think he helped.

DECISION MAKING BY UPPER MANAGEMENT

Just above middle management, the thought process is only slightly different. When a successful (he has survived) executive thinks he might be forced to decide something, his "logic" works this way:

1. Can I pass the buck?
2. How long can I stall so that if things change I won't have to make a decision?
3. Who can I get to join me? They won't blame me if it's a committee decision.
4. If I don't make a decision, what happens to me?

You can see that even if you luck into having a boss who's brave enough to submit one of your great ideas, you still don't have a chance of getting it approved.

Want your great ideas to be acknowledged and implemented? Play office politics better than your boss. Present your great ideas so that he (a) is not threatened (b) can see his own survival is enhanced (c) realizes he'll get most of the credit. Later, in *Get Promoted,* the details are explained. You'll understand why and how this makes you promotable.

If you want all the credit, present your great idea to your boss's boss in front of witnesses.

Warning! This will piss off your boss royally. You must have a very believable story for doing this as well as being prepared to take the heat he'll put on you for embarrassing him.

A final word on decisions. Most blatantly stupid decisions are made for high-level political reasons. Do not make a scene. Do not ridicule. That's the same as breaking the supreme unwritten rule, saying, "The emperor wears no clothes."

Let's make certain you understand exactly what's at stake by *Defining The Terms*.

We are all saying the same thing,
just using different words.
SEMANTICIST AND SLEEPING SENATOR S.I. HAYAKAWA

Defining The Terms

COMPETENCE: Pushing the paper from your In-Basket to your Out-Basket on time is half of "competent." The other half is relating effectively with other people. That means don't upset them so they can keep pushing their paper and don't get upset so you can keep pushing your paper. Competence is good. Super competence is bad. It makes everyone nervous, including your boss because everyone looks so bad compared to you. Hide your super competent light under a bushel until it really counts — you can save a big boss's bacon and he knows you saved his bacon.

EMPLOYEE: You are nothing more than one of the things needed to make the cow give milk. Some others are: trucks, desks, paper and raw material. The company, your boss and your co-workers will exploit you as far as possible, that means as far as you let them. Don't be a victim. Take Assertiveness Training.

GETAWAY CAR: Ten solid friends at ten other companies who can hire you is the ideal. Maintain contacts at every company you leave. Develop and maintain contacts at every business organization you belong to. Keep your resume up to date. Build a file of memos praising you, letters of appreciation and recommendation. Avoid exit-interviews with any excuse. If trapped, say nothing bad about anyone. Don't burn bridges.

GOOD AND EVIL: Good and evil exist in the minds of philosophers and preachers. Out here in the real world, *good* is enlightened long-term self interest. Anything else is evil.

GOOD WORKING RELATIONSHIP: It's nothing more than one pleasant enough so you can trade info and have the respect of others with the least amount of jealousy or obstruction. When someone comes to you with info he wants to trade, you've got the beginnings of a "good working relationship." If you don't reciprocate, eventually everyone will refuse to cooperate and you'll be blind, deaf, dumb and about to be fired.

HAPPINESS: According to your gender's brainwashing, it's a handsome, famous husband with millions, who adores you and your two beautiful children dressed in designer togs. In reality, only you can define this term. Ayn Rand says it's a man you love and a career you love. I say, Amen.

HOME BASE: The minimum to be independent: reliable car, safe, quiet place to live and enjoy living, presentable attire (the uniform), music, and most important of all, you owe no money to anyone, especially family. The young woman who reads this book establishes a home base in a few years. Those who don't read it never do, but you should see their clothes and cars. Wow!

INDEPENDENCE: They control you when you spend the money they pay you. You control yourself and become independent only when you have money, screw-you money. Most young women piss their money away on clothes, car payments and condo payments, remaining forever dependent on *them.*

INSUBORDINATION: "You wasted a lot of time. You chose the wrong person to do that job so he did it wrong." That's insubordination and that gets you fired. It's also known as telling the truth, as in "The emperor wears no clothes."

POLITICS: Characterized by shrewdness in managing, contriving or dealing. Shrewdly tactful and sagacious in promoting a policy. Keen and far-sighted with penetrating vision and judgement of the weakness and strength of an enemy or friend. Manipulating, expedient, practical. Deceitfully charming and treacherous, wily, ardent, cunning, deceptive and Machiavellian. Amen!

POWER: Territory is power and power is territory. Nothing else counts in the corporate world. How big your turf is determines your place in the pecking order. Turf can be office space, computers, people or anything called "resources." *Translation:* turf. To have great power you must be able to bestow turf.

PRIORITIES: The most important task you have is the one that your boss believes is the most important. Usually it's a report or something that's trivial in reality. *Priorities:* 1. Whatever your boss wants. 2. Whatever your boss's boss wants. 3. Whatever your boss designates as important by his historical panic. 4. Whatever your boss's boss designates as important because of his historical panic. 5. The actual important work. NOTE: Depending on the Jello content of your boss, priorities 1 thru 4 can take on any sequence, depending on the mood of his boss. Play it by ear.

PRIORITIES, REAL: Do the most important tasks first thing in the morning while you have all your smarts, your energy is up and your focus is on the job. On the way to work think about what's most important, then do it as soon as you arrive. Getting bogged down with low priority work lowers your IQ and dulls your instincts. Save that stuff for the end of the day.

REALITY: In the real world, reality is objective, that is, independent of the person looking at it. But corporate reality is subjective, dependent on the person looking at it. Reality is what the CEO says it is. He doesn't care if his reality isn't real. When his decisions, or lack of decisions, cause the company to go down in flames, he bails out with a golden parachute. What your boss thinks is real, is, for all practical (political) purposes, real until you go home at night. What your boss thinks is real and what his boss thinks is real are entirely different, neither of which is even slightly real. Your task is to pretend each one is "realistic" when you deal with either of them. Your reality, to others at work, is your image, the overall impression others have of you. Your attire, attitude and demeanor must loudly state, in terms they can grasp, that you are successful and powerful. If they perceive you that way, you are.

RIGHTS, WOMEN'S AND ALL OTHERS: Might makes right, period. Every right you think you have only exists if you can enforce it or get someone else to enforce it, like police, courts, or your 245 pound boyfriend. In the corporation or out, if you can't back up your rights with force, you have no rights. Oh sure, Federal law and the company's Policy Manual say women shall be considered equally for, fill-in-the-blank. That means nothing unless you can make them do it. That means using force, suing the bastards for millions with Gloria Allred handling your case.

SUCCESS: Being able to do what you want to do, when you want to do it, with whom you want to do it. Any other definition is foolish, dreamed up by your parents, yuppie friends, or strangers. Judging yourself by the standards of others such as Ann Landers, Helen Gurley Brown, or Gloria Steinem ensures that you will never be a success.

WORK: Something you are doing when you'd rather be doing something else. If you have to work, make as much money as you can, so you can do what you'd rather be doing decades sooner.

ZERO SUM GAME: There is a winner and a loser in every interaction in the jungle. The rule is — eat or be eaten. The python eats the wild pig. The tiger eats the python. If somebody wins, somebody has to lose. The corporate jungle is seen that way by ambitious corporate animals. To them, no interaction can be win-win. If she gets a raise, I can't. If she gets promoted, I can't. It's not true in many situations but that's the way every ambitious person sees it, no matter what trite slogans she mouths about team work.

Here are some *Helpful Hints*. They'll make your life instantly easier inside the bowels of General Cow.

By all that's good and glorious take this counsel.

Sardanapalus LORD BYRON

Helpful Hints

AIN'T NO JUSTICE: I saw only a few talented, capable, intelligent, efficient people get promoted in 30 years. Shocking? It certainly was to me the first 10 years. I was disappointed and heartbroken. Everything I believed in proved to be absolute horseshit. Hard work and ability counted for nothing. Half of the smart people I knew quit and started their own business before 35. Most made big money, like $500k. The other half endured the shit. Two of them are still working for the only company they ever worked for. Both are dead inside. One drinks until he drops, the other is fat and old at 46. In the corporate world there is no justice. Accepting this dismaying fact is the hardest thing you have to do. Once you accept, adjust your long range plans accordingly.

ALCOHOL IS AN APHRODISIAC: Drinking to excess is the end. Women can't drink as much as men. Don't compete on this level. Do not drink alcohol at any company function from going-away lunches to a formal dinner at the Division Manager's home. Booze loosens your tongue and lowers your guard. Don't even have a drink at lunch with a co-worker. It is even more dangerous when any guy from work is drinking around you. It makes him brave, Dutch courage, brave enough to make a pass at you. When rebuffed he becomes your enemy. Once you get way up there, you must socialize. Have only white wine with orange juice or grapefruit juice and make it last an hour. You can't control their drinking, only yours. The more he has, the better you look and the braver he gets. Time to go. If you do screw up and end up with a heavyweight on your hands, he can't sleep it off on your couch. If he stays, you go. Go sleep in the lobby or anywhere but don't fall for the too-drunk-to-drive-home routine. Maybe he'll get killed on the way home. Advancement possibilities loom.

CHRISTMAS CARDS: Send a happy, friendly, cheerful card to everyone on the department list. Add a personal note to your boss and his family saying you wish him and his family the happiest of holidays and other such drivel. It's hard to believe but the cretin actually thinks you mean it. These people are so insecure and so starved for love, they'll believe anything nice that comes at them. To him, you're a part of his imaginary, loving company-family. Send a card to all former co-workers and associates you think may end up on top someday.

CONTRIBUTE TO EVERYTHING: Someone is always retiring, having a birthday, in the hospital, having a baby, leaving the department or other excuse bored co-workers dream up to buy a present and send a card. Sign your name. Put your two bucks in the envelope. It's money well spent. The co-workers respect and admire you for your concern and thoughtfulness. The sheep who gets the card admires and respects you for your concern and thoughtfulness. There's always a charity drive no matter how crooked, such as United Way. Contribute the minimum with a smile. It's the same bargain and the same payoff.

DEALING WITH TOKENS: In 1994 there are some tokens here and there but in the future tokens will be everywhere. You must know how to deal with tokens, their co-workers and their boss. If the token is competent, no problem. However, most tokens aren't, but everyone pretends they are. Don't be first to say, "The token is incompetent." The token will blame you for causing his incompetence, claiming you're a racist or ageist or sexist and that frightened him, otherwise he could do the job. The company will side with the token because he can sue but you can't. If the token is making you look bad, talk with your boss in private. Make certain he understands what's going on. Do not ask him to fire the token. See if you can get the token transferred. If not, get procedures changed so you can bypass the token.

FAVORITE EXPRESSIONS: I'm up to my ass in alligators with the whole ball of wax that's a barrel of snakes becoming an accident waiting to happen. Just off the top of my head, it's just an idea, to run up the flag pole to see if it answers the mail. These phrases are used by your boss and his boss all the time. Work them into your vocabulary. They'll see you as one of them. Sounds dumb? Nah! They're such insecure, low-self-esteem people that anything works, no matter how blatant.

FORMULA BEHAVIOR: Smiles and nicey nicey. Unpredictable wackos. Yelling to intimidate and manipulate. Grumpy then pleasant. Whatever shtick they use, it's shtick, not reality. They have gotten where they are with a formula. They stay there using the same formula. They will die attempting to use the same formula long after it has become ineffective. Once you realize what someone's shtick is, you are able to wade right through it. If he always yells, he's going to yell about this, so what? If he's always agreeable and then does not follow up, you have to follow up. Just figure out what they do and use it against them.

GOOD OLD FEEDBACK: Ask your male friends, relatives, professors and associates what they think your business strengths and weaknesses are. Ask men what turns them off most about women at work, which ones they respect, which ones they hate and why. Ask anyone who didn't hire you, why he didn't. Say you need honest answers so you can improve. Don't defend yourself. Shut up and listen. The first time, the truth is between the lines, toned down. Say what you feel isn't being said and ask for feedback. Do the same when you didn't get the promotion. Talk in private. Say you want an honest answer. Shut up and listen. Remember, the truth is between the lines the first time. Say what isn't being said and get feedback.

LIVE AND LEARN: Experience as much of life as you can. Date as many different types of young and not so young men as you can handle. Travel. See what makes the rest of the world go round. Join the Army reserves. You'll learn more about how to manipulate the Fortune 3000 during your six months on active duty than you will working in them for five years.

LURKING LESBIANS: Many women I know were propositioned at work. The offer was so delicately put they were able to save the lesbian's face as they declined. One danger in becoming friends with a powerful woman at work is that she may think she's slowly seducing you with safe, subtle techniques. It happened to Martha, a young woman I was dating. The woman was a high-level camouflaged bisexual. Crushed to find Martha was offended when the overt move was made three months into it, she destroyed her chances at that company and attempted to destroy her chances at the next two companies. "Hell hath no fury like a woman scorned." *Office Sex* explains how to handle them.

MANAGEMENT CLUB: Some companies permit the grunts to belong. It's a good idea if you can stand being around middle managers when they are feeling powerful and euphoric from the booze. Any of them is extremely dangerous to your career if the booze leads him to make a pass. Rejecting one of these geeks destroys his "reputation" as a lady killer. These muddle-heads actually think they are attractive, believing you see them as men with real power and influence. At the Management Club, meet as many people as possible, no matter who or from which department. Avoid sticking with the safe, comfortable people you know. Volunteer for committee work. Do not volunteer for making flyers or cleanup or anything that labels you as a grunt. Make them see a dynamic, cheerful, hard-working, dedicated member who wants to become part of Management. In reality, you're looking to make contact with someone who can hire you so you'll get a promotion and raise much more quickly. As always, beware of other females. They are the enemy no matter what face they put on.

OLD BIDDY HENS: An old male who didn't get up the ladder has nothing better to do than talk about the disease-of-the-week TV movie. He has plenty of time to keep track of when each person arrives, leaves for lunch, comes back from lunch, who went to lunch with whom, who is not here today. He loves to generate problems, "Mary's running a bit late?" staring at her desk, hoping others will tsk, tsk with him. He's a bitchy little mutt, barking and snapping at anything to relieve the boredom of waiting for rigor mortis. He has a protector somewhere or he wouldn't still be here. Don't get into it with him.

ON NOT GIVING ADVICE: Don't give anyone from work advice. Giving advice is useless. If she follows your advice and it fails, it's your fault! If it's the right thing to do, but she doesn't have the courage to do it, she hates you for making her confront herself. If the advice works, she begins to see you as either her savior and shrink, then she comes to you with every problem or she resents you for being better than she is. No matter what happens, you lose when you give advice. Don't even listen to someone's problems. When you listen, they see you as their shrink, not as a co-worker, supervisor or subordinate. Roles get all screwed up and so does your work relationship. Some people want to talk about the problem, not solve the problem. To solve the problem, they'd have to do something self responsible like have the abortion, get divorced, move away from parents, put their mom in a nursing home. It's easier to whine than do what has to be done. Once they whine about it, they feel better, thus not motivated to do what has to be done. You don't help anybody from work by listening or giving advice.

For all the same reasons, don't give real friends advice. But, now and then, good friends need a shoulder to cry on, or someone to just listen, or some place to blow off steam. Be there for them, as they will be there for you.

POLITICIANS AT LUNCH: Cows love to attend department lunches to escape the boredom of the office. They pretend it's a real social gathering. Men hope they can penetrate your defenses when you let your guard down. Office politicians hope you let down your guard so they can figure out how to manipulate you.

REALISTIC ROMANCE: At your age you are still becoming the person you're going to be. Who you were at 20 is not even close to who you will be at 30. What you valued at 20 is inconsequential at 30. Remember who you were at 16? At 24, are you even half of what you were then? Begin your adult romantic life at 30. Pick a man who is not deluded about love, marriage, children and a tract home. Pick a man who knows it's impossible to be a single-family farmer in the suburbs. Divorced men over 35 are men, not boys, in every sense. They will see you and appreciate you. There's more on this coming up later.

SOCIAL EVENT ESCORT: At company social functions you must be escorted by an appropriate male. He must be from your ethnic group and be of the appropriate age and appropriate in every other way: attire, diction, grammar, intelligence et al. "Appropriate" means appropriate to 55 year old Northern European White Males and their neurotic, alcoholic 49 year old wives who have no life.

TEMPER OVER TEMPERATURE: Fighting over the thermostat is normal. It's the menopausal hot flashers against everyone else. They aren't rational because their brain chemistry is out of balance from the hormonal changes. These women hold grudges that last for years. Don't get drawn into this meaningless battle. Keep a sweater at the office.

YOU DON'T NEED HELP TO KEEP A SECRET: Never mention you're on your way as soon as you can get ten percent. Never mention you're working on a ten year plan of independence. Don't explain the reality of the corporate world unless he happens to be one of the "glowing" people. Why not? Remember what happened to the kid who told the other kids "There is no Santa Claus?"

WHO'S WHO: At work, when you ask someone a question and he pauses, ponders, then says, "I don't know," you've identified an honest, self-confident person. Add him to the list of people that you want to work for, or create a new list called "People I want working for me, someday."

WOMEN'S LIBERATION: After devoting years and millions of her own money to get her liberated hubby elected to a $28k job, she turned 50. He dumped her for a young woman. What should the most famous liberated woman have done? Stood by her feminist principles and blamed it on men, of course.

But Jane Fonda didn't stand up for anything she preached and fought for those 50 years. What did she do? Confessed her figure didn't get that way from aerobic workout tapes she'd sold to millions of adoring women. Admitted to buying a new body, a young woman's body — cellulite's been cut away, hips and thighs liposuctioned, tummy tucked, and breasts augmented. Conceded she'd also bought a young woman's face — neck lift, eyes fixed and face lift. At 55, she's everything her ex-sisters loathe, a busty, bleached-blond bimbo that billionaires wear on their arms as How-Studly-I-Am trinkets.

Betty Friedan is a housewife who wrote some books. Gloria Steinem is a writer who preached to the NOW choir for years. One never worked. The other, as CEO, bankrupted *Ms.* magazine. These two, and their clones, give speeches and go on talk shows posturing as experts on women in corporations. Methinks the Empress wears no clothes.

Don't throw in with a gang of females. There will be organizations like Women At GE or Fluor Corporate Women. Join if the unwritten rules say you have to. Keep your mouth shut. Do not promote the organization. Business sees Women's Liberation as completely discredited, run by lesbians, for lesbians who have destroyed the actual good that was accomplished.

Here's the most helpful hint of all, *Avoid Layoffs*.

Predicting the future by examining the past is like rowing down river facing upstream, steering based on where you have been. You will never see the waterfall.
UNKNOWN CRITIC OF STOCK MARKET CHARTISTS

There will be no layoff.
JUST BEFORE THE LAYOFF EVERY CEO

Avoid Layoffs

Every Fortune 3000 is inflexible because of its bigness, its military-like hierarchy and its bureaucratic structure. These organizations are always managed by a rigid Top Management team, stubbornly committed to historical methods of doing business. This means that sooner or later every company is forced to lay off employees.

The men who run a typical Fortune 3000 company cling to views of the marketplace that made their company successful and gigantic. To evaluate and analyze competition, they use models and standards that got the company where it is. When changes take place, as they always do, in the economy, in government regulations, in labor relations, Top Management continues to rely on what worked in the past.

If it ain't broke, don't fix it and follow time-tested recipes for success, is their mentality. In 1992, when the Russians surrendered forever, Top Management did what the Founder did in 1969 when industry slowed down at the end of Vietnam.

It never occurs to them that there has never been a situation like the one they face. They respond with whatever was done in the past. After those methods don't work, Top Management always blames the "general economic situation" or the "global economy." In a few months the stockholders demand someone's head. Top Management figures out who to blame, then sends them to the guillotine.

Beheading scapegoats doesn't work, of course, but they have stalled the inevitable while the CEO, CFO, COO and others fluff up golden parachutes and bail out. The new CEO and his crowd are stuck with sorting out the mess. To cut costs quickly so the stockholders get their dividend check on time, they lay off as many people as possible.

Someday you'll have to survive a layoff. It makes no difference why they happen, the main thing is to know, and accept, that they do happen. "Survive" means keep your job until hired by a different company.

SCREWED ONCE UPON A TIME

Brian was extremely bright and talented. We met in a class at the local junior college. His sense of humor was as dark as mine. My view of the universe matched his. We hit it off. I was 35 he was 18.

At 24, he stopped by, said he wanted to tell me something important he'd learned. He began by explaining that over the years he had kept his mouth shut when I'd rant about what slime companies were because he hadn't believed it, thought I was just a cynic with a grudge.

He said that on Friday at 2:30 the Editor of the newspaper where he was happily working as a graphic artist came into his department, flashed the lights on and off to get everyone's attention, then announced, "The paper has been sold as of noon. Clean out your desks. It's your last day."

Brian continued, "I trusted them. I liked working there. You always said, told me, everyone, to screw them because they'd screw me but I never even took a paper clip. What fuckers!" Brian wasn't letting his tears show but they were there. I agree, "What fuckers!"

It took Brian four months to get another job as a graphic artist because he wasn't working as a graphic artist. He had to work as a waiter. When he finally got hired as an artist, it was for 30 percent less than he had been making.

At the newspaper, not a single lower level person found out ahead of time the ax was about to fall. Top Management did a perfect job of keeping it secret. Of course, all top level people were hired at the headquarters of the new owners or they were given huge separation settlements.

A CHRISTMAS PROMISE

In most Fortune 3000s, they do it differently. At Christmas time, they have a giant party for employees. The CEO tells everyone how great next year will be, thanks one and all for such loyal sustained support, then, "About those rumors, I'm here to tell you there will be no layoffs. Everyone's job is safe and secure." The day after New Year's massive layoffs begin.

Why do companies big and small do this? To keep you from stealing or destroying their property until they get you off the property. They steal and destroy as much of you as possible but protect the company from you.

UNEMPLOYED MEANS UNTOUCHABLE

If you owned a company, would you recruit from the unemployed or the employed? People with jobs are automatically better than those without. Even those of us who don't run Personnel departments know that, right?

If unemployed, you're viewed by companies as worse than a leper with AIDS. It makes no difference if you got fired, laid off or quit. They believe that the only reasons for unemployment — you must be incompetent or irresponsible or a thief or a troublemaker or a druggie or a drunk.

In the corporate universe there are only two castes. If unemployed, you're an untouchable.

JUMP SHIP FIRST

Top Management does not lay off high salaried deadwood (old boys) until they've gotten rid of everyone else. Middle Management doesn't lay off deadwood who have been friendly and obsequious. Middle managers know what it's like to be incompetent. They know what's waiting out there in the real world for the nice deadwood.

Every piece of deadwood knows he is useless. To survive, he builds up sympathy in the eyes of his boss and the boss's boss. He makes certain everyone finds out about his prostate cancer, his alcoholic wife and his dying mother.

You're first when someone has to go. You're young, full of energy. You can easily find another job but the deadwood can't. He's kindly. You're capable. He stays. You go.

The instant you find out the ship is sinking, jump ship quickly before they throw you overboard. Timing is everything, so say the comedians. I say you can't jump too soon. If you have taken the correct steps, jumping ship is as easy as picking up the phone and calling a friend at another company.

QUITTERS NEVER WIN, WINNERS NEVER QUIT

Nothing in this book will do you one damn bit of good if you quit. Stay employed. Always have another job waiting. Don't be without a job until you have $30k in the bank.

NEVER BURN A BRIDGE

I'm swift to anger. I'm impatient. I despise incompetence. I hate injustice. But, I've only quit one job before I had another. It was the last non-freelance job I had! When I could stand it no longer, I announced that I was making a career change, becoming a freelancer. I thanked everyone, wished one and all well, then left.

In reality, I was so angry, my stomach hurt every night. I loved the work but hated the boss, had no respect for the boss, had to prevent myself from strangling him daily. Instead, I left without burning that bridge.

Six months later they begged me to come back as a consultant at nearly triple my old salary! Why? I didn't burn that bridge and they had a hot, CEO-level project that only I could do. After a short negotiating session, they accepted my single condition: the idiot I had worked for couldn't be involved in any manner.

The tactful explanation I used: "My style and methods of getting a project completed quickly seem to rub Albert the wrong way. I'm afraid with the short fuse and high visibility we have on this one, that would be too big of a risk for all of us." Notice the deliberate choice of *we, us* and *all.*

LAYOFF INSURANCE POLICY

Make all customers love and cherish you. Charm and win over every customer at every level. Have her, him, them, gush about you, in writing, to your boss's boss. ***Contradictory Advice:*** In this instance only, it is politically brilliant to use every one of your feminine wiles to woo and win your customer's favor. Of course, carefully avoid hurting feelings while keeping everything light and flirty, right? All's fair . . . .

SOONER OR LATER THE AX FALLS

Eventually, every company has a layoff. Even IBM, who proudly proclaimed for 70 years they never had one, managed to finally achieve organizational rigidity powerful enough to prevent any required changes from being made or even discussed until the ship was on fire and listing badly.

Don't burn bridges. Keep in contact with friends at other companies. Update your resume every few months. Those are common sense rules, not *Unwritten Rules*.

All I want is a fair advantage.
Never Give A Sucker An Even Break W.C. FIELDS

Laws are like cobwebs, small flies are caught but the great break through.
1618 FRANCIS BACON

Unwritten Rules

George Bernard Shaw said, "The golden rule is, there are no golden rules." No matter, there is an ultimate rule. Once you grasp all the implications of the ultimate rule, you understand the biggest picture of all, how the world really works.

At the upper levels of government and the upper levels of major corporations, nothing important is done by the book. This is not acknowledged and never mentioned.

Important things are done the way the most powerful want them done. That's what "most powerful" means. It's done this way no matter what Corporate Directives or Executive Guidelines require, no matter what the Constitution or any laws of the land say.

HOW THE WORLD WORKS

Following written rules interferes with the expeditious handling of important matters, not just in corporate offices, but in the Oval Office, FBI, CIA, DEA, IRS, Senators' and Representatives' offices and Pentagon offices. "Expeditious" means "secret" or it can mean "immense, illegal personal profit" or it can mean "getting re-elected" or "keep my job as CEO." In fact, it means any-damn-thing the most powerful want it to mean.

In Fortune 3000s, nothing important is done by the book. Everything gets done because of power, influence, negotiation and compromise. And, everything gets done without anyone mentioning unwritten rules.

Nothing important is written down — none of the taboos, none of the actual procedures, none of the understandings, none of the on-going turf battles, none of the truces, none of the alliances, nothing.

THE ULTIMATE RULE

Competitors in the eternal struggle for power near the top understand the unwritten rules somewhat clearly, but nobody completely understands them. That's why and how a palace revolt can be successful. But, each and every combatant clearly understands the ultimate rule.

The world itself, from the bottom of the ocean to the upper reaches of Mount Everest is governed by the ultimate rule. Nobody publicly acknowledges that fact, especially parents, priests, professors, politicians and office politicians.

The ultimate rule: The big fish eat the little fish. Other ways of saying the same thing: it's eat or be eaten, or might makes right. More to the point, power is everything. If you cannot defend yourself, you will be eaten.

How many divisions does the pope have?

JOSEF STALIN

WHEN THE POPE CONDEMNED HIS SLAUGHTER OF MILLIONS OF RUSSIANS

HOW THE CORPORATE WORLD WORKS

If everyone played by the rules, only extremely talented Boy Scouts would rise to the top. The written and unwritten rules in your office are no different from the rules in a football game. Most people follow them. But people who want to win, bend them as far as possible. Like W.C. Fields said at the front of this chapter, they only want a fair advantage.

Obeying the rules makes it impossible to climb quickly up the ladder. The big fish got where they are by bending and breaking rules, written and unwritten.

Anyone who wants to be considered a comer in the company is expected to show the big fish her shrewdness by being creative in interpreting the letter and spirit of the rule, written or unwritten.

Throughout this ten-year quest, form alliances with any big fish you can every chance you get. By associating with them, you learn many unwritten rules.

RULES OF THE GAME FOR BOYS

There are two things to learn about any game (a) what the rules really are (b) how far each rule can be bent, stretched or broken before you're thrown out of the game.

Boys play games governed by rules from the age of six. By playing, they learn that to win, they have to bend, stretch and break the rules because that's what the other team does. When opponents are somewhat evenly matched, if you follow the rules, you lose. Girls are never taught this crucial fact. They are taught they must get a husband.

RULES OF THE GAME FOR GIRLS

Women attempt to function in the corporation following rules they learned based on their gender's ultimate goal:

1. Never let any girl get ahead of you.
2. When another woman succeeds at anything, you lose.
3. Other women can never be your *real* friends.
4. The only rule when competing with other women is "There are no rules."
5. Do only what's best for you. She behaves the same way.
6. Only unattractive bitches make it to the top.
7. Beauty is most important. It'll get you a husband.
8. Emphasize your best physical attribute. Hair, eyes, legs, breasts, hips, whatever, dress to show it off.
9. Being popular is of extreme importance. One does this by being nice, helpful, kind, pretty and passive.
10. Being helpless is feminine. Courage is a man's virtue.
11. Real success is to marry well and be above it all.
12. You can love a rich one as easily as a poor one.
13. Never, never marry beneath your station.
14. You can always abandon your career and get married.

Following those rules makes it impossible for women to grasp what's going on in a company. I hope the quote below sounds familiar. If not, re-read *Dealing With What You Were Dealt:*

. . . squandering your precious, powerful years (a) playing in the wrong game (b) playing in the right game without knowing what the rules really are (c) changing games after you've lost nearly all your power.

TYPICAL UNWRITTEN RULES

In the list below, the first, second, third and eighth rules are the same in every Fortune 3000. The rest are only a representative few of the thousands of unwritten rules.

I. Thou shalt never say, "The emperor wears no clothes."
II. Thou shalt never whistleblow. Don't tell anybody how incompetent, irresponsible and illegal we are.
III. Thou shalt never put a female in charge of males.
IV. Thou shalt fill most token executive positions with black or brown females so we sin not against bureaucrats.
V. Thou shalt stall until it is settled out of court.
VI. Thou shalt never say what we are doing is unproductive, useless, unnecessary and wasteful.
VII. Thou shalt never complain about anything, especially reality. Reality is divinely revealed to us by reading between the lines of Top Management's oblique, obtuse, obfuscated communications.
VIII. What thou can get away with is what's allowed.

Some unwritten rules are sacred at Company B but they aren't even rules at Company C, such as: Thou shalt not be taller than the Division Manager. Thou shalt never swear in front of Little Dave. Thou shalt never mention UCLA.

SO WHAT? SHE SAYS

In the beginning, follow the rules. As you pay your dues across time, learn to bend the rules to your advantage. Later, learn how to ignore the rules that get in your way. Feign ignorance or give strong, common sense sounding reasons you ignored the rule. That's if you get caught.

You can take *Temporary Leave* and never get caught.

We would all be idle if we could.
SAMUEL JOHNSON

Truth is never pure and rarely simple.
OSCAR WILDE

Temporary Leave

If you set it up properly, and if you take acting classes as advised, you can leave Company D, work at Company E for a month and return without losing your job. Why would you want to do that?

AN OFFER YOU CAN'T REFUSE

After seven months at Company D, you stumble into a solid offer from Company E — company car, 28 percent increase. You know that you can do the job. It sounds too good to be true. Intuition tells you it's legit but you still can't believe it. What's a girl to do? There may be catch.

All of us doubt ourselves. All of us wonder if we really deserve the big break when it comes. Self doubt screws up our ability to clearly comprehend what's going on.

Here's a way to find out what's going on without risking four years of successful, ever increasing salaries. I've done it twice. Once the job was not what I expected. The other time the job was everything promised and more, much more.

Take the job. Find out for certain what's what. If the job's crap, you can return to Company D with nothing lost. If the job's great, you can keep it without burning a bridge at Company D. This is one of those rare situations that's truly win-win.

THE SETUP

After the second interview at Company E, you're seriously interested. Take your boss at Company D aside. With a worried look, tell him you need to talk with him in private. Sit down. Look solemn and distressed:

> *Mom's not doing so well. She's in the hospital. Dad's a mess. I'm tense and nervous. I'd like to go back home and help Dad for a week.*

He'll pretend to be concerned and caring with something like:

> *We'll cover for you. See Gracie. Tell her you need the Temporary Leave Forms. I'll sign them tonight.*

Look relieved and thankful, then slightly ashamed as you say:

> *I don't want to cause problems for you and the group. I'll brief Ralph so he can follow the Kramer Project. Everything else can sit. I'll stay in touch so that if he needs me I can help.*

For the next few days or weeks, depending on the progress with the too-good-to-be-true job, "Mom" can be getting better or worse. If you love the job, she gets "critical." You have to take a leave of absence to be with her.

If it was too good to be true, she gets better and you're right back where you started. Nothing's lost. After your return, you'll be viewed as tough, loyal and brave by your boss.

> *You were there when your family needed you. Now you're back with your other family.* (Don't puke.)

If you love the job, the leave of absence turns into a few months. Your calls get fewer. Then, "Mom" dies. Call. Tell your old boss you have to stay with Dad and help him get back on his feet. It looks like six months. You're sorry for letting your boss and the group down but you have to do your duty.

Not a plank in the bridge is burned. You can return should it become necessary. And, six months from now, your boss will give you a great letter of recommendation when you ask.

Nobody can check on this story. You're so "distraught" you don't know where or who or what. Besides, you always call from the pay phone in the "hospital."

After a few years and a few corporations this tiny piece of play acting won't seem hypocritical, it'll seem inconsequential compared to the lies, misrepresentation, broken promises, delays, excuses that each and every company pulls on you.

Take acting classes. You're going to need them.

Live together before committing marriage, that's what you do when working for a temporary agency. That's why *Temps Get To Choose.*

The knowledge of the world
is only to be acquired in the world, not in a closet.
LETTER TO HIS SON 1746 LORD CHESTERFIELD

Temps Get To Choose

Work for a temporary agency. That's the best way to begin this quest. You can bypass Personnel when you're just starting out. It's also a way to regain your bearings should you get sidetracked while on this quest.

Go from job to job, company to company for a year. You'll learn more in that year than women who work five years at the same company.

PAID TO LEARN

Many temp assignments require about only a fourth of your time and attention. You'll be able to read the *Must Books* while getting paid. Use their phone to stay in touch with contacts and friends from previous temp jobs. Rewrite your resume so it's slanted for the electronics industry or the shipping industry or whatever. Master as many new computer programs as possible.

LIVE TOGETHER FIRST

I was working as a temp at a 450 person division of a major company. After only a few weeks, they wanted to hire me, waving big bucks in my face. I held out for 20 percent more than the offer. They met me half way after a week of dancing. I declined, "Jeez. Sorry, Marty. I've turned down more than I'm asking. I'd love come aboard. There'd be plenty of challenges. It's a damn shame."

Had I not been there for awhile, I wouldn't have seen the situation clearly. I probably would have snapped up the offer.

Afterwards I'd have been kicking myself for not getting ten percent more to tolerate all the old farts in charge.

By working there, I realized the place was run by codgers. The 68 year old Division Manager was never there. In an emergency he could be reached at the golf course. Day-to-day operations were run by the Deputy Division Manager, age 65. Line and staff managers averaged 55. They did nothing. They wanted nothing. Most of all, they wanted nothing changed.

The guy trying to hire me was 40. He had delusions of taking over. His obvious plan was to build up a strike force of loyal Young Turks for a palace revolt.

As a temp, they look you over. You look them over. It's the chance to decide if you really like working there before you commit. It's a reality check like taking a used car to a mechanic before you open your purse.

MAKE THEM PAY

As a temp, you negotiate from a position of tremendous strength. You have a job. Plus, and this is the biggest plus, temp jobs pay a high rate because there are few benefits. If they want you, they have to give you a monetary reason. After they make a firm offer, turn it down.

> *I'm sorry. I really like working here. The people are nice and that position sounds pretty interesting but the salary just isn't something I can live with.*

Every company's first counter is to tell you about the great benefits and how that's worth 40 percent.

> *That sounds great. I'd love to have all those benefits, but the salary just isn't something I can live with.*

When they ask how much you want, say, "Right now I'm making (add 10% fudge) $27k," and shut up.

Usual response — shocked look, mumble, ". . . can't match that," followed by a reiteration of benefits worth 40 percent. As always your response is a sad, disappointed look, "So sorry, I really appreciate it, but I just can't possibly live with the salary, benefits or not. Gawrsh! I'm so sorry."

Some of them are smart enough to press you for what you'll take right then and there. It doesn't matter, stall. Even if you know the exact number, plus fudge, of course, stall, "I haven't given that much thought." Pause for effect. Wrinkled brow, chin stroking. "Let me think it over." That's how you keep all the power while they are courting you.

After a few days, if he hasn't approached you seeking an answer, call him and set up a private meeting. Tell him a number higher than you'll take and shut up. Being silent is a very powerful move in any negotiation. His move — stall by saying he'll have to "Take it up with Tom," or Personnel or the staff and get back to you. As a final manipulative move he usually adds, "I doubt if that'll fly."

If they want you, they'll give you nearly what you ask. Since they're trying to hire you, they obviously want you. They won't fire you for saying "no," at least not right away.

If they stall, do not chase them. Let time pass. They must come to you. The person who says "no" has all the power. You have all the power. Use the techniques described in the payoff chapter, *Get Promoted.* Have competitors and headhunters call and send letters to you.

After you get the position you want for the money you want, you'll have to attend meetings continuously for the next ten years. Here are some *Meeting Hints* to turn apparently wasted time into productive political gains for you.

One either meets or works.
PETER DRUCKER

A camel is a horse designed by a committee [in a series of meetings].
CONSISTENTLY IGNORED CORPORATE TRIBAL WISDOM

Meeting Hints

Thoroughly read *Win The Meeting,* listed in *Must Books*. The author explains exactly what's really going on in the endless meetings at major corporations. Here's the essence, but read that book once a year for the next ten years.

Meetings aren't about doing things. They're about figuring out how JB is thinking and *feeling* as part of paving the way for an effort that's still a few months away. (Emotion drives decisions far more powerfully than logic.) The idea is to edge everyone toward some eventual consensus. Of course, some people use meetings to grandstand, back stab, intimidate and establish their own power, so be prepared for that.

Even if the meeting is a meandering, muddle-headed mess, much valuable information can be obtained by the woman who attacks the environment with her eyes, ears and intuition. Simple facts can be useful in determining what's what and who's who. Who wasn't invited? Who didn't show? Who's late? Who's early? What does that mean in the larger view?

The boss may be feeling insecure and call a meeting just to show he's in charge. What does his insecurity do to your chances for advancement? Who's making him feel insecure, over what issue?

Staff members who don't show up or who are poorly prepared may be announcing they are about to jump ship or they've given up. Their jobs can be yours if you interpret the action correctly and plan accordingly.

Who's having whispered conversations in the hall before the meeting starts? ends? What does that mean, an end run? a palace revolution? As people return to their work areas, what are they talking about? What is the overall mood? What does all of this mean?

BREVITY EQUALS AUTHORITY

You'll be taken seriously if you express yourself clearly and to the point. Look over the meeting agenda and formulate your strategy. Figure out what you're going to say. Edit until you have a concise statement. Present your thoughts in a single 20-word sentence or even better, two 10-word sentences. Go last. You're remembered.

Your ideas are never subordinate. When speaking, do not act like a subordinate in body language, tone of voice or choice of words. Don't say, "In my opinion," or "Sir," or any other phrase that takes away from the authority of your idea.

Your ideas are from a suspect source as far as the men in the room are concerned — the mind of a female. Men are able and willing to fight for their ideas. Men actually enjoy the fight. They are going to attack you just for the fun of it as well as because they don't believe a female could think of anything useful. The odds are on their side, at least 8 to 1 in any meeting other than in the publishing business.

To talk without thinking is to shoot without aiming.
1732 TOMAS FULLER

Be well prepared and thoroughly ready to defend each and every idea you put forward. Think ahead. Anticipate what the objections will be and be ready to confidently respond to them. Confidently means without emotion, quietly, slowly and patiently no matter how much they bait you with questions or comments.

SELF INTEREST IS ALL THERE IS

No matter how they pitch their ideas, your rivals never have the organization's best interest at heart, only self interest at heart. In your own self interest, present your idea as if it's for the good of the corporation. The subliminal message of your pitch is, "If my ideas are adopted, everyone here will survive." *Kept Down And Out* has a much more thorough explanation.

NOBODY LIKES SURPRISES

Don't develop a great idea, then spring it on everyone in a meeting. Everybody will stall, trying to decide if their survival is at stake. If their survival isn't at stake, and your idea's great, they'll try to shoot it down because, by comparison, they look dumb.

Enlist the troops before the battle. Approach individuals ahead of time. Each of them wants a feather in his cap but doesn't want a black eye, just like in *Catch 22*. Explain your idea so it sounds like you'll take all the risk and they'll share the credit, without saying that, and they'll jump on board.

MEETINGS WITH YOUR PEOPLE AND OTHERS

When you and your subordinates meet, they do most of the talking. Just keep them on track, in the direction of a solution.

When you and your subordinates meet with your boss, you do most of the talking. Don't let him think you're not necessary. But, don't do all the talking, just key thoughts. Talking all the time makes him think you're impeding subordinates. He feels paternalistic, perhaps giving them an edge over you down the road. Hogging the floor also makes your workers hate you for denying them a chance to shine for the big boss.

AGENDA BREAKING DESTROYS HIS RHYTHM

There are some people who appear to be bright in meetings, with ready answers and tons of detail. Facts roll off their tongues. They spent their time understanding the small picture and spent all their energy preparing to look impressive for the published agenda. Outside the meeting, they are incompetents. These dullards are easily confused, thus discredited, if the agenda is changed at the last minute or if you can change it during the meeting by raising an important side issue.

PLACING BLAME NOT SOLVING PROBLEMS

After a major screw up such as missing the delivery date for a report, there's always a Who Shot John meeting. The purpose is not to discover what went wrong so that changes in procedures or assignments can prevent the problem from happening again. The purpose is to place blame.

If there is a witch hunt, a witch must be found and burned at the stake, if not, the person who started the hunt looks stupid. If a Who Shot John meeting is held, blame must be placed. People who don't attend are easiest to blame. Be certain you're there early, fully prepared to defend yourself and your boss. Have your facts straight and your temper under control.

UNDER FIRE

A few months after joining a new company, you'll be tested publicly. The guy who does it is a rival or an enemy. In a meeting where he thinks he has the edge, he'll ask a provocative question or make a provocative statement. He wants you to get angry, flustered or cry. All three would be paradise for him.

Eventually your enemy will attack. Before you go into any meeting, remind yourself that this may be when he strikes. Tell yourself that you'll breathe and remain calm. You'll remember to pause, look down at your papers and gather your thoughts before responding. When he does assault you, it'll be so much easier to keep cool. You knew it was coming. You just didn't know when.

PRETENDING YOU'RE THE SECRETARY

If you're the only female, men expect you to take minutes of the meeting because secretaries are female. The leader may even tell you, not ask you, to take the minutes. This touchy situation is known as a dilemma.

If you get all feminist huffy about it they dismiss you as a radical whacko. If you demurely accept the role, they no longer take you seriously. You're just another sweet, young thing who knows her place.

The solution is to ask politely, "Who took the minutes at the last meeting?" Pause for effect. Let the discomfort build. Remain silent. Look from face to face.

When someone finally answers, say without anger, "Next time it's not Ralph or me. Okay?" Pick up your pad and pen. Put a calm and relaxed look on your face and wait politely.

NUCLEAR COMBAT OVER MUFFINS AND COFFEE

When you do a good job as a menial person you are not considered for advancement. Being good at handing out towels in the locker room does not get you on the basketball team.

If you can't avoid being forced into the position of hostess or waitress do it cheerfully and horribly. Spill coffee on the least important person in the room, then drop the entire pot.

Nuke the muffins in the microwave until they are impossibly hot with the taste fully destroyed. When they laugh or snicker, smile and say, "My fiance says I can't even boil water." They'll realize you're more trouble than help. Someone else will do it next time.

FINAL MEETING TIP

When your rival's idea gets approved, stall, then stall some more. Suggest that a consultant be brought in to examine the decision process, conclusions and recommendations. Remember, when you're in a no-win situation, stall and hope for something to change. *Be Tough* and *Kept Down And Out* have much, much more on meetings.

Prepare for mediocrity unchained. In the perpetual meetings you must attend, there will always be *Middle Managers*.

My worst fear is that I'll find out I'm mediocre.
All That Jazz thru his alter-ego, Roy Scheider as BOB FOSSE

Middle Managers

They don't "manage" anything or anybody because they don't have a clue as to what anybody does. All they really do is sign time cards, approve vacation schedules, attend meetings, call each other with the latest gossip and spend the rest of the time covering their asses.

Middle managers are not mid-level management as commonly supposed. They are marginal, misplaced, mistake prone schmucks, stuck in the middle.

The company's stuck. It can't promote them further, because they'll cause even more damage. It can't fire or demote them because they'll sue. Gradually the responsibilities of the most inept are reduced so their damage is reduced.

CREATIVELY INEPT

Most Middle Managers are promoted by attrition. When one dies, he is replaced by someone who's not quite as dead. The replacement's sole qualifications? He's been there the longest without seriously pissing off anyone important.

Creativity is not why they got promoted. Conforming and kowtowing is. They have no idea how to create a better work environment or create a better paperwork flow or create a better atmosphere for communicating. Ideas? To them, being creative is putting blue tint on vu-graphs crammed with words that they read to the mind-numbed audience.

MANAGEMENT BY CRISIS

He has no power at home, he has no power from money, he has no creative power and he has no sexual power. Impotent everywhere except the office, these guys use work to hide from the terror of knowing how empty their lives are. Work distracts them from their emotions. Any work will do, even busy work.

Staying constantly busy prevents him from taking action ahead of time to prevent a crisis. He can only react to it after it happens. As soon as he puts out one brushfire, he spends all his time avoiding blame instead of figuring out why it started. It's only a matter of time until the next brushfire starts.

It takes a few management-by-crisis bosses before you can spot one who's dangerous to your career. If he's the type who can blame you, and make it stick long enough to get you fired, he's lethal. Telltale sign: he has thrown a worker to the wolves (blamed her for his mistakes) then shed crocodile tears in public.

HARD WORKERS NOT SMART WORKERS

The busy syndrome begins when he is first promoted. He works long hours, rushes from meeting to meeting with energy and enthusiasm, takes work home, comes in on weekends, calls other managers at home to discuss work.

Knowing he's incompetent, he feels guilty about being promoted. He tries to prove to himself, not others, he deserves to be the boss. If he isn't doing something, he feels guilty.

He produces reports and writes memos but never, and I mean never, figures out what's truly important. Since he does not understand the big picture. He has no method of deciding what's truly important, so every task is as important as every other task.

But a smart, new middle manager appears to do the same things. He takes work home, but only as a prop. He makes certain his boss and other important people notice his crammed attache case. On Sunday, he calls his boss at home to "touch base." They discuss a situation the new manager presents as a crisis in the making. Secretly, he already knows how to solve it. A week later, with much fanfare he "solves" it so he gets noticed, the first step to further promotion.

Smart middle managers move on up the ladder. If you spot one, finagle your way into his group. When he gets promoted, he'll take you along.

HELPING YOU ACHIEVE YOUR POTENTIAL

Middle managers, when they're young, say 35, actually believe they can motivate people to do more work in less time. They think they can change things and make them better, make the workers happier and more productive, improve the working environment and increase productivity.

They all attend Management Seminars run by pop psychology bullshit artists masquerading as management experts. At these gatherings, they pick up several idiotic ideas, then come back full of enthusiasm and try to impose the ideas on the workers. These jerks see themselves as "unleashing your creativity."

Don't complain. Don't tell him why it won't work and will piss everyone off. Smile and say "Okay," then do things the way you were doing them before the seminar and pray he doesn't attend any more this year. He'll forget about those great ideas in a couple of weeks.

MIDDLE MANGERS AT MANAGEMENT CLUB

At the monthly meeting, a con artist who calls himself a Motivational Speaker tells Middle Managers they can change their hopelessly empty lives and make a difference at the company. But that's not why they are there.

Management Club is Top Management's way of keeping middle managers happy and homogenized so none think about climbing up the ladder any farther. The secondary purpose is to get them all in one room so they can be examined closely for latent troublemakers and the dangerously incompetent. Another purpose is to give them an opportunity to seriously kiss some Top Management ass.

During the cocktail hour, a member of Top Management circulates. He "chats" with people in small groups, pretending he gives a shit about what they think as they wag their tails like dumb, slavering puppies. In fact, he's reminding them that they are low ranking slugs. The ritual keeps them humble and in their place, habituated as to who has all the power. It's like cardinals and arch bishops lining up to kiss the pope's ring.

THE FOUNTAINHEAD OF STUPIDITY

Can your boss become better than mediocre? Nope! He was born that way. Mediocre he is, and mediocre he'll die. Perspiration, inspiration, motivation and education are impotent unless one is born with talent and the courage to believe in oneself. Few, if any, middle managers have self confidence, even when they have talent.

After 20 years of frustration, futility and failure the only thing middle managers have left is fear. They have become hapless, helpless and hopeless. They distract themselves from reality in hundreds of ways, living as if there is no risk in being self blinded. This deliberate refusal to see is why most middle managers are such incompetents. They form the bedrock underlying the fundamental lack of common sense that's rampant in every Fortune 3000.

To successfully manage a boss, first *Understand The Boss*.

There are only two qualities in the world: efficiency and inefficiency and only two sorts of people: the efficient and the inefficient.
GEORGE BERNARD SHAW

Understand The Boss

Each boss just bumbles along, hoping everything will work out. Their primary concern is to avoid criticism from above after every crisis.

Although every boss has been sent to seminars that teach him how to plan, schedule, coordinate, cooperate and communicate, most can only react. They're not capable of planning ahead since they're not capable of doing the job at hand.

Most of them should not be in charge under any condition. Beyond not learning from past mistakes so they can identify problems ahead of time, they never have the right person doing the right job. People who are detail-oriented are put in charge of big-picture people doing detail work.

Most bosses are unable to choose the right person for the right job because (a) they can't see the big picture, (b) they don't know what the individual task requires because they've never done it (c) they don't have a clue as to how to judge anyone's strengths and weaknesses.

They never ask someone what she likes to do or hates to do, what she's good at or what she considers herself not so good at. When the timing is right, assert yourself. Tell your boss what you're good at and what you're not so good at while implying he'll look better because you'll do such a great job.

DADDY BOSSES

A boss will sometimes be fatherly. You know, worried about your health, concerned with your choice of anything and everything, then be rude enough to give you advice. He wants to protect you. You might be a substitute daughter in his subconscious. Don't encourage these twits by asking them for advice about anything personal, in fact, about anything.

Daddies are harmless if they are over 55 (often), happily married (rare), impotent (sometimes) and content to be where they are (common).

Being a daughter figure isn't useful. Daddy might be able to prevent your layoff if the recession hits while you're playing daughter. But Daddy doesn't give his daughter tough assignments from which she'll actually learn something. Move on to better things as soon as you have learned what you can.

BUDDY BOSSES

There are bosses who want to be pals with you. Under 40 or wannabe under 40. They want chummy conversations about college shenanigans, drinking parties at good old Omega My Thigh. These lonely, empty men thought business was going to be challenging, interesting and exciting. Disillusioned, they long for younger days when life was fun and full of hope.

These are the bosses who can promote you or get you a transfer to a hot, new department. They're doing their buddy a favor. They're also the ones who want to be your boyfriend. When he does have sex with his wife, he fantasizes about you. She weighs 40 pounds more now than she did in college and only talks about broken dishwashers, credit card problems, orthodontist bills and the new outfit she saw at Nordstrom.

Show him your "engagement ring" and beam. Talk about your linebacker boyfriend several times during the first few weeks working for this guy.

Once you're certain he won't make a pass, you can learn one hell of a lot from your buddy. You can close the door to his office and ask him to explain how the system really works, who you have to know, who you have to watch out for, what to do when Mr. Big Shot yells. In short, everything you need to know.

ENEMY BOSSES

There will be at least one woman hater. At first he seems like a toughminded all-business boss. No matter how great you are, he'll never take you seriously. He'll attempt to destroy you after you decline his pass, which he'll make in spite of your ring and your boyfriend's picture in his LA Raiders uniform. His secret view is that women were put on the planet to service men's sexual needs, period.

Spot this demented asshole quickly. The giveaway — to him, the new female VP is a castrating bitch but nobody else sees her that way. There's nothing you can do. Get out quickly, preferably to another company, before he makes a pass.

WHAT IS YOUR BOSS?

No matter how efficient and good he is at his job, no matter how well dressed, no matter how big his office is, no matter how much they pay him, he puts on his pants one leg at a time, picks his nose, reads on the toilet, has sexual fantasies just like you, me and everyone else. He's a person, just like you.

Women in general, young women in particular, have trouble seeing men-in-authority as merely human. This causes them to doubt their own intelligence, thereby delaying the onset of self-confidence without which they cannot proceed up the hierarchy at a rapid pace. Our patriarchal culture causes this misreading of reality. You're responsible to cure yourself.

SYMBOL IN PLACE OF SUBSTANCE

Corporate symbols of power seldom reflect the capability of the man possessing the symbols. This causes women to waste time.

As they were growing up, girls were taught to respect, obey and trust authority. Although boys were taught the same things, they were also encouraged to defy authority and to prove their courage by breaking the rules imposed by authority. That's why bright young men grasp that symbol-in-place-of-substance is company-wide and industry-wide much more quickly than bright young women.

The young woman I dedicated my first book to, Carla Ann, was at UCLA when she got her first job at a major company. She realized after only a few months that her boss was incompetent. She could see that he was only good at buffaloing subordinates and kissing up to his boss. She dismissed him as just one bad apple. After a changing companies, it happened a second time. She still did not generalize this discovery to other bosses and other companies. It took Carla Ann three companies and four years to realize that symbol-in-place-of-substance and ceremony-in-place-of-achievement is rampant. She's typical.

It usually takes a bright, conscientious young woman three years at the same company before she finally realizes most bosses are incompetent, not worthy of respect or admiration. That's if she is assertive enough to have transferred to several departments to escape one incompetent boss after another until she changed companies out of frustration.

Sadly, it takes her two more years to realize that it also applies to her new company. That's five years squandered, five of her most powerful years down the drain.

Assume your boss is incompetent until he demonstrates beyond doubt that he's competent. You'll waste no time.

IGNORANCE IS BLISS FOR CO-WORKERS

Most employees don't want to believe, or even know, that those in authority are not capable, not effective, not in control, not logical, not rational, not reasonable. They want Daddy to be strong. They don't want to know Daddy is a frightened buffoon.

Make certain you know it! Attack the corporate environment with all of your senses. Keep your mind clear and your eyes wide open. Evaluate. Analyze. This above all, trust your intuition. If your stomach says you are being lied to, you are. If your stomach says you are being used, you are.

KNOWLEDGE TRULY IS POWER

If you know the ship's Captain is a fool, you know what you must do to survive the imminent shipwreck, abandon ship. Change departments, divisions or companies. Or, be ready to take the helm once the Fleet Admiral realizes (with your anonymous help) the Captain is about to run aground. Or, figure out who the Admiral will anoint so you can join that alliance.

WHAT'S HIS STYLE?

Nearly every boss makes simple work complicated, tiresome and exasperating. Each boss does this differently. It depends on his own lack of ability, his own fears, and his own neuroses.

It makes no difference what bizarre concerns your boss has, identify his personal madness and conform. When you conform, he sees you as efficient and mentally healthy like he sees himself.

Every boss works a certain way. He has his neurotic, familiar, safe, secure rut. Do not attempt to create anything new. Simply figure out what his rut is, then feed whatever he wants into the rut.

They all communicate differently. If he writes memos to you, write memos to him. If he drops by and chats, then in an "Oh, by the way," manner tells you what he wants, that's how you communicate with him.

I had a boss obsessed with staple holes. If we had to replace an interior page in a stapled memo, he would spend several minutes aligning the new staple with the old holes in the top sheet! This guy's salary was $300k back in 1971. I never sent him a memo with a re-stapled first page.

FIGURE HIM OUT

Get your hands on his job description and an organization chart. Who's his biggest rival? his least worry? What are his priorities in reality? in his own alleged mind?

What deadlines does he face each week? each month? each quarter? What's the most important report he does? the least important? When are they due? How does he behave as the deadline approaches? Mark your calendar. To understand his methods, watch what he does as the stress builds.

What scheduled meetings does he attend? Who else attends those meetings. Which meetings are a big deal? which ones are a waste of time? Which ones make him uptight before he goes? after he comes back? Read this guy like a book!

When you are in his office, look around like a socio-psychological detective. Picture of the wife? Picture of the kids but no wife? No kids, no wife? Fishing trophy? Bowling Trophy? Degrees, certificates, awards? What does it all tell you about what he's proud of or about what he's hiding?

Is his desk a mess? Unanswered phone messages? Crammed in and out baskets? Either the guy is completely incompetent and disorganized or he's so busy that he should promote you to Administrative Assistant.

If he doesn't have any personal stuff around, he's left the job emotionally, mentally, psychologically, every way but physically. That's unless his boss's office is decorated the same way. In that case, he's merely mimicking his boss, who has left the job.

Notice! If either has left the job, someone will soon be getting a new job! What about you? If not you, trade this valuable insight for something you can use, like becoming Administrative Assistant to the guy who replaces him.

QUESTIONS WITHOUT END

Think about the answers you give to the questions below. Those answers will help you understand your boss and develop a strategy to control his view of you.

Is he having an affair with his secretary? One giveaway is that she calls him Mr. Carter but everyone else calls him Scott. If not, is he having an affair with anyone in the company, boy or girl? If he's involved, someone will be getting promoted or fired soon. Be in the right place to take advantage of the vacancy.

What is his general attitude? Is he an angry, frustrated, hurt, passed over lump that has it in for everyone? How much energy and time does he spend trying to get even instead of getting the job done? Use his desire for revenge. Suggest that if you were to take over the status report, he'd have Thursday afternoons available to concentrate on "more pressing matters." The information in that report will help you grasp the big picture. The people you contact for input are powerful new contacts.

Is he a fat, contented, castrated bull who has accepted his corporate fate? If he's just lying around waiting for the next load of hay, he'd be glad to have you take over the status report.

Figure him out. Your raise and promotion depend on it.

Some focus on the bad news, some focus on the good news, some ignore everything from below unless it presented as something "JB might get pissed about." Identify what gets his attention and use it.

Is this guy like Major Major Major in *Catch 22*? If so, you can do anything and he'll never catch on. Does he have an open door? If so, use it to bring him solutions, not problems and do it often. He'll soon realizes you're the best worker he has.

What do others say about him behind his back? Are they afraid of him? Do they respect him? Is he a barrier to your advancement? Use what you hear to plan your promotion even when it means changing departments.

The more insecure he is, the more he's worried about looking bad to his superiors. He gives this away by appearing terrified when his boss barges in. If he's insecure, present ideas so he sees your suggestions as improving his security. If he's ambitious and confident, present ideas so he sees your suggestions as earning him a feather in his cap.

Is he on the phone all the time? If so, is he socializing, or kissing up, or sharing gossip? I guarantee you that he's not communicating useful information.

How does your boss talk about anything that's work related? Is he emotional? Is he critical? Is he cold, rational and logical? Does he say, "This is a piece of shit," or does he make excuses for everyone? Once you decipher his general tone, you've determined how to present information to him. Do it so he realizes you share his view of the company and its problems.

Who comes by to talk with the door closed? Door-closers are sometimes co-conspirators. The level of the door-closers tells you something about what's being said. If the guy is higher than your boss, they're probably cooking up something. If the door-closer is lower than your boss, he might be the department squealer or the leading sycophant. If he's the same level, he could be conspiring or just whining or gossiping.

How fat is your boss? The leaner he is, the meaner and tougher his peers see him, as do his superiors. Fat men and women are disrespected at all levels. If he's thin and trim, he's serious about getting ahead. He can take you with him.

Does he interrupt his workers or let them finish? Interrupters are dreadfully insecure, always terrified the speaker may ask something they don't know or say something that reveals how incompetent they are. Interrupting is also his way of showing everyone he's more important than the speaker. Disgusting. Move on as soon as possible.

Does this neurotic bundle of conditioned responses worry about details (plastic or paper cups) or is he a big picture guy? When he reviews the budget, does he realize $47k for printing is way out of line? Or, does he add up the columns to check the math? If he's focused on trivia, your chances to have him authorize major, long range changes are enhanced. He'll only question trivial portions of the plan!

Trivia experts are the most common type of boss. They've been around for thousands of years. They'll be around for thousands more.

DEFEAT TRIVIA EXPERT EXECUTIVES

Michelangelo wanted everyone to know God as he knew and loved God. To Michelangelo, God wasn't the distant, angry, dark, inhuman, asexual, stylized God of the Dark Ages, He was alive, colorful, concerned and human-like.

To convert Christendom, everyone had to see his convention shattering images. Who could possibly put the paintings where everyone could see? Who could possibly pay for it? Only the richest man in all Italy, the pope.

Obviously, the pope's image of God was not changeable, so Michelangelo did not bother discussing images of God. But, he did intentionally create obvious, trivial mistakes, such as a hand that was too large, or a misplaced prop in the finished work.

When his boss, The pope, visited the Sistine Chapel for a progress review, he would immediately notice the "mistake," point it out, order it changed, feel smug and important then leave without noticing the big picture, Michelangelo's powerful, humanizing, world-changing, work of art.

DEFEAT "BUSY EXECUTIVES"

When I was 36 I wanted to be a film editor. I got a job at KNBC TV as a gofer, as in "Don, go fer coffee." I could learn quickly by watching and helping.

The chief editor was 50. He'd been there since he was 17. The documentary he was cutting had to be reviewed by executives. After he finished, he went to the front of the reel, rolled in two minutes and twenty five seconds. Just past that point, he looked at the edge numbers, called the lab and had another print made of that section. As gofer, I went and brought the print back. He checked it, rolled it up and put away. Then he deliberately made a long, tiny scratch in the finished film. I turned pale. He smiled and explained:

> *I figured out these suits. The assholes can't pay attention for more than a coupla minutes. Soon as they lose interest they say, "Stop." They make something up about*

whatever's around there and tell me to change it. I'm pissed off but I gotta do it, right? So I change it and the piece is screwed up.

The schmuck who's gonna review this knows jack shit 'bout story, knows jack shit 'bout rhythm. All he knows is he's gotta change something or he ain't earning his $200k. So I give him somethin' to notice, somethin' easy to change. He's happy. I'm happy.

DEFEAT "BIG PICTURE" EXECUTIVES

The department had never made its budget when I became Staff Assistant to VP of Business Development. Part of my new job was to control costs. I came aboard in mid-March and 40 percent of the year's budget was gone. The Who Shot John meeting blamed "those SOBs in Engineering" for the overrun, "charged too many overtime hours to proposals."

Nothing changed — no procedure to authorize charges, no computerized monitoring of charges as they occurred, no separate accounts set up for each effort. I couldn't control, I could only pass on bad news after the fact.

By mid-year, 70 percent of the budget was history. Corporate was extremely pissed. My boss had me calculate how much we needed for the rest of the year. I looked at it job by job. With contingency, it totaled $3.9M. He said, "Jeezus, I can't show Mike, he'll shit a brick!" He cut it to $3.3. He showed it to Mike, "Sumner! I can't show that to Jay! He'll have my balls!" Mike cut it to $2.5 and flew up to corporate to explain, apologize and beg for money. They gave him $2.0. We spent $3.7 by Christmas.

After another year of this, I realized what was happening. No matter how much cost history I had to backup the figure for each item in the budget, my boss cut the total. Mike cut the total Sumner showed him. When it got to corporate, Jay cut the total. ***Reality:*** we were not overrunning a budget. We were overrunning the wishful thinking of self-important executives.

The next year I worked up the real number for all the jobs we forecast, based on costs of similar jobs in the past, $6.9M. I invented jobs and added them in as padding. I raised the cost of each job so the total was $10.6. Sumner turned white.

He had me take out some jobs we had to do and jobs we knew from experience would "jump outda ground." He said, "I can show Mike $9.7." Mike cut it to $8.3. Jay cut it to $7.1. We made the budget for the first time. I was promoted, moved into a big office with frosted glass and received authorization for a walnut wastebasket. Everyone on the top floor had one!

These guys saw themselves as Big Picture Executives concerned with the bottom line. They never once questioned the cost of a line item. They never once questioned if the line item was necessary. "Cutting" millions at the stroke of a felt-tip pen made them feel powerful and important. "I just saved the company big bucks. That's why they pay me so much."

FEMALE BOSSES — AVOID AT ALL COSTS

Stereotypes are based in fact and on fact. Behind their backs, common nicknames are given to female managers: Dragon Lady, Bitch Witch, Dyke of Earl.

The fact is, women cannot get ahead unless they are TOUGH. Tough on their employees, tough on their peers, tough on everybody. Only the tough survive. Want to work for someone who had to toughen herself against everything to make it?

Feminist propaganda contends that women are different than men bosses: concerned, nurturing, try harder, more productive, less jaded, don't need flattering, don't play politics, believe in "participative management." Propaganda is just that, propaganda.

If you get stuck with one, beware! She's envious of everything about you. She resents your youth, your beauty, your education, your family and your lifestyle as she imagines it. She assumes you are a happy-go-lucky Scarlett with countless beaus at your feet. Make certain your engagement ring sparkles.

To survive, you had to learn how to control and manipulate males. Few, if any, of your skills work on tough females. Here's some sound advice I heard somewhere — obey her like a man but treat her like a lady. Makes sense to me, but I only had one female boss in 30 years. It worked on her.

To avoid career ending confrontations, chart her periods. After a few months, you'll see how her behavior and mood is affected. You'll know how to handle her during that time so she doesn't explode. It can range from pampering her for days to complete avoidance. It's just like learning to read the mood of your male boss so you know when to stay out of his way and when to ask for that choice assignment. The only difference, the calendar is useless in predicting his mood swings.

BISMARCK'S METHOD CAUSES PROBLEMS

As the company complies with government fiats to create gender equality, upper management positions are given to women who "know their place and won't get uppity." These women don't cause problems. They are content to be figureheads.

In the lower ranks, some women are promoted because they are women. These dolts will cause you endless frustration. As soon as you realize your boss is one of these tokens, get moving and get out. She's even worse than the bumbling man who would have been your boss if [1]Bismarck's method were not used.

AGE BEFORE BEAUTY

If you think you might want to stay in the corporate world even after you've accumulated screw-you money, you absolutely have to have a real mentor. Do whatever you must do to work for a bright, powerful old-timer, 60ish.

These guys are gold mines! You'll learn more from one of them than you will from all other bosses you ever have, combined. I learned more from my mentor in only two years than from all others combined! See the dedication page.

He may be difficult and cranky and grumpy and insulting, but he knows what it takes to survive and prevail. He knows how to run the damn company. He'll teach you how to do both if he judges you worthy of the knowledge.

To him, most young people are shallow, indifferent, selfish, lazy, spoiled, not worth a good god damn. He's right.

Stick around this guy for at least two years, more if possible. He knows everything. He doesn't want it to die with him. He wants to pass it on. But he'll only teach somebody worthy of knowing it, a loyal, married-to-the-company person. As Epictetus advised way back in *Your Goals,* do what you must do.

Be interested. Think. Ask questions. Challenge him once in a while. Win him over to your side.

Now that you understand middle managers and understand the boss, you're ready to *Manage The Boss*.

[1] Bismarck's method is explained shortly.

Son, to train the dog you have to be smarter than she is.

ON THE FUNDAMENTALS OF MANAGEMENT THE AUTHOR'S FATHER

There are only two races of people in the world, the decent and the indecent.

Man's Search For Meaning VICTOR FRANKLE

Manage The Boss

Your boss is responsible to his boss for the work you do. It's not your work, it's your boss's work, he merely delegates it to you. The only job you have is the one he wants done.

The person you work for day in and day out is your boss. He's automatically superior to you. He evaluates your performance, thus he decides your future.

Your boss is the most important person for you to control. That means control how he sees you. Control begins with the uniform you wear every day. It ends when you are promoted and transferred to the new office in Hawaii. Make him see that you are (a) no threat to him (b) valuable and promotable.

If your boss is a piece of deadwood going nowhere, shift your efforts to his boss.

RULES OF THE HIERARCHY

You must *appear* to be respectful and deferential to the boss no matter how many people know he's deadwood or an idiot or a bore or any other unpleasant type. In the military, this attitude is known as "salute the uniform not the man." Remember, the corporation is set up like a military organization.

If you don't know how the system works or if you ignore the system, you won't be considered for a better paying position. Mavericks don't get put in charge of anything or anybody. *They* have learned the hard way that if she doesn't play by the rules at an insignificant level, she won't play by the rules when she gets to a significant level (the magic number).

To be promoted up the hierarchy, you must play by the rules of the hierarchy. A major rule is that everyone must show respect for her superiors even when they are inferiors. You can never ignore, challenge, confront, disobey or criticize your boss. The military mind knows that if any disrespect is permitted, mutiny follows.

Another major rule of the hierarchy — nobody can go over her boss's head. The hierarchy cannot and will not tolerate it. In the military, it's called "respect the chain of command." The chain extends down from the Commander In Chief, the President, to the Secretary of Defense, to the Secretary of the Army, to the highest ranking general, then down through the ranks until it reaches the female private. The military mind knows that if any disrespect for the chain of command is permitted, mutiny follows.

After several years inside the corporate hierarchy, you'll learn to bend these rules with impunity. But, until you're used to working within the system, don't try to beat it, especially those two rules. *Unwritten Rules* explains many other key regulations you can't break.

STRAIGHT TALK?

Blunt, forthright talk is reserved for specific moments in certain situations. Straight talk is so unusual within the corporation that it's an extremely powerful tool you can use to your great advantage now and again. Knowing when, and to whom, is the essence, and art, of office politics.

You can only say what you really think behind closed doors, off the record, to an ambitious, talented, Machiavellian boss who trusts your judgement and who will act on your recommendation without disclosing that he heard it from you. There aren't many bosses like that. If you find one, hitch your wagon to a rising star and learn from a master.

Here's a situation where straight talk helps. Your intuition tells you that although you've done your best to not be threatening, your boss is still afraid you'll take his job. He sabotages your work, trying to make you look bad.

Tough position! Don't say anything to him. Don't acknowledge his fear. Quietly arrange an off the record, private meeting with his boss. During the discussion, show that you respect and understand the chain of command.

Although brevity is authority, don't be blunt. Get it down to short, clear sentences using only simple words. Rehearse.

This is awkward. I'm not trying to leave Dick out of the loop but you need to know the situation. Dick thinks I'm after his job. I'm not. Things aren't getting done right. It would be best if I went over to Eve's section.

Be prepared to offer examples of "things aren't getting done right" with dates and names. Do not blame Dick. If Dick's boss is even slightly above brain-dead, he knows that you or your boss has to go. You've given him the solution.

During the talk, pay attention to the listener. Search for clues as to how he's experiencing the information and you. Often he's pleased. Sometimes he even realizes you should do Dick's job and Dick should work for Eve! If he's average or above, what you didn't say will be understood. It marks you as tactful and indirect, two characteristics that show you are a knowledgeable team player.

Other situations that require straight talk are about a boss or co-worker who's drinking or drugging to excess, stealing, lying to customers or fill-in-the-blank of unacceptable behavior. Don't be a squealer. Be an off the record reporter of bad news.

You'll discover other moments to tell it like it is. Here are some. To your trusted but high-ranking associate, "I want that damn assignment. Who do I have to beat out? Who's the referee?" To a nosy gossip, so others hear, "How rude of you to ask such a thing!" At the department lunch, when nobody else can hear, to the person you want to work for, "I loved it when you rubbed Fred's ass kissing in his face at the meeting."

Always rehearse so you can pay attention to the listener instead of searching for the right words.

I BELIEVED IN STRAIGHT TALK

After a colossal, three-rung promotion, I had a heart-to-heart talk with my new boss, "The easiest way to deal with me is to come right out and say what you want. You don't have to beat around the bush with me. I believe in telling it like it is." There was an unbelievably long pause in which I could see he was struggling for the right words. Finally, "Son, I don't even talk with my wife or family like that. You're gonna have to get used to my style."

During the next few months, from that lofty position near the top, I got used to his style. It was the same style of communicating every man from his level on up used — subtle, oblique, obtuse, obfuscated. He was only four levels down from the CEO, knocking on the door of Top Management.

Epilogue: Every year he held a lavish Christmas Party for Top Management at his executive spread in the Pasadena hills. His alcoholic wife was in the shower struggling to sober up enough to fulfill her role as sparkling hostess. Thud, smash! she drunkenly crashed through the glass shower doors, cutting herself to the bone. Paramedics were saving her from bleeding to death as guests arrived. Two months later his son was busted for smuggling 10 kilos of marijuana. Communicating obliquely with him, Top Management never answered the door, the one he was knocking on.

Comment: Once in awhile there's some justice, a little.

THE ESSENCE OF GETTING ALONG

Adaptable, considerate, flexible, smart people get ahead. Stubborn, rude, ignorant people don't. Being flexible doesn't mean selling out, it means adjusting to fit in.

Behave exactly the same with everyone, from the mail room to the board room. You are polite, considerate, respectful. Everyone considers you fair, honest and straight. Someday, you're going to be a hero to those under you and to those above you. Act that way. Confident people don't lord it over anyone. Confident people don't kowtow or grovel. Defer, yes. Kowtow, no.

Sooner or later everyone must play "The CEO's New Clothes." They see nothing, hear nothing and say nothing no matter how obvious it is. When your turn comes, admire the CEO's taste in new clothes. Go into the rest room. Close the stall door. After you puke, say, "Where could I make $40k and do practically nothing while I accumulate screw-you money?" The answer is, nowhere. Once in awhile you must take shit and do shit just to get where you want to be.

DON'T KISS ASS, DEFER

Ass kissers beam when the boss comes into the room. They call him "mister" or "sir." Senior ass kissers say utterly repugnant, embarrassing things like, "That was a great talk, Mr. Colon. You take command when you're at the podium. You must have been a speech major."

When you notice an ass kisser, make a mental note to always and forever distrust him. While the kissing is going on, focus on the object of obsequiousness. Look for the reaction. If the kissing is appreciated, add that person to the distrust list. If the kissing offends, start a list. Put that person at the top. Title the list, People I Want To Work For. The other guy on the list is the one who said "I don't know."

Obsequiousness is odious behavior.
OSCAR WILDE

Ass kissers are universally hated and disrespected. If the ass kissing is ignored (a) the kisser's an idiot so everyone ignores him (b) the recipient is a good office politician who never acknowledges ass kissing. He knows that if he's rude to the kisser he may make an enemy. At the same time, he realizes that if he's even civil to the kisser, he'll make enemies of everyone in the room. More data is necessary before you can decide who's who.

When others praise and flatter you, smile politely, then flush it down your mental toilet. It is worthless, a blatant, manipulative move. Words are cheap. Action requires courage and character. Believe only deeds. (This is just as true in romantic relationships. I had to learn the hard way, twice, before I accepted it.)

Now and again it's politically brilliant to give quiet recognition to your boss's extremely modest talents. Pick out something he did right. Acknowledge it. He's starved for recognition. His boss never pats him on the back. "I liked the way you handled that guy from Manufacturing, right to the point." Generic, universal, safe, meaningless compliments are also useful. "I liked working on that Ride Share Plan. Thanks for giving me the chance." Develop a list of generic pats.

Many corporate males think women who admire them want to express more admiration while horizontal. Anything beyond polite, simple acknowledgement marks you as a potential sex partner. The instant he thinks you believe he's great, he sees a worshiper who can be called in to service the lord. That goes for every male at or above your level.

ON NOT FIGHTING WITH THE BOSS

Do not disagree publicly, loudly or in any other way with your boss. Do not snipe or back bite your boss or his boss. You can share your opinion with your boss. You can exchange views on a topic but don't fight. Every fight has a winner and a loser. Your boss is the winner, automatically.

You're not playing by the rules if you don't play along when stupid decisions are made at or above your boss's level. Exposing the obvious is considered traitorously disloyal. Remember, never say, "The emperor wears no clothes."

After the furor over the stupid decision dies down, figure out a better solution, not obvious to everyone. Make certain your boss knows you want him to use it. Say, "Modify it anyway you want so it's acceptable to Arnie and Fred. We'll all be better off with this than what they laid on us."

He'll change it and thereby own it. It makes no difference. He now sees you as a concerned, bright, team player.

WIN WHEN THE BOSS WINS

When dealing with your boss and other superiors, after you've stated your case firmly, but they disagree, you must defer. This is mandatory. Let small minded people win the small battles. Save your power for the big ones to come. When your boss wins a small battle, he feels powerful and beneficent, especially if you acknowledge his victory and congratulate him.

Shortly after this moment passes, sometimes an hour, sometimes a day, you can get just about anything you want from him. He's still deluded about his competence, he feels magnanimous and generous. Take your ideas to him when he's still feeling brave. He might even actually change something!

BODY LANGUAGE SPOKEN HERE

Encourage your boss to keep talking by listening attentively. Sit up, lean forward, nod, a few "uh huh's," raised eyebrows, tilted head. Keep you hands off your face and mouth. Don't cross your arms in front of your chest. Don't steeple. Don't cross and uncross your legs or any other courtship body language.

Overstaying your welcome in his office makes him see you as dull, inattentive and not getting the work done. When he's done talking, he looks at his watch. If you miss that, he straightens papers, then looks at the papers not at you. If you still don't get the hint, he puts his palms on his knees as if he's about to stand. If you're still babbling like a bimbo, he turns his chair and faces the door. If he stands up, you're a dimwit in his eyes. Time to change companies.

Buy and read every book on body language you can find except *Body Language* by Fast. He's a writer who interviewed experts then masquerades as an authority. "Success" book authors do the same thing. The writer does not know how, and has not done, what he's telling you how to do. Pure crap!

MANAGING MANAGEMENT BY CRISIS

In Chinese writing the character for crisis and opportunity is the same! Most sheep and cows see crisis as dangerous. Learn to see a crisis as the opportunity to shine.

Remain calm and rational amidst the chaos. Show concern, thoughtfulness and steadfastness while the project burns to the ground. Do the best you can. Don't yell or get angry. When your chief rival goes off half cocked, you'll look like a pillar of strength.

Pompous, blustering buffoons think yelling and threatening can cause the impossible to happen. Sometimes The Big Boss wants the impossible, or the VP's son wants the impossible. Even worse, sometimes your boss wants the impossible.

When this happens, adopt and maintain a posture that says "I'm concerned and calm." Then, in a concerned tone of voice, apologize for not being able to do what the twit wants done. Absolutely DO NOT say you'll try. If you try the impossible, guess who's blamed in the inevitable Who Shot John meeting?

Don't be buffaloed, bullied or bullshitted into saying you'll try. Simply say, "I'm sorry, that can't be done, no matter how much money we spend, no matter how many people help. There's just not enough time."

When the person who wants the impossible is not a buffoon, you can sometimes make the point with humor. "Look at it this way, Arnie. We can't make a baby in a month even if we get nine women pregnant!"

Lack of planning on your part
does not constitute an emergency on my part.
SIGN IN CORPORATE REPRO DEPARTMENTS

Explicitly do not say, "If you dumb shits had done only a teeny bit of planning and a tiny bit of communicating, this wouldn't have happened."

A very toned down version of that can be presented at the inevitable Who Shot John meeting. This can be done only after you know which person in authority is genuinely interested in preventing the problem from happening again. You won't know who that is until you have attended a few Who Shot John meetings at each company. ***Caution!*** Don't make your boss look bad when you present the solution which is a new procedure to be followed by one and all. Have him clued in ahead of time.

CORPORATE BUREAUCRATS

The bureaucrat inside and outside the corporation, worldwide, does not care about what makes sense, what needs to be accomplished or what works. Never attempt to be reasonable with a bureaucrat. Reason, logic and common sense are not part of his job description. He lives by rules and policy.

It makes no difference what you want from Office Services, Shipping, Purchasing or any other bureaucracy. Fill out the form. Get it approved or sign it yourself (my favorite ploy). The bureaucrat has no idea if the scrawled signature is genuine. He's happy. He has his form and you have the computer or printer or desk or whatever you wanted.

Forms are his world. Forms are his boss's universe. The Chief Bureaucrat judges his workers by examining the completed forms they turn in. If the forms are correctly filled out, the bureaucrat is doing a good job. Reality does not count.

If you are not able to get something your boss wants done because of a bureaucrat, let your boss know. But don't take responsibility for not being able to accomplish the mission. Explain the situation. Say what has to be done.

Sorry, Dick. Tom, in Office Services, says he can't call the repairman unless we have JB sign a WTF-1130c. I brought one up. Want me to get JB's signature?

MAKE IT EASY FOR HIM TO DO WHAT YOU WANT

Think. Plan ahead. What will have to be done so you can get that transfer to Public Relations or whatever. What will your boss have to do? Can you make a few preliminary phone calls to "line up the ducks?" Does he have to speak with someone in person or on the phone? Is that person on vacation or on a business trip? Which forms have to be completed?

Middle managers like to pretend they are so busy and overworked they can't spare the time to do what an underling like you wants done. Make it quick and easy for him. Keep it simple [for] stupid (KISS) to prevent him from chickening out.

Write the memo for him. Have it final typed. When you go in to complete discussions on your tuition refund, have the memo with you in a folder so it's not obvious. When he says, "I'll have Rebecca prepare that memo, but I can't spare the time right now." You say, "I know you're busy, so I had her get it ready," as you slide it over to him.

THE BOSS'S BOSS AND YOU

Your boss is extremely happy when his boss says something good about you. That takes time. Here are the fundamentals.

Your boss's boss judges you solely by what you look like, because he has no idea what you do. He notices you are at your desk earlier than the starting time. He notices you take brief breaks. He notices you are back at it before lunch is over and you don't rush for the door at quitting time.

He approves if you don't turn heads, his or others, as you blend in with conservative attire in good taste. To him, your tortoise shell, slightly too-large stage glasses make you look intellectual, someone to be taken seriously.

He subconsciously notices that when he's talking, you listen attentively, sitting up, leaning forward, head tilted slightly, as if you really are interested.

When you don't understand his orders, you're not intimidated. You say, "Sorry, I'm not certain what I'm to do after I run the hours vs foreign dollars report. Let me have that again, please."

You know what's important to him. Even if it's foolish, you play along. That is, you conform to his idiosyncracies, without a funny look on you face.

SUPERB PERFORMERS ARE TREATED THE SAME

Most managers don't have a clue as to what's really important. They attained their status by doing as they were ordered. Now they blindly enforce rules that make no sense. Here's an example from the Fortune 3000 world.

Cathleen Black, publisher of USA Today, says managing salespeople brings special problems. "Good salespeople are very wily. They'll always push to see how far they can go and what they can get away with. They try to beat the system and push for special case status. 'Just look at my numbers,' they'll say. 'I'm doing great so it shouldn't matter what hours I work.' But nobody here works 9:30 to 4:30 no matter how good the numbers are. You must show them the limits."

Translation: You smart ass productive workers think you're better than everyone else! You think you deserve more because you produce more! I'll show you who's in charge. Behave like all the other cows, or you're outta here!

Is that insane or what? Sales make everything else possible! As my boss used to say, "Nothing happens until somebody sells something." Dimwits like Black run Fortune 3000s.

Be at your work station when the opening bell sounds and stay there until the closing bell rings. That's a "good worker." A quiet cow, in her stall, ready to be milked, not mooing.

WORKING HARD AND WORKING SMART

The Protestant Work Ethic is what made America the most powerful nation ever. It's not what Fortune 3000s are about. You must work hard, don't get me wrong. But the hardest work is establishing in the mind of others, your boss, his boss and any other members of management, that you're a hard worker as well as a loyal, dedicated, team player.

But you really must work your ass off, put in the long hours, do the grunt work and endure the drudgery. Otherwise, how will you ever stand out enough to get noticed if you're like all the others? The first step to getting promoted is getting noticed.

Once you get good at your job don't expect to any pats on the back. Your boss isn't interested in the bottom line, he's interested in appearances. He doesn't care if you do your job at half the cost of your predecessor. He cares if you're in your seat at 7:58 AM and are still there at 5:06 PM.

WORKING HARD FOR YOU

When you come in on Saturday to straighten out that mess you didn't get to, you're not doing it *for* them, you're doing it so you look better *to* them. Helping the lazy new girl finish on time, explaining to the dumb guy until he finally gets it, doing extra tasks for your boss. No matter what you're doing, it's *for* you, so you look better *to* them. By working hard, you're taking care of you, not them.

Everyone thinks you're Superyoungwoman. Get a big increase by leaving them. A year later, they'll beg you to come back if you stay in touch with everyone.

KEY FINAL THOUGHT

Getting the job done *in spite of* your boss is what separates the girls from the women. Whatever it takes is what's required. Obstacles are there to test you. Overcoming the obstacles makes you stronger and smarter.

That which does not kill me makes me stronger.
FRIEDREICH NIETZSCHE

Be prepared. Plan ahead. There will always be obstacles, *Rainy Day Woman.*

Shit happens.
UNKNOWN WISE PERSON

You can't step into the same river twice.
Only change is constant.
HERACLITUS

Rainy Day Woman

Fate, kismet, destiny, luck, karma, the winds of war. Life interferes with the best laid plans of mice and young women. A betrayal of love that crushes your heart and spirit may render you unable to work for a month. The engine from a DC-10 may fall out of the sky and kill the best boss you ever had.

Smooth sailing is not possible. There are storms at sea. There are storms in life. Disease, death, divorce, abortion, treachery, insanity, who knows what it will be, but it will always be something. You cannot escape life's natural and normal problems.

PASSAGES OF LIFE

Everyone's life, including yours, goes through a major upheaval every six to ten years. You're due at 24 if your life hasn't been completely disrupted since you were 19. Weathering the storm in a snug harbor is what you must be able to do. Snug harbors are made of money.

By the time your third major upheaval strikes, say about 32, you should have put away at least $20k to weather the storm. You must be ready to care for yourself when the upheaval comes, as it will. You can't survive with your integrity or self-esteem intact if you have to beg for help.

Trouble comes storming across the plains of your reality when you least expect it. That's simply the way it is. Caution! If the company ship is sinking, women and children are thrown over the side first because they can't fight back. You must be ready with a plan and contacts should the ship begin sinking.

REMEMBER TO STAY HUNGRY

You may be comfortable and feel secure at your third company, deciding, "this is my niche." You'll become complacent and satisfied as you ride the gravy train. When rainy days come, all gravy trains stop.

Save for, and survive, rainy days that always come. Provide for yourself. The more companies you left who wanted you to stay, the more shelters you have when the inevitable storm comes.

THEY WON'T PLAY FAIR

If they feel benevolent, you get two weeks notice before you're set adrift. Usually they wait until Friday afternoon, "Due to circumstances unforeseeable, Mr. Bootit announces this Division will permanently close as of 4 PM today. Good luck and thank you for your loyal service. Unemployment counselors will be available at 123 Upyourz Street on Monday at 8 AM. That is all."

It doesn't do any good to pretend this won't happen to you or your division. Shit happens. Only the prepared survive.

KEEP YOUR OPTIONS OPEN

Once someone is promoted, he holds that position like a Supreme Court Justice, until death. This reality baffled me when I first discovered it 25 years ago. It baffles me today. For a thorough explanation of this insane policy, read *The Peter Principle,* listed in *Must Books*.

It's of the ultimate importance to always have options outside the company. Never stop looking. Never for a second think you'll last more than another month.

Things change that fast in the corporate universe. Why? Because, just like in the military, the foot soldiers don't know what the sergeants know. Sergeants don't know what the officers know. Officers don't know what the Generals know. And nobody knows what the Commander In Chief, the CEO and his inner circle know, not even the Board of Directors.

The company can be bankrupt for months before anyone finds out. When it becomes known, the big fish eat the little fish.

Contingency plans are mandatory. Death comes when least expected. If a manager is caught with a VP's wife or son, he dies of sudden resignation. Prescription pills, cocaine, speed or alcohol flatten two of the Fortune 3000's biggest wheels every month.

If it happens to your boss's boss, things get nasty in a hurry. The wild dogs begin circling the hyenas who are circling the jackals who are circling the lions as the vultures watch and wait. Each wants to rip off a piece of the corpse's territory.

DEATH IS THE GREATEST TEACHER

Sooner or later, someone will die unexpectedly. You'll get to see the mad scramble and all-out battle for his spot. If you're lucky, the corporate jet will crash, killing ten VPs.

Lucky? Yes, because all subtleness disappears when there are ten big-time promotions available. Blatant office politics begin. You'll learn much, and learn it quickly, watching the blood-letting among pretenders-to-the-thrones as they plot and counterplot while mouthing platitudes and feigning respect for the dead.

You'll grasp the true nature of your co-workers as they wring their hands, literally, in abject terror of what the future holds. You'll see a hypocritical, phony stance of religiosity and piousness infest everyone.

Quickly you'll realize not a single person gives a good hoot in hell about any of the dead. They only care about, "What's going to happen to poor little me?"

Sanctimonious pronouncements of, "What a great guy Joe was," fill conversations. ***Reality:*** he was incompetent but predictable. Everybody knew what could be done and couldn't be done when that "great guy" was alive. Each person knew where he stood. Now everything's up in the air.

Fear and doubt, especially self-doubt, are rampant. The truly incompetent people who worked for the "great guy" shamelessly suck up to anybody and everybody they think has a even an outside chance to take over. In their dark little hearts they know their survival under the great guy was possible only because he was so blind and stupid. Now, they are facing transfer to Guam and a demotion, at a minimum.

Seeing this hypocrisy up close will convince you way down in your guts that you want more out of life than pushing paper for General Cow. It will strongly motivate you to save your money and plan your future.

If you're really lucky, the jet won't go down until your fourth year. By that time you'll have learned enough to realize exactly what's going on. You may even know how to maneuver into a position so that you can hitch your wagon to one of the rising stars.

CHANGE IS FOREVER

Times change and people change. Nothing lasts forever. Knowing that gives you a giant edge over fellow gravy train riders who think the train never stops for fuel and water or, more important, to drop off the dead VP of Production and pick up a new VP of Production.

Sunny days come, and sunny days go. Corporate raiders buy the company. Divisions get closed. Assets get sold. Contracts get canceled. Elections go the wrong way. CEOs die or get caught doing insider trading. The good ship Lollipop sinks. Nothing is constant except change.

CHANGE COMPANIES TO INCREASE OPTIONS

You can't be protected from change. Change is the only law. Obey the law and change. Change companies at every opportunity until you are have enough money in the bank to survive the eventual rainy days. Keep changing until you have enough money in the bank to decide what you really want to do with your life.

52 Random Truths didn't fit in any of the chapters or they deserve repetition. Fit these truths into your store of knowledge so you can end up with a ton of screw-you money.

Ye shall know the truth
and the truth shall make you free.
JESUS OF NAZARETH

If you can't stand the heat [of office politics]
get ***into*** *the kitchen.*
PARAPHRASING PRESIDENT TRUMAN THE AUTHOR

52 Random Truths

1. When it's crucial, do it yourself. Don't delegate. Don't depend on anyone.

2. Only 1.2 percent of taxpayers make over $200,000 a year. That small group earns 15 percent of all income. Only 20 percent of the workforce earns more than $50,000. Two out of three working women earn less than $22,500.

3. Being in charge of others does not make you a good person, it makes you responsible for them. To find out if you are advancing look at your income tax return. Is the number written in the box labeled "Taxable Income" bigger than it was last year? That's all that counts. The rest is imaginary.

4. Stay slim and trim to be taken seriously. Fat people are not respected, never taken seriously.

5. Fake it until you make it.

6. Everyone wants to feel important. Make everyone feel important.

7. Most working women with degrees majored in English, Psychology, Sociology, Literature, French and such. If you have a degree in English, tell everyone it's Communications. If your major was Psychology, say Industrial Psychology. Nobody ever looks it up except Personnel on the first job.

8. Eventually, all who remain within corporate America lose. They lose their health, sanity, potency, orgasmic ability, drive,

lust and passion. They become pastel nothings as they passively await death.

9. If you don't know, say, "I should know that, but I don't. I'll find out and get right back to you." Go find out and get right back to him.

10. Read corporate symbols. Expensive is good. Utility is bad. The desk must be made of expensive material: marble, ebony. Not tasteful, expensive, which announces, "I am important." Other symbols:

The less visible, the more important.
The farther away, the more important.
The less accessible, the more important.
The less available, the more important.
The bigger the plants, the more important.
The wider the hallways, the more important.
The bigger the door, the more important.
The closer the parking space, the more important.
The more costly the trappings, the more important.
The higher in the building, the more important.
The closer to the corner, the more important.
The corner offices are most important.
The NE corner office is the most important.

11. Be on time. Not early. Not one second late. Early means you're anxious and needy. Late means you don't care. On time means all business, capable, focused and organized.

12. God created man and woman. Sam Colt made them equal.

13. Basic requirements for the success of any organization: confident, experienced leaders; clear, practical goals; coherent plans; realistic schedules; reasonable budgets; well defined roles for all team members; respect among team members for each other; respect for and confidence in leadership; willing to compete; willing to be flexible; willing to take risks. Bright men who work for small companies learn this before they're 30. You'll never see this at a Fortune 3000. If you get the chance to work for a lean, mean business machine, it's wonderful! Small companies can't afford to discriminate against females or anybody else. They're in business to make money. If you make money for them, they reward you.

14. Health insurance, profit sharing, dental plans, glasses, pension plans and other benefits are useless to a young woman. High pay is useful. Abandon the Fortune 3000 for any small company if they'll pay you big bucks. In this context, that means a 15 percent raise. Change back to a Fortune 3000 as soon as you can get a 10 percent raise. That's 25 percent, overall!

15. Women consciously and subconsciously approach the corporation as if it isn't going to be forever. They're waiting for Prince Charming. Stop waiting to be chosen, invited, persuaded, asked to accept. Start acting. Stop waiting to be told what to do. Take the initiative. Learn new skills. Volunteer for more work. Show you are motivated. Show you'll take risks. Squeaky wheels get greased. Being an impatient, ungrateful pushy broad is the kiss of death.

16. Never let them see you sweat. Emotions, to men, are frightful things. Control your emotions at work. They think emotionality equals a lack of rationality.

17. Girls are socialized to never show anger. Boys are socialized to never cry. So, when a woman gets angry, she cries. When a man gets hurt, he roars! This may help you understand us men better.

18. If you are a minority, never put up with a racist who is on your ass either directly or subtly. Take him aside. Tell him to cool it. He'll claim he's joking. Get in his face, "Not fuckin' funny!" That usually ends it. If not, publicly and loudly do the same thing. That ends it, and him.

19. Quality circles, management by objectives, one minute manager seminars, participative management, team concepts, total quality management or whatever drivel is trendy gets instituted every few years by high level fools. It is resisted and sabotaged until it is discarded in favor of nepotism, old boyism, and whatever was working before. "working" defined as the cow is upright and giving milk. McDonnell-Douglas destroyed the *Douglas* portion of itself doing this in the mid-80's. Look it up.

20. Never tell or delight in ethnic jokes no matter who's telling them. A polite smile if it is your immediate boss or his boss if not, no reaction. Do not get tagged as a liberal or as a racist. Either is corporate death.

21. As a female, your brain wiring[1] makes it easy for you to read people intuitively. Use this, your biggest advantage, at all times. What they are really thinking and feeling is available to you if you tune in and focus on your emotions. Trust your feelings, use your natural advantage. Come up with the right thing to do then go around and gather facts to support your intuitive idea. Intuition is good. Saying it's intuition is bad. Don't tell anyone you figured it out using intuition. Say you've been working on it for weeks. Males don't trust or believe in intuition. They think you're kooky if you tell them you use it.

A woman's guess is much more accurate than a man's certainty.
RUDYARD KIPLING

22. Japanese corporations operate differently because their worldview and their culture is radically different from ours. You do know how women are seen and treated in Asia, don't you? Avoid Asian owned or controlled companies unless you can get a dynamite raise. It's smart politics to be their token for a short period if the salary is big enough. Jump back as soon as possible, even two months. If asked why so quick, say they're prejudiced. They are.

23. Criticism is not death. Take it without crying, whining or trying to shift blame. *Take it like a man.*

24. When you don't know what someone's talking about, say so. When you don't know what to do, ask. Struggle to understand. Don't be afraid to say, "Sorry. I didn't get that. Please explain it again." That's for job instructions, not something your boss or a manager says in the staff meeting. If you don't understand what he said, wait. Ask a co-worker later. Often what the boss says in meetings doesn't make sense and nobody understands. So, don't embarrass any superior in public.

25. Asking questions makes you the child and the other person the parent, teacher or adult. Make statements like, "I can't figure out how to pull the manhours off this estimate. Please run through it again."

26. Winning the war does not require winning every battle, just the crucial ones, those that determine the ultimate outcome.

[1] Brain wiring differences are explained and documented after other innate characteristics of men and women are presented.

27. No matter what anyone at work says about team spirit, company morale, for the good of the department, for the good of all or any other such bullshit, everyone is motivated solely by self interest. Do not get sucked into or talked into self-sacrifice for any reason other than to save your children.

28. A well worn prostitute doesn't ever consider what he's doing. He just does it, that's all. Only in the beginning does a prostitute consider alternatives. Once bending over becomes routine, he never considers other ways of being. It's exactly the same at your company. Once someone gets used to bending over, he never thinks about what he's doing. Guys who've been middle managers for years can do things that would make you puke if you tried. They sold their souls long ago, lost their self-respect long ago. To them, it's business as usual, another day, another dollar, whores who do it without shame.

There are lies, damn lies and statistics.
MARK TWAIN

29. Numbers are just like resumes, discountable by up to 50 percent. Don't believe any numbers in any report or any forecast your enemies and rivals present. Don't believe any numbers your subordinates develop. Mentally discount the numbers based on the political skill level of the presenter.

Round numbers are always false.
SAMUEL JOHNSON

30. A no-man always says "no." That's the easiest and safest way to survive. If he said "yes" he might have to explain to a no-man higher up why he's in favor of the project. If he says "yes" he might have to work on the project rather than pretending to be busy all day. Even more dangerous, if he said "yes" and the project fails, he gets blamed. If someone higher up approves the project it doesn't matter. He won't be asked to work on it because he was against it. And if it goes down in flames he'll be blameless. When the project becomes a solid success, not many remember his "no." If someone does remember and asks him to explain why he was against it, he says that the way it was originally proposed was absolutely impractical. It turned out to be a success because it was revised properly after receiving much healthy criticism.

31. If it is written, it is so. The written word is much more powerful than the spoken word. Once it is "down in black and white," it takes on a mantle of credibility beyond all reasonable expectations. When it's on company letterhead or memo form, it comes "from on high." Anything you want emphasis added to, write it down and promulgate it. Those who publish memos do not perish.

32. Learning anything requires making mistakes. Learning to function in a hierarchial organization requires making mistakes. The great thing about following the ten year plan set forth here is that mistakes made at Company A are left behind when you move to Company B. By the time you arrive at Company M you appear to be someone who never makes a mistake, Superyoungwoman.

33. The Procedure Manual was not written by people who know how it really works. It was written by clerks who take notes from some underling assigned to "get the input ready for the Policy Manual." As long as the Procedure Manual doesn't give away how it really works, it is approved. It is always out of date and incomplete. That is not an accident. Being out of date means *they* don't have to do what it says. Since you don't realize it's out of date, you must do what it says.

34. As a female, you may show excitement, enthusiasm and fist-pounding anger over a lost client or contract. You may not show catty anger toward another female, ever. If you slip, in front of men, cover it up by exaggerating and making fun of cattiness. Men see cattiness as silly and un-executive like. That's also the way all men, including me, see moods, crying, pouting, whining, bitchiness, snootiness, sadness, weepiness, self pity, helplessness, hopelessness or fatigue.

35. Fear of success is a common female affliction. It's up to you to determine if you've got it. How do you know? You get "sick" just before the big presentation. You're "accidently" late for an important meeting. You only screw up the big assignments. If you're afraid of making it, you won't, so don't worry. One great way to destroy your chances is to discuss, with anyone at work, the possibility that you may be sabotaging yourself. Just mention self doubts and you'll never have to worry about succeeding again. You're responsible for curing yourself.

36. Dale Carnegie and positive thinking classes are great if you don't become a true believer. Take what you like and shitcan the rest. Having positive thoughts is good, even great. It works.

37. Nazis got Jews to go quietly into the gas chambers by telling them they were going to get showers and deloused. The Nazi's in charge at your company don't want you telling fellow employees the company doesn't give a shit about them, considers them chattel. Fellow employees don't want you saying that 99 percent of them are going nowhere, ever. They especially don't want you to tell them the company will trash them like a used condom when crunch time comes. They want to believe they are going to get deloused and a shower before being "reassigned."

38. Most people make decisions using the same process they use when buying a new car. They buy to one that gratifies them emotionally and temporarily fills the void in their self-esteem. Then they scramble to find facts and figures to convince themselves and others it was a rational decision.

39. The USMC says you can't lead unless you can follow. You must be able to take orders to give them. That's true and that's the way it works in the real world and in the Fortune 3000. You must do, or have done, what you're asking your troops to do, if you want their respect.

40. Pavement pounding, casting couch propositions, long hours, grunt work, bit parts, walk on's, cattle calls. Big biz is the same as showbiz. Breaks come after you have paid your dues. *Translation:* After you have worked for four different companies and have three years of experience in the same industry and know what you are doing.

41. *Corporate Bullshit:* Everything is going to get better. After the annual Board Meeting things will improve. We can't accommodate that right now but soon. There will be no layoffs. The pension plan is sacrosanct. We're not moving the division to Iowa. It was out of my hands. The check is in the mail.

42. Bosses will say anything to keep you from taking another offer except pay you what you are worth. After a particularly dishonest, double-dealing political move cuts her out of a promotion, she becomes disillusioned and tells her boss she moving on. He reassures her.

I know you should have gotten it but company politics prevented it. Right now there is a lot happening behind the scene I can't tell you about. But everything will be changing, and soon. Let's just say there's going to be a major reorganization. Once that's decided, things will fall into place. Great things are ahead for you. Be patient. Your time is coming. You have a great future here. In just months the new division will be opening. You can transfer over there and probably get more than General Bull offered. We need you and you're such a great person. You must be patient. Everyone likes you. Dick, himself, said he sees good things for you right over the horizon. Think it over. But if I were you, I'd turn that offer down. You've got friends here who will make it worth your while, once they get their team in place. Take a couple of days off. You've earned them. This is a compilation of actual sentences my first seven bosses laid on me. I believed the first two guys. It cost me seven months the first time, four months the second time.

43. *Myth:* The company is concerned about its employees and is dedicated to their welfare, so you must be loyal to the company. *Reality:* There is no written contract at your level. Only Big Boys get contracts and golden parachutes. You're chattel.

44. You learn more about business by working than anything else. While in college, be a waitress. Be a clerk. Be anything you can. Work in the bookstore, library, cafeteria. Do anything, everything. You'll find out how to get along with people and how to communicate. That's all you need to make big money from Fortune 3000 cows. They teach you the rest.

45. To whine is to die.

46. Nothing changes from the bottom up. Change only happens from the top down. Change only happens when it hurts enough. *Translation:* The company is losing so much money that changes must be made.

47. Today, September 2, 1992 on page one of the LA Times there is a sob story about "unfair corporate practices" during a big layoff. Hughes announced January 2 it would cut 6000 jobs before the year was over. What are employees doing on

September 2? Filing lawsuits! Can you imagine anyone thinking his job was safe when 6000 jobs are to be cut? Can you imagine anyone sitting around for nine months instead of getting his ass out there and finding another job while still employed? $250k attorneys will get continuances for years. Unable to get jobs at other companies, ex-employees with air-tight cases will settle for a dime on the dollar. Ex-employees with dubious cases will be countersued for filing frivolous lawsuits.

48. In my industry, an illegal roster of troublesome ex-employees is circulated. Anyone who takes a company to court is blacklisted, win or lose. It makes no difference how legitimate the lawsuit was: exposing racial discrimination, unsafe workplace, illegal dumping of toxics, anything. That person is never hired again in the "biz" or by its major subcontractors. Every industry has a similar blacklist. Raquel Welch hasn't worked in the moviebiz since she sued and beat the producers of *Cannery Row* for firing her 12 years ago.

49. Obeying all the rules is as stupid as flaunting all the rules.

50. The corporation is racist, sexist, ageist, anti-homosexual, anti-semitic and anti-everything not Northern European White Male. So what? The rest of society is the same. Play the hand you've been dealt or fold it.

51. Half the population is of below average intelligence! Shocking? The definition of average tells you it's true. Half the population has an IQ above 100, half has an IQ below 100. The vast majority, 60 percent, has an IQ between 90 and 110. Only 20 percent have an IQ below 90. Only 20 percent has an IQ over 110. That means 80 percent are not bright, follow the drift?

In any organization, 80 percent of the work is done by 20 percent of the group. When you become boss, identify the 20 percent. Reward them. Dump as many of the 80 percent as possible. Your profits will soar, and so will you.

See Random Truth 2. Which 20 percent makes over $50,000? North America and Europe have 20 percent of the world's population but create 80 percent of the world's wealth!

52. You're on at all times. Be an actress.

The *how-what-when,* everything's that's come before, is the foundation, the bedrock of knowledge needed to *Get That Raise,* the central purpose of office politics.

Money talks. Bullshit walks.
EVERY POLITICIAN'S CREED

*The greatest of evils
and the worst of crimes is poverty.*
GEORGE BERNARD SHAW

Get That Raise

Knowing how much you should be paid is the first step to getting paid more.

How much your predecessor made is crucial. The simplest way to find out is to ask him. If he's still in the department or company, he usually won't tell you. You'll have to snoop as described below and in *Spying*. If he's left the company, only a few amenities are necessary, since he feels no need to be secretive. Figure out how to contact him. This person is dynamite.

I was working as a temp and being courted to replace the guy who had left the company on short notice. I found his home number in the Executive Directory. His wife answered. I told her I needed to get in touch with Dave to wrap up some key items. She gave me his number at the new company.

He was more than happy to tell me since I put it this way, "Herb mumbled about canceled contracts, offered $57. I stalled. What do you think?" He said, "Nah, that Manager of Proposals title's good for $65." I got $64 and lasted almost a year.

UNEQUAL PAY FOR EQUAL WORK

Do you know the going rate for your position in the industry? Find out. Research want ads in trade journals and the Sunday paper. On the phone, ask "What's the salary range?" You already know what they pay at General Bull because you brought it up with your counterpart at the trade show. A headhunter or agency can tell you the going rate.

Men in a similar position, with the same amount of experience, are probably getting more than you are. Have a male friend call the same headhunter or answer the same ads. See how much he's worth. Use his number, not the female number, for negotiations.

If your company pays males who do the same job more than they pay you, that's illegal and that's great! It's the proverbial ace-in-the-hole. It's a weapon nearly as powerful as the nuclear weapon of sexual harassment. If your company pays most other people doing what you do more than they pay you, that's a king-in-the hole, not a weapon, just a guaranteed raise.

HARD EVIDENCE IS GOOD TO FIND

A xerox copy is hard evidence. Hard evidence prevents injustice. The regular secretary sometimes hides keys to the file cabinets where a smart woman might look. The files with the personnel records have the hard evidence.

Sometimes when the secretary goes on vacation, the temp girl has no idea where anything is. Help her look for whatever. Start in the file cabinet with the personnel records.

You know everyone. Help the temp pass out the checks. If Tom, Dick or Mary is sick, tell the temp to put the check in her desk. Work Saturday. On Monday, the regular secretary will complain that somebody opened the envelope! Don't forget, paycheck stubs sometimes end up in the wastebasket.

LET'S BE VULNERABLE, YOU GO FIRST

A trustworthy male friend on your level will sometimes tell you how much he makes. This kind of vulnerability is possible only if you become vulnerable first. Tell him how much you make in a complaining, not whining, way. Say you think they're screwing you but you don't know how to find out. If you could find out, they'd have to give you a good raise. Wait a few beats.

Wait a beat more. Then look him right in the eyes and say, "Jim, how much *more* do you make?" We men do the strangest things when challenged this way.

ANNUAL RAISES, THE BOSS'S VIEW

From the pool of money for raises, your boss, in cahoots with his boss, gives the incompetent, competent and outstanding employees the same four-percent raise, plus or minus a percent or two. He secretly divvies up the remaining money among favorites, buddies, main squeezes and the ass kissing incompetent whose wife has cancer.

Every penny your boss keeps from you is his to spread around as he chooses. You won't get a penny unless you fight for it. As a preview, read this quote from *Reality Check.*

> *Damned few, if any, in Top Management care if you, your co-workers, your boss or even his boss are treated unfairly or abused. In the upper reaches, everybody knows that most employees are as expendable as a sheet of paper and replaced as easily.*

That's what you're up against if you appeal to higher authority empty handed. Top Management does nothing about grievances concerning injustice or favorites. They mumble "We must back up our managers and their decisions," as you're quietly branded a troublemaker. (Read *The Caine Mutiny* for the horrifying details of this universal fundamental, listed in *Must Books.*)

However, Top Management would be delighted to instantly overrule those same managers if your complaint were written on the back of a piece of hard evidence. Don't let it become necessary. Once you play that ace-in-the-hole you're empty handed and your days at that company are numbered. After you make your boss, his boss, the department, the section and the division look bad for underpaying you, they will get rid of you, and may even blacklist you.

START OUT EASY

In a casual way, mention to few co-workers that you saw the hard evidence and what it showed. Don't let them know you have the hard evidence. Word will spread. About two months before the annual review, talk with your boss in private, off the record. In a concerned tone of voice gently let him know that you know.

> *I've uh, heard* [from pretty reliable people] *that men (most other employees) are being paid more. I'd appreciate it if you'd check and see how I rank compared to the men (most other employees) doing this work.*

Skip the words inside the brackets. If he asks who, hesitatingly add the words inside the brackets as you hint at the consequences.

I've uh, heard from pretty reliable people that men are being paid more. I'm only concerned about equal pay for equal work. I don't want this to get, uh, blown out of proportion, Personnel involved. I'd appreciate it if you'd check and see how I rank compared to the men doing this work.

Check back in a week. If he stalls, subtlety has failed. He does not want to pay you as you should be paid. Worse, he's confident he can get away with it. It's time to change companies.

GET AN ABOVE AVERAGE ANNUAL RAISE

To get a raise beyond the standard four percent, convince your boss his money is well spent. *Translation:* It's in his long-term self interest to keep you happy.

What convinces him? Everything in *Managing The Boss*. First, and most important, you do one helluva a job. Second, you make him look good by doing a helluva job. Third, you credit him as the basis for your great proposals. Fourth, you make him feel important by acknowledging his limited capabilities. Fifth, he thinks others are trying to hire you.

COURTSHIP LETTERS FROM COMPETITORS

He thinks others are after you when you let it be known they are or you make it look like they are. Have the competition's empty envelope sitting on your desk. It only contained the standard "we'll keep your resume on file" bullshit. Co-workers don't know that and they gossip.

At several different companies, I had friends who worked for the competitors send me, via certified mail, a letter in their company envelope with Personal and Confidential typed on the outside. To make certain my boss knew, I had them send it "incorrectly" to his mail station. Twice the boss, himself, brought it to me.

The one who was a great office politician dropped it on my desk, then said nothing as he waited for me to reveal something. I glanced at it, set it aside, looked up and said "Thanks," and waited for him to reveal something. He didn't.

The other boss was a typical upper middle management dweeb. He said, "This came to my office. Looks important." I took it, set it aside and thanked him. He stood there befuddled until I said, "What's happening with the Snavely report?" He recovered, responded appropriately, then left.

I got a twelve percent raise from the politician. He appreciated me. I stayed another nine months. The dweeb came up with apologies, promises and six percent. I moved on a month later.

Certified mail gets everyone's attention. It looks official. It has to be signed for. It intimidates your boss. He's afraid to open it. He's afraid to throw it away.

COURTSHIP PHONE CALLS FROM COMPETITORS

Be out at the prescribed time. Before leaving, forward calls to your boss's secretary. Have a friend call and ask for you. Your friend says, "Please have her call me at General Bull." If asked, "May I say what it's about?" Have your friend act like she's covering up and say, "It's, uh, personal."

I am asked all the time by temp agencies if they can call me at work. My answer is an enthusiastic "Yes." It keeps the reality of the situation clearly focused in my boss's mind, "Don can pick and choose. I must treat him with consideration."

Use headhunters the same way. After saying that it's fine to call you at the office, "accidently" give them your boss's extension instead of yours. When his secretary tries to transfer it to you, politely ask her who's calling. Have headhunters send letters to the "wrong" mail station, too.

Conduct these ploys a month before the review period. That gives your boss time to realize you have options, unlike the rest of his herd.

SAY WHAT YOU WANT

You'll never get anything handed to you. You must reach out. Ask directly, once you've shown the boss that you're worth every penny and more. Be positive, upbeat and interested in helping him look better and making the company better.

When you turn down a guy who asks you out because you really had plans, then he never asks again, what conclusion do you draw? Well, when your boss says "No raise," or he says "four percent," no matter what words or excuses he uses, if you don't persist, he doesn't think you're serious. He feels free to give an eleven percent raise to Debbie Doubledees. Persistence is necessary to convince him you're serious.

Silence is the virtue of fools.
FRANCIS BACON

Persist by relying on everything you learn from *When I Say No, I Feel Guilty* and in your Assertiveness Training. The essence is asking for negative feedback. "What do I have to improve to be considered . . ." Read that book. Get it down. Persist but don't be pushy.

When the answer is still "no" and the reason given is there just isn't any money, listen with only slight disappointment showing. Say with conviction, "I understand the situation. Please keep me in mind when things improve."

If you don't get a raise by asking for it, you get respect. You never get fired for asking. You get fired for issuing ultimatums or demanding.

Being an impatient, ungrateful, pushy broad is the kiss of death.
THE AUTHOR

Sometimes there is no money for raises. That means layoffs are coming. Update your resume. Start looking in earnest.

Never let anyone know you are dissatisfied. They talk. Should a layoff be required, you'll be first to go since you don't like it here. Should your boss be an insecure lump, most are, he sees your dissatisfaction as disloyalty. You'll get transferred to the warehouse. Again, you don't need help to keep a secret.

WINNING THROUGH INTIMIDATION

The ultimate power you have is saying "no." You must decide ahead of time, "Either I get this raise or I take the offer from General Bull." That must be heartfelt, not an act. You must be willing to walk away. Ringer's advice is not bullshit. Those who have the power are those who say "no." If you're not genuinely willing to walk away, he can tell and will call your bluff. At that point, he loses respect for you. Next review, two percent is what you'll get if he's feeling benevolent.

Be prepared. Think about what you are going to say *when* you don't get what you want, not *if* you don't. Do not attack. Do not accuse. Do not blame.

As explained, my mentor taught me, "When you have to say 'no,' cry a lot before you say it, then they're not angry. They feel sorry for you!" It works. I've cried, figuratively, many a time. Nary a bridge was burned when I said "no."

THE ANNUAL REVIEW SHAM

Once a year, you are forced to participate in an appallingly disgraceful exercise. You'll be given some complex, hard-to-understand forms with vague instructions and told to criticize yourself in writing, identifying the areas you need to improve. Next, you are asked to set goals to improve yourself. Then you must endure an extremely awkward hour, or more, behind closed doors with your boss discussing what you wrote, negotiating wording that will appear on the official final version.

Everyone with a three digit IQ is embarrassed by this MBA nonsense but everyone must submit. Why? Because government bureaucrats are protecting us poor, helpless workers from those mean, nasty, dirty old capitalist pigs who own the company. These forms, to the bureaucratic mind, prevent exploitation and make promotions fair.

The boss doing the evaluation has nothing to gain and everything to lose by writing a less than excellent review of anyone who works for him. Why? Because his boss will want to know why the less than excellent employee has not been helped or fired. The boss can't say his workers are a bunch of incompetents. It reflects on his judgement in hiring them or spotlights his inability to manage them effectively. Your boss will never admit to having anybody on his staff who is less than excellent. So, everyone gets about the same raise.

In reality, everyone in the department knows who the best workers are and who the incompetents are. Everyone knows Joanna does three times more work than Carla. Everyone knows Tim gossips half the day. And yet, the boss rates them all excellent.

The difference between the raise Joanna gets and the raise Carla gets is only one or two percent. The difference between what Carla gets and what Tim gets is about two tenths of a percent.

Some of this injustice is caused by your boss wanting to give a big raise to Debbie Doubledees. Some of this injustice is caused by the boss not wanting to admit he's incompetent for hiring and keeping incompetents. But, most of this injustice is caused by Top Management not wanting to get sued by an employee, so they have an unwritten rule, "On paper (hard evidence), everybody's equal."

IF YOU GET LESS THAN EXCELLENT

Do not sign a less than excellent evaluation under any circumstances. Once you sign, it becomes part of your permanent employee file. You don't want anything negative that can be used against you in the future. Who knows, you may want to come back here in a few years. Making waves is necessary. Before they can fire you, they must grade you down and you must sanction their lies.

Your boss and all other middle managers are cowards to the core. They survive by being rabbits, and rabbits they'll remain. They won't stand by a less than excellent evaluation if confronted loudly in public.

You can't always get what you want
but if you try hard enough, you get what you need.
MICK JAGGER

A Tower of Jello always backs down when challenged. Don't attack him personally or his character. Demand an explanation of how he arrived at his evaluation.

The guy has no backup data. He has no hard evidence to convince anyone up the chain of command you're not as good as everyone else. He's all bluff. You're in the driver's seat.

In a loud voice say, "There are no facts to back this up. These are personal, obviously prejudiced, opinions."

He'll find some face saving way to back off and give you the same excellent evaluation he gave everyone else. That gets four percent added to your salary before you move on, which you must do. After winning a major skirmish like this, he begins collecting the hard evidence needed to fire you, even if he has to lie, cheat and steal. Move on before two months pass.

A FLURRY JUST BEFORE THE BELL

In a boxing match, judges watch each round in its entirety, then mark their cards, awarding the round to one fighter or the other, or rate it even. The judges cannot help being impressed by strong, concentrated attack just before the bell. That was the last thing they saw. It sticks in their minds and influences their decision.

Do the same thing as a smart boxer. Give it hell in the quarter just before the evaluation bell. Look good, work hard, cooperate, stand tall, fight the good fight, reach down for something extra and all other cliches you can think of.

Volunteer for everything. Overload yourself. This sometimes gives a Tower Of Jello the courage to give you seven percent instead of the standard four. Convince your Tower Of Jello to be even more liberal with his money by having the department's busybody overhear you talking with an imaginary headhunter on the phone just before the annual review.

If your boss thinks you're being courted by others, he'll have to hire and train someone to replace you. That costs him time and money and the work might not get done. He might get criticized. Fear combined with the flurry before the bell convinces him he's got to do something to keep you happy.

WHAT HAVE YOU DONE FOR ME LATELY?

Bosses forget. Come up with a nine month long list. Prove your worth. Without evidence you get the standard four percent.

Give concrete examples of your contributions. You finished the Greek Report ahead of time. You were under budget on the San Francisco Presentation. You have not taken one sick day off. You trained Edna and Jamie in only two weeks. Talk about what you have done for him. Don't talk about what others haven't done. Don't knock the competition.

Cases of your brilliance need to be documented. Memos from another department commending you impresses your boss more than anything you can cite. Make this happen by asking for the memo directly after you do something for someone. When they thank you, say, "Thanks, I enjoyed working for you! I'd really appreciate it if you'd drop a note to my boss, let him know you liked my work."

Months later, during the evaluation meeting, hand it to your boss, "Here's that memo JB wrote thanking me for supporting him at the Long Beach trade show."

PROMISES, PROMISES

Your boss said during the interview that you'd get a raise after 90 days. He has no reason to remember it. On day 75, "You mentioned I'd be getting a raise after 90 days. Do I have to fill out some kind of form or anything?"

If the Personnel geek said it, on day 75 tell your boss. "Jim, the guy from Personnel, said I'd be getting a raise after 90 days. Do I have to fill out some kind of form or anything?"

FUN AND PROFIT

They don't pay you to do your job because it's fun. They pay you because it's not fun. The object of my brand of office politics is to get paid as much as you can, so that some day you'll have enough money to do what you want.

Happiness is getting paid to do what you enjoy doing. Doing something you'd do for free and getting paid for it is paradise.

SUMMARY OF GETTING THAT RAISE

If you want to be a Supervisor, dress for that part in the play from the beginning. Determine where you stand compared with the industry average, department average, versus men or whatever. Show how underpaid you are.

Keep a record of accomplishments. Demonstrate success in concrete numbers: dollars, manhours, percent. Develop a file of letters of commendation from customers and in-house VIPs. A month before the annual sham make certain he thinks headhunters are after you.

Make an appointment with your boss and review all of this. Absolutely don't wait for those ghastly forms to appear. Once that sewage starts, it's hard to stop.

Write it all down in a *one page* memo. Detail your accomplishments in concrete numbers and concrete examples. List the people, with their titles, who have commended you. Explain how you determined the average pay. Don't send the memo, use it as a guide during your talk. Hand it to him at the end of the discussion, "Here's a summary of what we talked about."

Ask for the raise. Be specific, $2,900 a year or eleven percent, whichever way your company gives raises. Pad it so there's room to negotiate. Specific numbers prevent vague promises such as, "a substantial raise."

MANIPULATIVE MOVES

Some managers think they can intimidate you by asking a manipulative question. He'll pop it immediately after realizing you want a raise to interrupt you and throw off your timing,

"Why should I give you a raise?" or some version asking you to justify yourself. Your answer, "My motivation will remain high because I'll feel my enthusiasm and efforts are appreciated." Don't wait for his response. Pick up right where you left off and continue with energy, enthusiasm and conviction that his money will be well spent on you.

Getting a raise is bartering, negotiating, dickering over how much you are worth to the company. Strategy, tactics, moves, end runs, intimidation and time outs are part of it. You're the seller, he's the buyer. Sell yourself.

There's much more than selling yourself required to *Get Promoted*. In short, office politics is what it takes.

All rising to great places is by a winding stair.

A wise [woman] will make
more opportunities than [she] finds.
1620 FRANCIS BACON

Get Promoted

The quickest way up the hierarchy is to win the favor of a high ranking executive. The only way you can win his favor is to be noticed. The best way to be noticed is to work where he works.

EXPOSE YOURSELF

Figure out which departments expose you to Big Boys. Try these: PR, Business Development, Advertising, Legal. In your own department, volunteer to work on proposals, annual reports, five year plans, quarterly reports, house organs. Big Boys have to review and approve these.

No matter what level you are, finagle a job in front of the biggest boy you can. As you move up the hierarchy, keep increasing the size of the Big Boy you expose yourself to.

If you can't maneuver into a job with exposure, a Big Boy usually oversees the arrangements for the annual golf tournament, the United Fund drive, the semi-annual executive retreat or some such effort. Volunteer for those task forces.

Get informed. Know the outside interests of all the Big Boys. Create an impression others can't.

As you work nearby the Big Boy, remember all he has to judge you by is your uniform and your all-business attitude. Anybody can wear the uniform. Anybody can have that attitude.

Anybody can make small talk he considers drivel. But, because of *Big Picture Research* and *Spying,* you alone can make small talk he's interested in, so he becomes interested in adding you to his staff. Get informed and stay informed.

EXPOSING MYSELF STORY

The biggest boy I exposed myself to was the biggest boy in our division, Issac, Vice President and Division Manager, salary $4M, yes, million. His only outside interest was USC football. A total fan–atic, he and his cronies flew the company's Gulfstream to South Bend just for the Notre Dame game.

Early on I discovered Issac's obsession. My boss, a workaholic, griped about having to waste valuable time listening to Issac's replay of Saturday's game in the Executive Staff Meeting every Monday morning. The company was paying my tuition at USC. It was easy to bone up on Trojan football.

There is no such thing as luck,
only preparation meeting opportunity.
COACH VINCE LOMBARDI

In the fall, I was directing the final production of a $2B, yes, billion, proposal due to the customer in the morning. Issac drove to the office at midnight to approve the cost section and the transmittal letter before they were printed and bound. The proposal team leader, project manager, chief engineers, VP of finance and I were sitting in Issac's big corner office waiting for Repro to bring us a review copy. Small talk abounded.

The team leader was a UCLA grad. I boldly told him Scarlet and Gold Trojans would kick Powder Blue Bruin ass on Saturday and baited him with a $10 bet, offering the spread. He hemmed and hawed, complaining about 8 points. Issac smiled. I offered 9 points, upped the bet to $20, adding, "A poor young proposal manager like me, being taken advantage of by . . ."

A few days later I went to Issac's office to get his signature on the secret Prime Prospects Report. He took it, speed read it, changed a percent, then without looking up said, "Whadya spend Dan's $20 bucks on?" Without missing a beat I said, "Gave him double or nothing, SC against the Ducks, even. He took it, the fish!" Looking up and smiling, Issac said, "Good boy!" (Yes, they really are that patronizing!)

After that, he'd talk football with me when he had the chance. In less than a year, my salary went up three grades and my office went up four floors, to the top floor.

PREPARED TO PERFORM

When Ms. Opportunity presents herself, you must be prepared. But after you're promoted, you must perform. That's easy. Whoever had a hand in getting you promoted has a stake in your success. He'll help if you need it by pointing you toward people who can teach you what's needed to do your new job. Don't ask your sponsor for help until you've done everything else you can think of. Show him he was right.

SECOND FASTEST WAY UP

If you don't have a friend who has the ear of The Prince, you must solve problems. Begin in your department. Understand the big picture, known in military jargon as your department's mission. Develop an understanding of the work flow. Identify who does what. Figure out which organizations deliver input and which ones use your output.

Start with casual conversations among co-workers, move up to supervisors, then your boss. Later, for refined knowledge, strike up conversations with people who are responsible for what comes into your department and those who receive its output.

Fully grasp just what it is your department does and how it gets done. Don't let on you are doing anything more than, "Just curious, couldn't figure it out." For Christ's sake don't say you're thinking up ways to change things! Panic alarms go off in everyone's insecure heads and hearts. Incompetents freak and tattletale to your boss.

To completely understand the big picture you'll need policy and procedure manuals, job descriptions, organization charts, five year plans and such. Insecure twits insist on keeping everyone in the dark. That makes these hard to locate. If, as advised in *Spying,* you become friends with secretaries, it's easy to get your hands on these.

TAKE SOLUTIONS TO YOUR BOSS, NOT PROBLEMS

Draw a diagram of the work flow the way it is. Color code each step so you can see whose toes might be stepped on by changing it. Study your sketch. Ponder it. Find a way to improve it, but in so doing, make certain you become more important.

Write a proposal to improve the system. Be certain to Keep It Simple [for] Stupid, KISS. Use short sentences and simple words. Don't use "change." Use "improve." Brevity is authority. Describe the problem. Propose a solution. Have everything on a single page: Problem, Solution, Consequences of not *improving* it, Plan, Schedule, Cost, Benefits, Conclusion.

If you can't tell me in one page
what has to be done and why, it won't get done.
HIS IRON CLAD RULE ON MEMOS IN THE NUCLEAR NAVY ADMIRAL RICKOVER

Put it away for a few days. Edit so it's shorter, clearer. Have friends from outside read it. Ask for feedback on how to make it better, more to the point, then make it better. If you have people you trust with your career at the office, have them read it. Have friends from previous jobs do the same. Don't get defensive. Don't argue. Listen, then make it better.

Finally, when it's as good as you can make it, get this thought in, "Boss, it was your idea, I just formalized it." Sometimes that can be in the opening, "Based on your idea from our talk about work flow in July, we should bla de blah to *improve* . . ." The last thing is a request for action, "Can we go over this Wednesday at 2:30 in your office?"

Send him the proposal. Make certain he knows there are other copies out there. Don't send a copy to his boss unless that's SOP, military jargon for Standard Operating Procedure.

After getting screwed twice, I sent a bcc, blind carbon copy, to someone I trusted who had a moderately plausible reason to be informed. "Blind" means the bcc addressee's name does not appear on the memo. The key recipient doesn't know it exists. This procedure is called CYA, also from military jargon, Cover Your Ass. Don't get screwed from behind.

While we're on this military stuff, another word you'll hear is SNAFU, pronounced snah-FOO. It's colorfully descriptive and accurate about Fortune 3000s. In the military it means Situation Normal, All Fucked Up.

TYPICAL SOLUTION-NOT-PROBLEM

If your boss is a Tower Of Jello, tell him there is a "situation" not "problem" regarding the Hot Prospects List that goes directly to Big John. Subtly describe the "situation" so he realizes that his ultimate fear might come true, Big John himself will criticize him if the "situation" is not corrected. Matter of factly, with slight urgency, say

One of these times we're gonna miss the deadline, then our tail will be in a crack with Big John. The reps don't give me their input until Tuesday. They don't think it's crucial. The copier broke down at the last minute. We barely got Big John's copy in the pouch!

Save him from his worst nightmare by telling him how to "correct the situation." The solution, of course, increases your power and responsibility. He'll show great relief and you'll hear, "Fine. Do that."

If your boss is a control freak who wants to decide every-damn-thing or someone who thinks he's a hot shit executive and shows everyone how decisive he is by making a decision a minute, each one different than the one before, give him three options to "correct the situation."

For example, ". . . barely got Big John's copy in the pouch!" We have three ways to correct the situation: 1. bla. 2. bla de bla. 3. bla de bla de bla.

Put the most obvious solution, the one increasing your power and responsibility last. Wait quietly while Mr. Hotshit makes his decision in your favor. The first two solutions are realistic but don't go far enough, or go too far and Big John will criticize your boss.

The real skill in writing them lies not in finding a solution to your problem, but in finding a problem to your solution. The solution is easy — it is a list of all the means by which you want to increase your own power and status and freedom and security while shedding uncongenial work and unwelcome responsibility. The skill lies in making it appear that all these are merely the inevitable steps toward the solution of a genuine and pressing problem which concerns the whole department or the whole company.

Management and Machiavelli* *ANTHONY JAY

HOW TO ESTABLISH PRIORITIES

Obey your last order first, that's the military's way of establishing priorities. Do that unless you have asserted yourself and asked your boss how he wants *you* to determine priorities. For example, Jack hands you a draft report and tells you to complete it today. Later, Cindy hands you an estimate and tells you it's more important than Jack's work.

Check with your boss as soon as Cindy leaves. "I don't know how to tell which of these is most important. Jack gave me this report, Cindy gave me . . . How should *I* decide?" The crucial wording implies you are the one to decide. You're merely checking with him to find out what criteria *you* use to decide.

His answer reveals much about Cindy, Jack and your boss. The real pecking order will be disclosed. The actual importance of reports versus estimates will be disclosed. And, your boss's decisiveness will be disclosed. You'll learn a lot.

Most people write badly because they cannot think clearly. The reason they cannot think clearly is they lack the brains.
H.L. MENCKEN

IF IT IS WRITTEN, IT IS SO

Once something gets written down it takes on importance and proportions beyond all reality. People react to something on paper as if it were from The Prince himself. I don't understand this phenomenon. I use it.

Don't expect that writing one-page proposals will be easy. In May of 1992, I spent two full days writing and rewriting one and I've been doing this for 30 years! Distilled, to the point, carefully phrased writing is the most powerful tool you have to persuade those with the power to promote you, to do exactly that.

Great plays aren't written, they're rewritten.
GEORGE BERNARD SHAW

Get thyself to writing classes. Writing fundamentals are the same no matter where they are taught, so unless the company's paying for it, a Junior College is fine. Take Business Writing, Copy Writing, Speech Writing, Composition 101. Learn to express yourself clearly on paper, then persuasively on paper.

Being able to write it down, have it understood, accepted and executed will take you far, far up the ladder. This skill, all by itself, adds another $10k on top of whatever else you make the first five years.

As Mencken said, most people lack the brains. Volunteer to draft memos or anything else for your boss and co-workers. They'll appreciate your help. You'll get lots of practice. The more you write the better you get.

GATHERING INTELLIGENCE

In your group, offer to revise the Five Year Plan, Procedure Manual and Job Descriptions. These documents are rewritten to match reality about once a year.

Nobody enjoys revising the Procedure Manual because of the intense political pressure applied by competing groups to have the wording favor their interests. Simply say, "I'll take that up with *Mister* Wilson and the Executive Review Committee on Tuesday. I'll certainly point out your concerns." Subtle emphasis on Mister, right?

After you don't do what they want, they try to make you look bad by stalling, so you are replaced with someone they can manipulate. They miss due dates, don't return review copies and skip meetings to delay the project. The longer they keep the new book from coming out, the more time they have to lobby powerful people who are sympathetic to their cause.

The second time I was in charge of revising a Procedure Manual, two different groups were dragging their feet. Instead of confronting them, I sent a Status Report to the VP in charge of the effort, with copies to one and all. The VP didn't have to kick ass. Just seeing their names listed under *Input Late* motivated everyone to be prompt.

Don't wait until you get burned by stalling tactics. In the kickoff meeting announce that you'll be "sending a status report to Richard," look in the direction of the VP and nod, "every Tuesday morning, so we can stay on schedule."

The stakes are high. Once it is written, it is so, at least until next year. By writing and producing it, you will see how everything gets done, the big picture. Without understanding the big picture, you'll never get up the hierarchy.

WHO DOES WHAT TO WHOM

The same thing happens when revising job descriptions, but the political pressure is far less. You're only revising an individual's responsibilities but it still scares the crap out of some people and pisses others off.

The good news is you get to rewrite your own job description, adding and deleting whatever you want. Do yours last. Pick and choose from what makes you more important and more visible. The best news is you find out what each person does and who reports to whom, how the big picture is organized. Without understanding that, you'll never get up the hierarchy.

Sometimes job descriptions reveal that your boss, and even his boss, are overstepping their bounds or they are not doing what they're supposed to be doing. This information is useful. Later on, when you need something valuable to trade, you've got it.

THE ANNUAL FIVE YEAR PLAN

All Fortune 3000s have a Five Year Plan. It gets written every year as strange as that sounds. The concept is worshiped because a Stanford MBA convinced Big Boys at corporate HQ it is useful.

People at the top of your division think it's foolish but it's their chance to lobby for a much bigger budget next year. To get their share of the limited money pie, they have to look as good, or better, on paper than other divisions.

Big Boys at every division will be blowing optimistic smoke. Trying to match other division's bullshit causes everyone to paint ridiculously rosy pictures of the future, no matter what reality is. Don't let on you know. That's like saying "The emperor wears no clothes."

Working on the Five Year Plan exposes you to the biggest Big Boys. Even better, you see the big picture of the entire company and how your division fits in. That's something very few people get to see. Why?

You know that if everyone knew where we're trying to go and how we're trying to get there, we'd have a better chance of making it. That's not how Top Management sees it. Knowledge is power. Knowledge withheld is power withheld. That's how Big Boys defend against attacks from below.

CIRCULATE TO ELEVATE

Being able is useless if you don't know anyone who wants your ability. How do you match your ability and interests with a job? Find someone who wants both. How do you find them? Circulate.

The best opportunities for a big promotion are outside your department. Discover them. Get up off your duff and meet people. Start with those you mail things to. Hand carry the package to Building 433. Find Wally Wilson. Introduce yourself. Say something about liking to put a face with a name. Shake hands like a business woman on the rise, not a demure, nice, little girl. You're savvy, smart and someone who's going places. Search out the people you talk with on the phone. Do the same things.

Join every company organization. Attend a few meetings. If there's no exposure or important contacts possible, drop out.

Also join Toastmasters, as dorky as they are. Get used to speaking in front of a group. As a beginner, you want to make the mistakes you can learn from in front of dorks, not important people.

Participate in social events, work on special projects and task forces, join company athletic teams and clubs. Attend training seminars, internal and external.

Join every outside professional and trade organization you can. Drop the ones you don't like. After you join the Society of Paper Pushers, volunteer to head up committees or work on the newsletter, anything that puts you in touch with people from other companies.

Become the president of the organization. Get your picture with the VP of Employee Services in the house organ. Getting noticed is what you are doing. Meeting people with lots of stripes who can pull strings and cut through red tape in your company is what you are doing.

Join everything business oriented: lunchtime organizations, trade associations, professional societies, seminars. Attend conventions and trade shows to meet the competition, and later, join them.

Successful job seekers: 63% because of personal contacts 11% by answering an ad, 2% sending unsolicited resume.
How To Swim With The Sharks HARVEY MACKAY

Join all professional associations. Subscribe to trade journals. Figure out a presentation you can give. Get up in front, let them look you over, see you, notice you, remember you. Expanding contacts increases your opportunities. We remember what Vince

Lombardi said about preparation meeting opportunity, don't we, Lucky?

Do-gooder stuff such as collecting canned food for the poor who live near the office is not what you volunteer for. It's too much like girl's work. There are no important people involved. Donate money and beg off.

IT REALLY IS WHO YOU KNOW

At meetings, circulate. Sit in a different location every meeting so you can easily meet new people. Get up and introduce yourself around during breaks. Chit chat. Keep your ears open. Find people you like. Become friends. The first step to getting a big raise and promotion is having a friend in another company who can hire you.

Volunteer to attend in your boss's place for activities such as the United Fund, Blood Drive, Christmas Charity Drive or whatever. Most people hate to attend these.

Anywhere, anytime you talk about yourself and your job, do so with animation and self confidence. You never know who's listening. He might need someone like you.

Only two percent of the people you meet will be of any use to you. So what? It only takes one person to save you from another month with your boss, Dick Brane, and give you a 20 percent raise to boot.

COURT THE COURTIERS

Those around the court can get you a promotion the quickest. They have the ear and confidence of the King. Barons and Dukes, although powerful, are seldom in court. Their dominions are the in the outlying provinces. Getting close to the Staff Assistant to the VP of Administration is extremely valuable. He knows all the other staff assistants.

Ally with the Courtiers. They have the real power in the corporate realm just as they have it in the White House. Figure out who has the ear of any Big Boy. Often it's his staff assistant. Often it's his secretary. Sometimes it's his deputy manager, but not often. The Big Boy sees him as a threat.

OVERALL QUALIFICATIONS FOR PROMOTION

Remember, *they* all assume "She'll get married, get pregnant and leave." You can only progress if the guy who really counts, your boss's boss, sees you as a good worker, a team player and committed to the company. He sees you as someone in it for the long haul if you make certain everyone, everywhere knows you are in it for the long haul. To him, the key qualifications for your promotion are:

1. Your uniform and look matches his.
2. You are deferential and respectful toward all superiors no matter how inferior they are.
3. You are respectful of the sanctity of the chain of command.
4. You get along with just about everyone.
5. He knows from experience that you have the ability to make decisions and use common sense.
6. You imply the promotion is best for the department first, the company second, you last.

YOUR BOSS'S REQUIREMENTS FOR PROMOTION

To get promoted, make the boss see he's the one who's benefiting. Your promotion won't cause a tiny ripple in the day-to-day efficiency of the department because you have already trained a replacement. If you're training a replacement all the time, it's easy to move up and out of the department. Simplify everything. "Rick's been working with me for three months. He's thorough and dependable. He's ready."

Long ago you made it clear that, if necessary, you'll do your old job and the new one at the same time to ensure a smooth transition. Even after you're gone, you'll be happy to support your replacement, making certain he adapts smoothly.

Reassure the boss that your rivals won't rebel when you get promoted. Say, off the record, "Sure, Bernadette will whine the way she always does. That's to be expected, right?"

"PLAN B" IS NECESSARY

Always have a Plan B. For example, you go to your boss with a foolproof plan to get promoted but for some reason or other he can't do it although it makes perfect sense and he knows you deserve it. He apologizes and agonizes.

Don't let it become "yes" or "no." Plan B, suggest a well above average raise instead. Plan C, suggest a transfer to Contracts where you'll get an automatic promotion. Plan D, suggest time off to attend a convention in his place or whatever. Always have ways to save face, his and yours.

OTHER PROMOTION POSSIBILITIES

Pregnant women get replaced. As a female, you can detect a pregnancy much faster than males. Don't go off half-cocked and say anything. She may get an abortion and stay. She may sue the Division Manager for child support. Don't be the one who announced her condition.

As a woman, you can spot office lovers long before men. The look is unmistakable. Promotion possibilities loom. One of them has to go, usually the woman. She may quit, get fired or get transferred. Again, don't go off half-cocked.

Important things: What's her job? Do you want it? Where do you have to be to get it? Who can give it to you? Figure out what you must do, then do it.

BURN PROOF BRIDGES — HAPPY GOODBYES

Say these kinds of things with a straight face.

> You're solidly grateful and appreciative for the chance he gave you and the confidence he showed in you. You'll apply much of what you learned from him to your new job. He's a good coach and teacher. (He taught by letting you sink or swim.) You'll be checking back from time to time to see how he's doing.

They believe this inane, generic stuff and love to hear it. Trust me.

WHY YOU WANT PROMOTED

More money. You'll learn new skills so you become worth even more to your next employer. You're bored stiff. You may have a shot at one of those rare positions that's actually fun and enjoyable.

It makes no difference what your motives are. Relentlessly upward is how you make enough money to get out!

WHAT AND *HOW* ARE NOT ENOUGH

Okay! You now know the *how,* but before you can master office politics (make the really big bucks) you must understand the *why*. The corporate world is merely a microcosm of the real world. Principles that govern the real world also govern the corporate world.

One of the hardest things you have to do to succeed in the man's world of corporations is to understand men. Before that is possible, you must *Understand Yourself.*

> ***Caution!*** The next six pages challenge you to take an honest look at your most cherished beliefs, values and goals. This may be unpleasant, this may be disillusioning, but this is mandatory. If you don't understand yourself, you have absolutely no chance of understanding men, thus no possibility of succeeding in their world, the corporate world.

Before you begin, remember, you have options. This is from the first chapter:

> My goal is to have you (a) understand the reality of being female in the corporate world (b) accept the reality of being female in the corporate world. Once you understand and accept, you'll be able to use the techniques, strategy and tactics in this book to make enough money so that you can:
>
> (1) Leave the corporate world and follow your bliss
>
> (2) Stay in the corporate world and make $150k
>
> (3) Stay in the corporate world and make $60k doing a job you enjoy while easily defeating office politicians who try to make your life miserable.

What's taught is what's known.
Nowhere To Stand kd lang

Know thyself.
400 BC SOCRATES

Understand Yourself

Before any goal can be reached, you must know what the goal is. Before any journey can begin, you must know where you are going. To get to your destination, you must know where you are. To understand where you are right now, you must know how you got here.

THE PERFECT JOB

Suppose a genie popped up and offered one job wish. Any job you want, $100k. What do you wish for?

Some women might say "executive for a large company" but they don't really know what they're wishing for. The exact definition from somebody who was one:

> *As everyone knows, an executive has practically nothing to do, except to decide what is to be done; to tell somebody to do it; to listen to reasons why it should not be done, why it should be done by someone else or why it should be done in a different way; to follow up to see if the thing has been done; to discover that it has been done incorrectly; to point out how it should have been done; to conclude that as long as it has been done it might as well be left where it is; to wonder if it is not time to get rid of a person who cannot do a thing right; to reflect that he probably has a wife and a large family and that certainly any successor would be just as bad and maybe worse; to consider how much simpler and better the thing would have been done if one*

had done it oneself in the first place; to reflect sadly that one has to spend two days to find out why it has taken three weeks for someone else to do it wrong.

***Forbes Magazine* MALCOLM FORBES**

If the genie asked me, I'd edit movies for Stanley Kubrick, George Miller or David Lynch. I'd work 12 hours a day. And, I'd do it for $15k. But then, I've been alive long enough, done enough, seen enough, tried enough, hated enough jobs, loved enough jobs to know exactly what my dream job is.

A man's just got to know his limitations.

Magnum Force DIRTY HARRY

To prevent wasting your precious short time, you need to know (a) what you like to do (b) what you have the ability to do (c) what you *don't* have the ability to do.

If you don't know what job to wish for, begin to pay attention to your daydreams and night dreams. Talk honestly with close friends about what you wish you were doing instead of what you are doing. Next, go to a junior college. Enroll in *Choosing Your Career* or whatever they call it.

Take the aptitude, interest, personality and intelligence tests. These identify areas you're qualified for based on the combination of personality, abilities and interests. I doubt the results will show your ideal career is pushing paper for General Cow Corporation. If they do, at least you'll know it when you're young so you can set your sights on the best paper pushing position.

Also, you'll get exposed to hundreds of jobs you never knew existed. The teacher has recruiting literature from hundreds of companies. Your options are increased, always a wise move.

THE BIGGEST QUESTIONS OF ALL

There is no pencil and paper test that can tell you:

WHERE AM I GOING?
WHO'S COMING WITH ME?

These are the two most crucial questions life ever asks us. Trouble is, most young women strongly believe the second question must be answered first.

Until *he* signs on for the journey, she seldom considers where she's going in this life. Once he's committed, she follows *him* toward his destination. In which sequence do you seek the answers?

WHERE DID YOU COME FROM?

What is your relationship to the world? Are you John's fiance, Ann and Frank's daughter, Debbie's best friend, Eric's sister? Our culture teaches you the entire time you are growing up that you are something to somebody, not an independent, autonomous person who must work until she retires.

Boys are taught from day one to be independent, autonomous, self-reliant people who must work until they retire. Girls are taught from day one to be dependent, but they may have to work until someone marries them. Then they are free, free to serve children, keep house, shop, prepare food and stand by their man.

JUST WHAT DO YOU BELIEVE?

Do you believe what they want you to believe? Or, have you looked at the world and decided for yourself? Take this short true or false test to inventory your beliefs.

1. Justice will prevail.
2. I can trust *x* with my secrets.
3. There is such a thing as luck.
4. A Volvo wagon, a beautiful house, two cute kids, and a wealthy husband who loves me is what I need to be happy.
5. Half the population is below average in anything that's measured, even intelligence, that's what average means.
6. Life is rough and tough.
7. Racism, sexism, ageism and religious discrimination have all but disappeared from corporations.
8. Hard work, ability and honesty will be justly rewarded.
9. Having children and being a good mother will fulfill me and make me truly happy.
10. Honesty is the best policy at work.
11. I cannot be bribed with sex, money or power.
12. What goes around comes around.
13. The Company is concerned about its employees and is dedicated to their welfare. I must be loyal to the company.
14. If I were in charge, I could be just and honest with my subordinates and wouldn't have to manipulate or threaten.

15. Problems are punishment from God, from bad karma or whatever.
16. There are no completely evil people. Everyone has something good about himself, even Charles Manson.
17. My boss and his boss know what they are doing.
18. It feels like I will live forever but that doesn't affect my decisions.
19. Getting married before I'm 30 is a good idea.
20. A high GPA is useful to a corporation and worth bucks.
21. Just about everyone except me is confident.
22. People with MBAs know something useful.
23. Helen Gurley Brown, Frances Lear and Gloria Steinem know a lot about the business world.
24. Ethnic diversity will strengthen the company.
25. Men are kinda like women.
26. Money will make me happy.
27. Given a chance, most people will play fair.
28. I'll always have my health is how I feel, but that doesn't affect my long term decisions.
29. My friends will never betray me.
30. My boyfriend will be a good husband and we'll live happily ever after.
31. I can trust most people.
32. There is only one correct way to do something.
33. Corporations are logical, profit seeking enterprises.
34. The government is run by intelligent men who rationally plan what they do.
35. Everything is supposed to go smoothly.
36. When in doubt, tell the truth at the office.
37. Committees make the best decisions.
38. Everyone believes in the same God (values).
39. Most people in the office don't do much work because they are not motivated properly by management. I could get them to work hard.
40. What people think (out of the office) is important.
41. I don't need to exercise.
42. I won't end up like people in this office if I stay 10 years.
43. I can believe what most older people tell me about life and business.

44. I must do what I have to do so that someday I can do what I want to do.
45. My boyfriend/fiance knows what he's doing.
46. University learning applies to the real world.
47. Expensive, fashionable clothing helps my career.
48. Fair play and talent will carry the day.
49. Love is all you really need.
50. Professors know a lot about the business world.
51. Happiness is work you love and a man you love.

Office politicians know which ones you believe. That's how they manipulate you. Only 5, 6, 44, 51 are eternally true. Only time will tell if 30 becomes true.

Ye shall know the truth and the truth shall make you free. Here's the truth.

Life is an expedition with no destination, no purpose.
No matter which goal you seek,
the trail is blocked by a series of obstacles.
How you deal with the obstacles
determines your worth as a human being.
In the end, you can only win self respect.
You, alone, are responsible for winning or losing.
THE AUTHOR

In the most simple terms, *there is nothing to achieve other than a joy in living.*

Unlike most people, I didn't find the truth devastating. To me, it was liberating. I discovered it with the help of a great shrink at age 32. To me, it means freedom. It means everything is up to me. Everything is in my hands. I'm in charge of my life. I, alone, determine how much self respect I have. I, alone, determine how much fun to have during my trip to the coffin.

Can I convince you this is true? Methinks not. When I was young, I believed in truth, justice and the American Way. At your age, you don't yet want to believe in yourself, your mind, your heart, your spirit. You believe someone or something from outside can, and will, make you happy and successful.

PEOPLE MAGAZINE DEFINITION OF HAPPINESS

I could be wrong. Perhaps a handsome millionaire will sweep you off your feet and into his limousine. You will live in a mansion with servants and have celebrities for guests. Your children will love and appreciate you. Your family will all see how wrong they were about you. They will apologize, from the heart, for treating you so badly. Father will admire and respect you. Mother will love and adore you. Sister will be your truly best friend. Brother will take your side and be at your side forever.

That's a mocking, even cruel, paragraph! Your emotions are value judgements. Emotions tell you "good for me" or "bad for me." Take a moment. What do you feel? What does the adrenaline have to say to your intellect? Which movie script will you live, *Cinderella* or *Working Girl?*

UNDERSTAND YOURSELF TO UNDERSTAND MEN

Do you understand yourself better now than you did six pages ago? I'm forcing you to understand yourself, even if I have to be rough. Why?

If you don't understand yourself, you don't have a prayer of understanding men. If you don't understand men, you'll never make the big money Fortune 3000s can, and will, pay you when you understand men.

Men own, men run, men control, men decide. The corporation is a man's world. To be successful in their world, you must understand them. Everything coming next is from Anthropology 101, History 101, Sociology 101 and Joseph Campbell's, *The Power Of Myth.*

When confronted with these facts, gender-neutral politically correct professors refuse to make the obvious connections. Feminists refuse to draw the obvious conclusions. They don't *want* to understand that men are, and always have been, *Hunters Not Gatherers*.

Attention! Many manuscript reviewers were shocked and disoriented by the next four pages. Please adjust your attitude so that you can grasp all of the implications. No matter how much gender-equality propaganda feminists and liberals generate, these facts explain why men behave as they do at your office. But the most important thing these facts explain is why the corporate world is, was, and always will be, a man's world.

The battle of Waterloo was won
on the playing fields of Eton
a hundred years before.
DUKE OF WELLINGTON

Hunters Not Gatherers

Team sports saved the world from Napoleon's dictatorship, as the Duke's quote acknowledges. The values a nation wants its future soldiers to hold dear (be willing to die for) must first be instilled in its young men. At Eton, and other British schools, all young men must participate in athletics.

Millenniums before team sports, there was the hunt. The values and attitudes needed by a team of men to score the winning touchdown are the same values and attitudes needed by a team of men to track, surround and kill a dangerous beast or to ambush and slaughter a rival clan's war party. Team sports are a microcosm of the hunt.

AFTER WORK GATHERINGS

Men from the office don't invite you, or any females, to join them in their after work get togethers where corporate intelligence and gossip are shared over drinks. This information is crucial. If you know it, you can be in the right place to get the new position Fred was authorized. Or, knowing that Jake is drinking too much means Tom will ship his ass to Saudi and Eric will get his job. Those who get close to Eric will move up quickly.

Feminists claim women are not invited to these vital-to-your-career sessions because men don't want competition from women. But then, feminists believe in glass ceilings for the same preposterous reason.

MEN ARE ANIMALS

To really understand men at the office, you must understand men as animals, who, like all other animals, are the result of evolution. The male of our species has characteristics and traits derived from evolution's maxim — survival of the fittest.

For the past 250,000 years men have excluded women, children and non-hunting males from after work gatherings. In these hunter-only groups, they build camaraderie and share survival information. Even more crucial than sharing information, these gatherings allow each hunter to bond strongly with every other hunter. Bonding was, and is, fundamental for the survival of any group that must confront danger every day.

Before we get into why bonding is required to survive danger, it's necessary to understand why men are the hunters and women are the gatherers.

LABOR DIVIDED PRAGMATICALLY

Females, on average, are smaller, weaker, slower, narrower of shoulder, have less testosterone and a slower metabolism than males.

Being larger, stronger and faster obviously gives males the advantage when killing a dangerous animal for food or driving it away from the clan.

A less obvious advantage is given by testosterone. It causes one to be aggressive in general, to resort to violence quickly. Those are desirable traits for anyone rescuing a clan member cornered by a wounded animal. They are mandatory traits for anyone defending the clan from attacking human enemies intent on carrying off women and children as slaves.

A higher metabolism creates a higher body temperature, causing one to be more energetic as well as producing a felt urge to get up and move around. Clan members value these characteristics in anyone who must go out into a driving winter storm in search of food for the clan.

Broader shoulders give men increased mechanical leverage in their arms. Greater leverage means men can hit menacing animals or attacking human enemies harder with clubs. It means men can throw spears harder and farther. It means men can draw a stronger bow, driving arrows harder and farther. Spears and arrows driven the hardest, kill charging, fierce enemies and animals quicker and farther away, best for the survival of all.

Contrary to the audacious rhetoric of feminists, the historical division of labor between the sexes was not sexist or political. It was pragmatic, period.

IF HUNTERS SURVIVE, EVERYONE SURVIVES

For the past 250,000 years, the clan's hunters, eight to twelve men, young men and older boys, armed only with wooden spears, courage and allegiance to one another, have killed wild animals to feed everyone. As a team they track, corner, attack, wound, then struggle to kill fearsome beasts several times each month. The same team fights off attacks from enemy clans several times a year.

For eons, every night (after work) they have gathered, telling and re-telling stories of bloody hunts and bloody battles. Younger males learn critical survival skills and team values. Every hunter has his knowledge reinforced.

Tales honor bravery and shame cowardice. Details in the story indirectly emphasize where spears must be driven to kill quickly, less dangerously. By recounting events that led to a battle barely won, each man is reminded that strangers are deadly enemies.

By repeating the tales they learn what to do and what not to do when a wounded bear attacks. They learn to stick together as a group. They learn to depend on each other. Gathering unto themselves every night, they see themselves as special, a singular unit, a team.

On the hunt, when an enraged boar wheels and charges the nearest hunter, his survival odds increase when every man, without hesitation, attacks. Eight men in a blood rage, stabbing and slashing, overwhelm the beast. Not a man flees. They become brothers in blood, brothers in battle.

When all hunters survive, they are stronger than if one dies. A complete team of hunters increases the odds they can supply meat for the clan. Meat, a compact, portable, rich source of calories, increases the odds that the clan survives.

Survival of all hunters guarantees a stronger defense when enemies attack, increasing the odds for the survival of the women and children. Their survival insures more children are born, aiding the clan's survival.

TO DIE FOR, BONDING.

In the civilized world, men who face danger as a part of their occupation: soldiers, sailors, cops, firemen, even gangsters take part in men-only gatherings after work. The meetings are no different from those of primitive hunters. It ensures they bond. They become willing to die for each other. In turn, that increases each man's chances of surviving the dangers they face together.

SURVIVAL OF THE FITTEST — THE RESULTS

Men who face only the dangers of office politics also gather after work. If you push your way into the group they may talk with you, but in this setting they are only able to see you as a sex object. They do not consciously choose to see you that way. They do not consciously choose to gather after work. Evolution, survival of the fittest, chooses it for them. It is primal. It is inherited. It is inevitable. You can never be part of this prehistoric ritual.

Even if you can discuss the point spread on this Saturday's USC versus UCLA game, you won't be accepted. They are genetically incapable of accepting you. Save your self respect. This is one barrier that never will be broken, no matter which woman is elected president!

MEN ALWAYS HAVE BEEN DIFFERENT FROM WOMEN

After 30 years of feminist propaganda, a few men and many women believe males and females are the same.

During the rise of mammals over the last 60 million years, evolution created the essential male and essential female homo sapiens. Survival of the fittest dictated the primary characteristics of each sex.

Males developed characteristics that are best for the survival of everyone in a hunter-gatherer band of 25 humans. Females developed characteristics that are best for the survival of everyone in a hunter-gatherer band of 25 humans. Survival of the fittest determined that males must be aggressive and competitive. Survival of the fittest determined that females must be submissive and nurturing, unless defending their young.

These characteristics don't disappear because the corporation isn't a 25 person hunter-gatherer band. Every male and female at General Cow has these fundamental characteristics. These characteristics dominate everything inside and outside the corporation. These characteristics cannot be legislated away, educated away or forced away at bayonet point.

YOUR TIME REALLY IS SHORT

Remember, your time is short. Don't spend it trying to be one of the boys at the bar after work. Even more important, don't spend it banging your head against the *Mythical Glass Ceilings* feminists believe in.

Warning! The next twenty plus pages are unforgivingly frank. You are about to learn some harsh truths. These facts explain the *why* behind office politics.

> *The man who knows how will always have a job*
> *but the woman who knows WHY will be his boss.*
> UNKNOWN WISE PERSON

Please remember this from the first chapter as you read. Keep it in mind should you become disheartened:

> *Each of us must choose our own future. You, alone, must decide what to do with the powerful knowledge, and sometimes disappointing truths you are about to learn. After you have money, you can choose to stay in the corporate world or you can choose something else, like starting your own business or starting a family or becoming a consultant or whatever you want. The point is, you will be independent. You will have choices. You will never be a wage slave.*

On Brain Wiring. Several times I said female brains are "wired" differently, causing them to have a different worldview as well as a different perception of the people sitting at the conference table. The connection between the right brain and the left brain is much larger in women. Thus, women can process and integrate rational information from the left half with sensory and emotional information from the right half and know something accurately without concrete evidence — intuition. The larger connection also is the source of women's ability to discern extremely subtle changes in patterns. Thus, women are far more (40%) proficient at gathering edibles for the clan than men. But, women don't efficiently process strictly rational, spatial information that arises in the left brain because the larger connection permits interference from the right brain. This causes a lesser ability to find their way in the wild, or in today's world, to understand maps and blueprints. The smaller connection in men seems to make them far more proficient (40%) at hitting a target with a thrown object, such as a spear. The differences in ability between the sexes is scientifically demonstrable from the age of two! *Time, 1-20-92, Sizing Up The Sexes, Christine Gorman; Scientific American, 9-92, Sex Differences in the Brain, Doreen Kimura.*

If it were easy to be a chief, everyone would be a chief.
ATTILA THE HUN

In two words: im-possible.
METRO GOLDWYN MAYER SAM GOLDWYN

You can have any color you want
as long as it's black.
HENRY FORD

Mythical Glass Ceilings

Competition, life-or-death competition, determines who eats whom at the top of the food chain and at the top of the corporation. It's the same at the top of everything — organized crime, organized religion, showbiz, government, office politics. Combatants have no principles. "Whatever it takes" is their creed. Pragmatism dominates. Machiavelli rules. Only the strong survive.

To explain why there are no female CEOs at the head of a Fortune 500, libbers claim that men conspire to keep women out of top management because they're afraid to compete against females for the best jobs. Do men conspire to keep women out of the best jobs in the mafia? Of course not. Women don't have what it takes to run a mafia family or a Fortune 500 company. There is no conspiracy. There is a lack of testosterone.

Females, by their *biological* nature, are not aggressive enough, belligerent enough, fierce enough, vicious enough, ferocious enough or brutal enough to take, then hold, power at the uppermost reaches of business, government, religion, education or military organizations.

As a homo sapiens who happens to be female, you are about 90 percent the same as a homo sapiens who happens to be male. The difference is inconsequential when pushing paper. The difference is mandatory to rise above middle management. The male's natural aggressiveness is the difference.

If two people compete for the same job and they have equal talent and political skills, the most aggressive competitor wins. Does that seem like news? Will it change if politicians pass thousands of laws enforcing "gender equality?"

But the glass ceiling isn't solid testosterone. At the same time you were being conditioned with "Don't fight girls! Play nice!" your male counterpart was being conditioned with, "Slide with your spikes up, you pussy! Take him out going into second!"

Team sports are a microcosm of reality, corporate reality in particular. Sports reveal a timeless truth — the more aggressive one is, the greater advantage one has. By playing on a team as young men, corporate males learned a crucial lesson — the tougher, harder, meaner you are, the more often you win. You win the right to play or you sit on the bench. If you have to sit on the bench today, tomorrow you must get more aggressive.

And, the glass ceiling isn't made out of testosterone plus conditioning. Of females who join a Fortune 3000 company at 22 years old, 1 in 20 is seriously dedicated to a business career. "Seriously" means truly willing to forego all other interests for 20 years, especially children, work 50-60 hour weeks without complaint, constantly manipulate and maneuver to gain the slightest edge over every rival, ferociously fight for every possible promotion, and all the while present a friendly "team-player" facade to the corporate leaders. In other words, that 1-in-20 woman is ambitious, loves competition, is tougher and politically smarter than any guy she comes up against.

When that 1-in-20 woman is 37 years old, she's finally made it to the upper level of middle management, where the route to top management actually begins. When she looks around, there isn't another woman in sight. She's the only female who was willing to endure the sacrifices necessary to reach these heights. Trouble is, there are 30 men who were willing!

OLD BOY CONNECTIONS REQUIRED

It gets worse. For her to make the quantum leap into top management, those in top management (men) must genuinely believe she (a) is the best qualified (b) has the best business and social connections (c) will go along to get along.

Take another look at (b). As my boss once summarized the philosophy of big business, "We only do business with friends."

To become a member of Top Management, one must have connections that provide access to high level, powerful people with the authority to make agreements at other companies, at City Hall and in Washington DC. Those people are men, well connected men, from a long line of well connected families. The old boy network stretches back into history as far as ten generations in some industries such as shipping and banking.

Members of Top Management do not discuss important topics or make significant deals in the office. Discussions and deals are held and made: on the golf course, at the charity fund raising ball, while cruising on the company yacht, after dinner at the private club, over lunch in the company hunting lodge and on the company jet returning from the Redskins-Raiders game.

Rarely is a woman connected well enough socially and politically to move in those circles. If she is, she comes from a well connected family or she married a well connected husband. If so, she doesn't need to be, and probably wouldn't want to be, a member of Top Management. As explained in *Get Promoted,* it really is who you know.

When only 1 woman in 20 has only 1 chance in 30 but still doesn't have the connections, glass ceilings are not necessary. You can have any job you want, as long as it's a "woman's job." *Translation:* not top management.

A WOMAN'S JOB

Remember, you're on a quest to accumulate capital. Get the highest paying job you can. Enter the race where *they* can accept the fact that a woman's in charge: Personnel, Corporate Benefits, Public Relations and such. The politically smart woman looks over the organization chart and figures out which positions don't feature competition from males: Staff Assistant, Project Administrator, Project Coordinator, Scheduler, Cost Estimator, MIS Technician, Benefits Administrator, Travel Coordinator, Communications Manager, Training Support Manager, Office Services Manager or Marketing Support Services.

WOMEN IN CHARGE OF MEN?

Even if doubly qualified, it's foolishness to get in the race for a position that requires supervising mostly males. It's career suicide to win that race. Why? Just competing for any promotion creates enemies but you create twice as many by having the audacity to compete for a "man's job." The odds against you are tremendous, 75 men against 1 woman. It gets worse.

At the beginning of Women's Lib, companies learned the costly way that men thoroughly resent taking direction from a woman. In those days, when women won this type of job, the men they supervised, in an undeclared guerilla war, conducted slow downs and innocent looking sabotage until customers demanded a change. The companies replaced them with men.

Humiliated, the women sued. After long, costly legal battles, with not one man testifying in their favor, they often lost. If companies won, they still lost hundreds of thousands in legal costs. Worse, they lost millions because pissed off customers never came back. But worst of all, they lost mega millions because the negative publicity drove away future business.

Nowadays, companies don't let it get to that stage. They unofficially make certain a woman never ascends to a position where she supervises men. That's not a glass ceiling, that's The Great Wall Of China made of glass.

BEGINNING OF THE END

It isn't just Old Boys and walls of glass, in 1994, a little publicized study shows a sharp rise in white male absenteeism with a corresponding drop in profitability as women and minorities are promoted to comply with government mandates. This won't destroy your chances for promotion immediately, but it does not look good in the long term. I agree with Janis Joplin, get it while you can.

MONEY IS THE ONLY REASON

I'm certain what I've just told you is disappointing, disheartening, discouraging, disillusioning and dismaying. At least you won't waste years of precious youth believing you can achieve the impossible. Time is money.

It's not possible for a woman to make it to top management. So, the only reason to work for a Fortune 3000 is because that's where you can make the most money during the next ten years.

If you understand the *why* behind office politics, that will be easier. It's time for a *Reality Check*. Your professors didn't understand what's on the next few pages or didn't want to tell you. You decide. Then decide how, or if, you want to use this knowledge.

After stubborn negotiation and long delay, grant the least radical demands of the revolt's leaders. Believing they won, their followers celebrate, then go back to their villages.
ON DEFUSING REVOLUTIONS OTTO VON BISMARCK

If you took all the money in the world
and divided it equally,
in 20 years the people who have it now
would have it back.
AMERICAN FINANCIER BERNARD BARUCH

Reality Check

Young women have been taught that everyone would be equally capable if everyone got the same pre-natal care, early childhood nurturing, housing, nutrition, education, health care, transportation and self-esteem training. Young women have been taught that poor people are no different from anyone else, they just don't have money. Young women have been taught that rich people are no different from anyone else, they just have money.

THE GOLDEN RULE

The people with the gold make the rules. It always was that way, it is that way, it will always be that way. Those with gold (power) have it because they are smarter, more ruthless, more cunning, more fill-in-the-blank than the rest of us.

The only way their position at the top of the system can be threatened is to first upset the status quo, then start a revolution and change the system. In 1776, the American Revolution first upset the status quo, then changed the system. In 1789, the French Revolution first upset the status quo, then changed the system. In 1917, the Communist Revolution first upset the status quo, then changed the system.

REVOLUTION DESTRUCTION

In 1968, America's anti-war and civil rights protests were reaching their peak. Blacks rioted. Students rioted. Police rioted. The country was polarized. There was no consensus. The first step to revolution had been taken. The status quo was threatened!

Martin Luther King was assassinated. The civil rights movement fell into disarray. *Result:* no threat to the status quo. Robert Kennedy was assassinated. The anti-war movement lost a candidate who could have won the election. *Result:* no threat to the status quo. In 1972, George Wallace was shot and paralyzed. The candidate who could force the election to be determined by the House of Representatives was eliminated. *Result:* no threat to the status quo.

MOST POWERFUL, DEFINED

The most powerful (richest) people in the world answer to no one. They do whatever they want, whenever they want. That's exactly what "most powerful" means.

The people at the top of Corporate America are members of that same ultra exclusive group. The people at the top of Corporate America are all males, Northern European White Males, to be exact.

At the top of corporations, old, gray haired Northern European White Males will be replaced by middle aged, graying haired Northern European White Males. That status quo will never, ever change no matter what Congress and the Federal Commission on Gender Equality do.

REVOLUTION CASTRATION

In the 70s and early 80s, revolutionary liberals, socialists and radical feminists began to disrupt the status quo, demanding minorities and women be made part of business and government leadership. The heads of big business and big government followed Bismarck's advice. After stubborn negotiations and lengthy delays, some minorities and women were promoted to figurehead top management positions.

Followers of the radical feminists and radical left celebrated their victory, then went back to whatever they were doing before the status quo was threatened. That "victory" rendered the women's movement impotent.

In the 90s and beyond, studies and statistics produced by big business and big government show "progress" continues. The message: "Things are continuing to improve. Your 'victory' is safe." With a straight face, the media reports the results. After all, no matter how liberal, big media is also big business. (See the *Preface* and *Status Quo Forever* for more on this.)

So what? You can't change or control that, or them. Make certain you don't waste your short time trying to change the status quo instead of accumulating capital.

WHO PAYS TAXES

The rich get richer . . . is an unchangeable, eternal fact. In the end, the Communist Revolution collapsed because it was out spent by the American Revolution.

Review Baruch's quote at the beginning of this chapter. Who actually pays when grandstanding politicians increase the taxes on "greedy corporations," or ensure "free" heath care for everyone by forcing employers to pay for it. Do corporations dip into their profits or do they raise prices, the prices you and I pay? Think about it. Follow the money.

LIMOUSINE LIBERALS

These hypocrites ride through the ghetto in armored, stretch limos. While sipping champagne, they look out at the squalor and proclaim, "The government must do something to help these poor people."

To pay for their "social programs" government can only get enough money by raising the income tax. Teddy Kennedy is the best known hypocrite. He has no income, per se. The Kennedy billions are in a trust fund that cannot be taxed.

Other limousine liberals are the offspring of real Capitalists. Like Teddy, their wealth (capital) is preserved where it cannot be taxed. Their last names are sometimes recognizable: Fleischman, Ford, Dupont, Busch, Rockerfeller et al.

Those who already have massive wealth do not want others to accumulate capital in large amounts. Their reasoning is sound. It goes like this.

> Takes money to make money, right? If anyone accumulates big money he will be able to make more money. With that, he'll make even more. Soon he'll have so much money that he'll be able to compete with us. Let's have the government

raise taxes so high that nobody can ever accumulate enough money to get started on the road to threatening us. We don't have to pay because the megabillions we already have can't be taxed. We don't care why they raise taxes, but if we make it sound like it's a noble cause, we look like saints. Let's advocate helping the poor, sick, retarded, crippled and aged. Who will dare protest?

The rich didn't get that way by accident. They don't stay that way because they're stupid. The poor aren't that way because you, me, business and government don't give them something.

JUSTICE FOR ORDINARY EMPLOYEES?

Damned few, if any, in top management care if you, your co-workers, your boss or even his boss are treated unfairly or abused. In the upper reaches of all major corporations everybody knows that ordinary employees, in fact most employees, are as expendable as a sheet of paper and replaced as easily.

The graveyards are full of irreplaceable men.
CHARLES DEGAULLE

Don't waste time trying to force The Company to be fair. They'll simply replace you, then blacklist you forever within their industry.

WHY SUCH BRUTAL HONESTY?

Jousting with windmills owned by corporations instead of accumulating capital is a waste of time. Only after you have capital can you dream the possible dream, then live it. If you missed this quote back in *Dealing With What You Were Dealt,* don't miss it now.

Books will speak plain when counsellors blanch.
1607 FRANCIS BACON

Don't waste your short time dreaming the impossible dream, fighting the unbeatable windmill, Donna Quixote. Concentrate on the portion of the universe that you can change and control, your life and career choice. Concentrate on taking care of yourself. In the end, she's all you've got.

The truth of what's been said on the previous few pages is hard for most people to accept, even harder for young people. Knowing with your intellect that it's true is one thing, but to accept it in your heart and in your guts is much harder. Until you accept it, you won't concentrate on accumulating capital.

Without capital (money), others will decide your future. Want enough money so that eventually you can do what you want, with whom you want, when you want? Fortune 3000 companies have that kind of money. They will gladly give it to you if, and only if, you'll *Be Tough* all the time.

Caution! Some manuscript reviewers saw themselves as incapable of behaving as prescribed. First of all, you don't really have to *be* tough, you only have to *act* tough so they will believe you are tough. Secondly, you only have to act like this if you want to make the really big bucks like $150k.

Compassionate note to the reader: Nearly every manuscript reviewer told me how difficult it was to accept what was said on the previous twenty plus pages. But, to a woman, they reported that somewhere in their hearts they had known it was true before they read it. Confronting it in black and white made it inescapable. Many said it left them disheartened and feeling completely hopeless. PLEASE! Take heart. So what if that's the way it is? None of us can change it. We can only understand reality, then go on about the business of living. As a reminder, this is from page two:

> *Once you* understand *and* accept, *you'll be able to use the techniques, strategy and tactics in this book to drive your salary high enough so that you can (1) leave the corporate world and follow your bliss (2) stay in the corporate world and make $150k (3) stay in the corporate world and make $60k doing a job you enjoy while easily defeating office politicians who try to make your life miserable.*

And this is from page six:

Take what you want and pay for it, sayeth God.
SPANISH PROVERB

The wisdom of that quote means that each of us must choose our own future. And, no matter which choice you make, there's a price you must pay.

Let's get tough!

SUPER BOWL XXIII JOE MONTANA

DOWN BY 3 POINTS, 92 YARDS TO GO, 3:20 LEFT, THAT'S ALL HE SAID IN THE HUDDLE

Tough times don't last. Tough people do.

UNKNOWN WISE PERSON

Be Tough

Angry, frustrated, hurt, confused, disoriented, disbelieving, she bursts into her boss's office crying and screaming she deserved the promotion. He sees only a hysterical female. While patronizingly consoling her, he makes mental preparations to get rid of her.

Your toughness will be tested three times as often as a male your age and position. Promotions come your way only if your boss respects you because men only respect and reward toughness. If you have a female boss, she respects toughness too, but she won't promote you. Why? Because there are only a few high paying slots for females. Only a tough female will make it. She limits the competition by holding you back.

As explained in *The Play's The Thing,* to get paid like the men, dress like the men. Tough is just like that. To get far enough up the ladder to make the big bucks you have to be like the top men, tough. If you aren't tough, you stay on the lower rungs of the corporate ladder forever, even if you change jobs again and again.

HOW TO BE SEEN AS TOUGH

Acting tough and talking tough is all there is to it. But, at this point, you don't know how to talk tough or act tough.

Tough People Don't Lose It. They are cool, logical, rational and relaxed in the face of pressure or danger. But everybody has a breaking point. Once that point is reached, we all lose it. Each of us loses it differently but we all lose it. Oh sure, afterwards everyone makes apologies and excuses and pretends all is forgotten. Nope! You're *kaput* at that company.

Once you display hysterical female behavior, no matter how provoked you were, no matter that genuine assholes drove you over the edge and everyone knows that, you're finished. Losing it makes you a non-pressure player, thus non-promotable.

You'll cry or whine or scream or throw things or whatever your beloved manner of losing it is. I haven't lost it for years. Since I work as a temp employee, my ego is not involved and my future is not at stake. However, when I do lose it, my eyes narrow to slits, my nostrils flare. I grit my teeth, clench my fists, tense my shoulders and neck so tightly veins stand out on my face. I become murderously pale. I glare. In an ominously cold voice, "Get the fuck out before I strangle you."

It makes no difference how you lose it. Once you do, they realize you are not management material. The end. No more promotions. Minimum raises or none.

You can only learn how to not lose it, by losing it quite a few times. Screw up during your early jobs when and where it doesn't count. After three or four companies you'll know how to prevent yourself from acting like a "typical hysterical female." You'll realize the type of person and what kind of situation causes you to lose it. You'll be able to prepare or withdraw before it becomes impossible to control yourself.

Tough People Are Not Kind. Kindness is seen as weakness. To the cows in the corporate pasture, a strong person is a tough person. To them, a kind person is just another cow, someone that can be taken advantage of.

Don't do kind things for people on your level, immediately above or below you. Without people knowing, do kind things for those way above or way below you. Helping those beneath you causes them to see you as wonderful. They're used to being treated like animals, so they are most appreciative. Later, they'll die for you in corporate combat if you ask. Being kind to those way above you gets you noticed, the first step to promotion.

Tough People Don't Ask If They're Doing Their Job Right. Asking how you are doing indicates a lack of confidence. Don't ask your boss, co-workers or subordinates if you are doing okay. Asking someone, anyone, how you are doing is asking for his approval. That makes him the Daddy and you the child. But it's important to explain to your boss ahead of time that you want to know when you screw up so you can learn from mistakes.

Tough People Admit Their Mistakes. When you make a big mistake, tell your boss before someone rats on you. By so doing, you show him that you're tough enough to admit it when you are wrong.

Tough People Don't Whine. Only little girls and Jewish American Princesses whine. Whining is death. Respect is lost. Whining grates on everyone's nerves. No one likes, respects or promotes a whiner.

Take a tape recorder to work. Just let it run. Listen to yourself. Do you whine? If so, raise your self-awareness. Monitor and control yourself. At the same time, get a new job. You're known as a whiner here.

Tough People Don't Give A Shit About Other People's Kids or Grandchildren. If trapped, listen and be civil. With your boss and above, ask about children and grandchildren only if they have pictures displayed. Should he mention them during casual conversation, show moderate interest.

Tough People Don't Let People Cry On Their Shoulders. Don't listen to anybody's personal problems, ever. Discourage all whining unless you're learning something useful about who's really in power or such.

Tough People Are Loners. Do not become friends with anyone. You can socialize with particularly influential women if it will produce a quick promotion. Keep it superficial. Reveal nothing. Do not socialize with males from work, period.

Tough People Don't Discuss Their Personal Life. We all have personal problems from cheating boyfriends to noisy, nosy neighbors. Leave all that at home. At the office you are all business and no bullshit. If an enemy knows you have personal problems he spreads it around immediately. When you're out sick, he gets management to write you off by saying, "Donna? Home feeling sorry for herself. Got dumped again."

Tough People Don't Quit. They persevere and they're in it for the long haul. Talk as if you plan to make a career at the company. Quit as soon as you have a new job with a ten percent or better raise.

Tough People Live For Work. You have a boring social life as far as everyone at work is concerned, even if you're fulfilling perverse fantasies every night. When pressed, say you finished Von Clauswitz' *On War,* then went to bed early. You are a dedicated company man who happens to be female.

Tough Women Don't Like Women. Don't become "one of the girls." Be pleasant but don't become one of them. They are losers, stuck in menial jobs forever. Women in misery love company. Be on guard if you offend them. They will band together to make certain you don't succeed.

Tough Women Don't Have PMS Or Periods. The first few months at a company don't miss a single day because of PMS or cramps or blues. Somebody, usually a rival, is trying to track your periods. Suck it up. Get in there and do your job. Don't leave early. Don't be late.

When females miss work, men are pissed off because they believe women get special consideration. An enemy, male or female, can destroy your image with a single sentence, said in a joking manner, if you miss the scheduled staff meeting. "Donna? Must be all cramped up. Missed a month ago, too." His tone of voice says, "What a puss. Can't depend on her when the going gets tough." Use Motrin 600s to ease the pain. Keep them in your car's glove compartment, not in your desk. Rivals and enemies go through your desk looking for hard evidence.

Although makeup is restricted severely elsewhere, a tiny bit is required to disguise zits but not for vanity's sake. It keeps others from realizing that PMS may be the cause when you snap at someone. With severe problems, see a doctor. Depo Provera injections eliminate periods and PMS as long as you get your shot every three months. If I were female, I'd love it.

Tough People Scrap For Every Penny. Don't compromise and split the difference in any negotiation, no matter if it's a raise or the price of the new computer you have been tasked to get by working with Procurement. People respect you only if you are hard-nosed about money because of all the psychological and mystical power money carries with it. There's more in *Temps Get To Choose, Get That Raise* and *Personnel* about negotiations over money. The best tactics are in *Winning Through Negotiation,* listed in *Must Books*.

Tough People Don't Fall For Flattery. In a meeting a guy tries to kiss up, "That was a great job you did on the parking plan." Just look at him, nod, then go about gathering your papers. The pregnant silence tells everyone you don't play that shit.

Tough Women Fight Back When An Ambitious Underling Makes His Move. Whack someone's balls good now and again to maintain your position as his superior. Call him in. Say something like, "Jim, about that car pool study . . . uh, oh, never mind." Say nothing. Wait. He says, "What about it?" Long pause, thinking, mulling, "Oh, never mind." Look down at your papers. Let him stand there awkwardly and wait. Look up. Your face says, "Are you still here?" No matter what he says you reply, "Never mind," then go back to work. He'll leave with mental wheels spinning. He will be so busy wondering what you didn't say he won't have time to be overly ambitious for at least another week.

Tough People Don't Have Psychological Problems. Telling co-workers you ride with Dykes On Bikes every weekend is less damaging to your career than saying you went, or are going, to a shrink. Although we all have problems we can't cope with at some point in our lives, don't tell co-workers. They see a walking time bomb, so unstable you might blurt out, "The emperor wears no clothes."

Why? These co-workers know on some level that they, themselves, are crazy. If you say, "I was crazy and I got better," they'll have to confront themselves. That's the last thing they want. They're so busy distracting themselves from their feelings they have no idea how whacked out they are. The longer they deceive themselves, the crazier they get.

Tough People Don't Discuss Some Topics. When someone tries to ask you something personal or is rude enough to ask what you think about a religious, political or racial topic, you say, "That's something I don't discuss."

If he presses with, "Why not?" Your reply is, "I just don't." If he continues, "But why?" Glare, letting indignation show.

Say, "It's not appropriate." If he dares to push farther with, "No, really now, why not?" Stare at him. The astonished look on your face reveals how amazed you are that an asshole has begun to grow right between his eyes! Slowly repeat, "That's just something I don't discuss," turn and walk away or rise from your chair, closing the conversation.

Never debate anything. Don't even discuss emotion-producing subjects: abortion, civil rights, welfare, sex, politics, well, you get the idea.

Tough Women Don't Have Cute Names. Take a moment and think of a strong woman's name. Ann Bancroft, Elizabeth Taylor, Lee Grant, Joan Jett, Meryl Streep, Barbra Streisand, Joan Crawford, Chris Everett, Cloris Leachman, Lana Turner.

Here are some others: Carla, Jo, Carol, Jean, Susan, Linda, Jane, Jean, Jan, Norma, Helen, Gale, Lou, Olivia, Mercedes, Donna, Audrey, Dana, Margaret, Rita, Ruth, Eileen, Frances.

Names that ends with an "e" sound, make you, and keep you, a cute little girl forever. Cathy, Debbie, Cindy. Never let anyone call you Missy, Suzie or such. Politely but firmly say, "I prefer Melissa."

The corporate world is Northern European White Male with no tolerance for ethnic or foreign names. There are no positions with high visibility if you insist on an unusual name: Setaeran, Latifa, Billyjo, Guadalupe.

Pick a new name. One that can be a man's is best: Dawn, Jo, Lauren, Kris, Jean, Sandy. Initials are better: JJ, PL, KC.

When you change companies, change your name. If the bureaucrats in Personnel insist on using your official name for company records, don't raise a big stink. Just introduce yourself as DJ. If someone calls you Donna say, "I go by DJ."

Tough People Take Care Of Themselves. Open doors, carry packages, re-arrange furniture yourself. Do everything unless a guy beats you to it, then be gracious. Don't lecture. Take what's forced on you and do the rest yourself. You are strong, tough and independent, not a castrating bitch. You're absolutely not helpless, ever, under any circumstance.

Tough People Pay Their Own Way. Remember, money has psychological and mystical power. When you go with "the guys," pay for your own lunch. If they object, insist. Do not back off. This is not like opening the door yourself. If they pay they feel superior, even if they are just trying to be gentlemanly. Apologize if necessary, "Sorry, guys! This is a big deal to me. I pay my own way."

The subtle message is, "If one can't pay one's own way, one can't do much for the company. I carry my weight. I don't mooch. I am tough."

Buying anything for someone makes them beholden to you. Buy lunch for anyone, anywhere, anytime you need to have him in your debt. That's the only time you buy for others. You're tough, not an easy touch.

Tough People Don't Borrow Or Lend Money. Once again, money has psychological and mystical power. Never borrow money, even $3 for lunch because you forgot to go by the bank. The message is, "I'm irresponsible or forgetful or incompetent." Never lend money to anyone unless you want him beholden to you. When people don't pay you back, they feel guilty and hate you for causing that. Lending money to real friends is usually the end of the friendship.

Tough People Don't Flirt. Always be civil and polite. Don't hurt anyone's feelings unnecessarily. If you flirt, you're a girl, just a cute girl who might be a great sex partner. Tough people don't need the attention of the opposite sex to boost their egos.

Tough People Take What They Want. If you want something, take it. It won't be given to you. The only person who'll fight over whatever you grab is a rival or enemy. He'll cry foul and tattletale. When your boss comes to you about it your response is, "I'm just trying to do a better job. If I don't have to wait for the printer, I can get twice as much work done. Sorry if that's tramping on someone's toes." Wait. Make him force you to return the printer.

Tough People Are Practical. They say things like, "I have no control over what the board of directors does. I only concern myself with things I can control." They act that way, too.

Tough People Don't Laugh Much. Tough people are serious. They never giggle. Clowning around is something boys do so the girls laugh and think they're cool. Telling jokes is something that salesmen do to be liked and wannabe comedians do to get attention. Business is no laughing matter. Polite, appropriate smiles are how tough people express humor. If you didn't notice this quote before, notice it now.

Women are like tea, you don't know how strong they are until you put them in hot water.
DUCHESS OF WINDSOR

Tough People Don't Request With "Please." They just say what they want done.

Tough People Don't Yell. Dirty Harry doesn't yell. He speaks quietly, with self-assurance. He repeats his command until it is complied with. Yelling is what insecure broads do to make people think they are tough.

Tough People Aren't The Department's Fire-Safety Geek. Firmly decline the silly hat and vest and bullhorn and flashlight and first aid kit. Everyone sees the person designated for this role as a loser. They're right.

Tough People Never Admit To Being Weak Or Even Appear to Be Weak. Never make desperate, weak, helpless looking moves, statements or even adopt a weak posture.

Do you understand yourself better than you did hundreds of pages ago? Why do I ask? As a woman you must make *the* toughest decision life asks anyone. What about *Children?*

He that hath wife and children has given hostages to fortune; for they are impediments to great enterprises, either of virtue or mischief.

1624 FRANCIS BACON

Children? Now, Later, Never

About 30 pages ago, the two most important questions that life asks each of us were put to you. I don't know what your answers are. But, children? That's the most important question life asks females. Before you answer, remember, if you don't know where you came from, you don't know where you're going.

Caution! This chapter is frank and direct because young females in our culture never are given a chance to consider why, or even if, they should become mothers. The information is meant to help you decide: *now, later* or *never* as well as to prepare you for the attitude corporations have toward women with children. Every young reviewer reported that she was forced to seriously consider, for the first time, the consequences of deciding to become a mother. You, alone, must choose what to do with this information.

NATURE VS BRAINWASHING

You were raised to achieve a single goal, marriage, so you could fulfill your ultimate purpose, motherhood. You were taught, brainwashed, pressured, conned, hoodwinked, schnitzeled, convinced, persuaded, manipulated, maneuvered, punished, rewarded, pushed, pulled, coerced and coaxed until, deep down in your ovaries, you, yourself, accept this.

They taught you to accept their values by telling fairytales about Cinderella, Sleeping Beauty and Rapunzel. They reinforced them with movies like *Pretty Woman, Officer And A Gentleman* and other variations on Cinderella, then doubly reinforced their values with TV shows like *Cosby* to perpetuate the myth that happiness is a nuclear family, even in the late 20th Century.

We've been poisoned by these fairytales.
End Of The Innocence DON HENLEY

Our entire culture is permeated with this version of "a woman's purpose," so permeated that only a few percent of women ever question it, let alone reject it.

Biological alarm at age 28? In the natural state, primitive cultures, females are two-child mothers by 14. It's hard to conceive, pun intended, of a biological alarm waiting 14 more years to go off just because we're civilized! A biological clock? A brainwashed clock is far more plausible.

GONE WITH THE WIND

Two hundred years ago the economy was agrarian, so most people were farmers. Life expectancy was 42 years. It made sense for young couples to unite in until-death marriages. It made survival sense for them to have children as quickly and as often as possible. They needed help with the endless, hard, physical work necessary to survive on an isolated, pre-industrial, single family farm.

Today, that pre-industrial society's marriage system, reproductive goals, and the social norms devised to enforce them, are virtually intact and mindlessly instilled in America's youth, generation after generation by our culture's institutions: church, school, family and, most powerfully, by television.

In the late 20th century, we live 75 years in a highly mobile, urban society. Our economy is service, information and high technology. We have needs, goals, values and dreams that bear no resemblance to those of pre-industrial farmers. What it takes for us to survive is drastically different from our forefathers. And yet, every year two million young couples unquestioningly unite in until-death marriages then unthinkingly reproduce as if children were needed to work the fields.

Yes, in a time when overpopulation is the cause of nearly every one of our problems, the culture blindly enforces the social norms and reproductive values of a society gone with the wind.

GREAT SCHIZOPHRENIC EXPECTATIONS

Unfulfilled expectations lead to disappointment. The higher the expectations, the deeper the disappointment. The harder you try to meet the expectations, the greater the disappointment.

When a woman tries to meet her own expectations and the expectations that her husband, and her parents, have of what a wife and mother should be, she behaves like a farmer's wife.

However, she behaves as unlike a farmer's wife as possible when she tries to meet her own expectations, her husband's and her business colleagues' expectations of what a suburban career woman should be.

After a woman valiantly tries, then fails, to meet the impossible, conflicting expectations hammered into her head and heart, the pain and disappointment she feels is real. It's just as real for her husband, for her children and for her parents. Pain and disappointment lead to feelings of betrayal which lead inexorably to indignant rage followed by bottomless despair.

This double-bind, schizophrenic, contradictory predicament is exactly where every woman puts herself when she tries to live up to the expectations of a culture gone with the wind. Sadly, it results in divorce but, most disheartening, it results in children who begin life with deep self doubts and low self-esteem.

CHILDREN WITHOUT PURPOSE

Children who were born between 1961 and 1975 became Generation X. They share a common soul with today's children. They serve no purpose at home. There is no work for them to do. They serve no purpose in the economy. There is no work for them to do. They have nothing to do but pass time.

By their teens, many kids begin to realize they have no purpose and suspect they're unwanted burdens. In turn, they feel indignant resentment toward their parents. In turn, the parents feel unappreciated and offended. Hurt, anger, guilt, blame, remorse, rejection and neuroses run amok!

If you ignored this quote before, read it now.

> *Ninety percent of families are dysfunctional*
> *and the other ten percent are in denial.*
> JOHN BRADSHAW

The solution? Have realistic expectations. But, try to tell that to a young woman who is selecting her wedding gown and planning the honeymoon trip. In *Helpful Hints,* I offer a reasonable alternative.

YOUR CHOICE, YOUR RESPONSIBILITY

You cannot change the way society views itself and how society attempts to ensure its long-term interests are served. Only time can do that or a national crisis larger than Vietnam.

You, alone, must choose what your "real purpose" is. You, alone, must choose what to do with your life. I strongly urge that you take plenty of time to search your soul for the truth. Separate what you believe from what *they* want you to believe. It's okay to be confused, but it's not okay to confuse yourself so that you don't make a conscious, responsible choice.

WHAT ARE THE ODDS?

The average marriage lasts 9.1 years — death or divorce. The divorce rate is 52 percent. The divorce rate of re-marriage is 67 percent. That doesn't tell the whole story. What about the couples who don't divorce? How many are genuinely happy?

If you want children, it's prudent and responsible to have job skills you can use to support yourself and your children, should Mr. Rite turn into Mr. Hyde after 9.1 years.

A GOOD MOTHER IS HARD TO FIND

If you choose to become a mother, it's responsible to do so only if you can be a good mother, not a second-rate mother like today's confused women who are part-time mothers as they attempt to be full-time career women. Those poor souls swallowed, then acted out the Big Lie feminist gurus were spewing in the 70s — you can have it all, career, children and an understanding husband who respects and supports you.

In the 90s, these betrayed, bewildered women are multiple-child mothers of kids who are troubled and trouble. The women are exhausted from 50 hours at the office just to keep their jobs and another 100 plus hours at home. The understanding, supportive husbands got fed up after the second child. Most left. But when fed up, angry, bitter, disappointed husbands stay, those marriages are neurotic pretenses that damage the children forever.

Wait until you can be a caring, nurturing mother. Do it right. Have a child because that's what you want, the real *you* wants, not the you *they* created. Beyond that, money must not be, and never will be, a problem because you might end up in the 52 percent who don't wait until death to part.

THE COMPANY'S VIEWPOINT

Because the Women's Movement forced the government to force companies to pretend they are concerned about women with children, this is an unwritten, unstated position.

> *We don't give a damn if your child is sick. You are supposed to be at your desk. The men are. You will no longer be considered for promotion.*

FINAL ADVICE ON CHOOSING TO BE A MOM

Nearly all men and women avoid talking about and thinking about the long range consequences of fundamental life-changing choices: dropping out of college, marrying, getting pregnant or quitting a job.

> *There are few, if any, accidents.*
> SIGMUND FREUD

Everyone hopes the necessity to choose goes away if one doesn't focus on the magnitude of the consequences, doesn't discuss pros and cons, doesn't allow oneself to feel, then evaluate the meaning of the powerful emotions connected with the choice.

> *Not to decide, is to decide.*
> UNKNOWN JESUS FREAK

In reality, most people choose by not preventing the "accident" from happening. The payoff? They avoid blame and responsibility by pretending *it just happened* to them, they didn't decide, *it just happened.*

Read that quote by Freud again. Thousands of females get pregnant "accidentally" every day and every night. She says, "I forgot to take my pill," or "Got too stoned, didn't know what I was doing," or "The rhythm method didn't work." And, millions of other rationalizations for "accidents."

Current research shows that many women in unhappy marriages or relationships have a baby so they have someone to love and someone who will love them in return. How heartbreakingly, horribly sad.

RATIONAL DECISION MAKING

Make your decision to have a child only after long, serious, mutual self disclosure sessions, soul-searching and fact-weighing discussions with your husband. Consider the lifelong consequences, the lifelong costs and the lifelong risks. Be logical, rational and realistic. Above all, be honest with yourself and with him.

Take a moment: The information and advice in this chapter and the other *why* chapters are for the women who want earn $150k. If your long range goal is different, only use the portions of this book that help you achieve that dream.

So, *Now What?*

You've got to walk that lonesome valley,
You've got to walk it by yourself.
HANK WILLIAMS

I'm Leaving It All Up To You
Sung by Linda Ronstadt TERRY HARRIS

Now What?

You now have the tools, techniques and the strategy needed to pile up enough screw-you money to live life on your terms. But, now that you know the truth about office politics and the man's world of corporations, you may decide it's not worth it. Before you decide what to do, please remember these few key points.

There is no finish line in life. There's no place to get to. There is only living and loving and laughing as much as possible between now and the time they close the lid on your coffin. That takes money.

In the real world everyone must compete for what one needs to survive. What everyone needs is limited: air, water, food, sex, security, love, self actualization. The corporate world is just like the real world. What everyone wants is in limited supply: money or jobs that are fun. You must fight for them.

DECIDE BASED ON REALITY, NOT DREAMS

Consider the facts of biology, sociology, anthropology and history presented.

Realize that, because of biological differences, a woman's sense-of-self is different from a man's sense-of-self. Remember and understand that a woman's brain is wired differently from a man's brain. Women and men, do not, and cannot see the same world. Thus, they will never see eye-to-eye, especially in the man's world of corporations.

Weigh the fact that in *real* management (not PR, Personnel and such) men outnumber women 8 to 1, in Top Management 50 to 1. Calculate the probability of a woman winning a top spot in the corporation.

Nature to be commanded, must be obeyed.
ISSAC NEWTON

By their very nature, males love to compete. They can't help it. Women, by their very nature, love to nurture, they can't help it. Men run corporations. I say, take the money and run!

I'M LEAVING IT ALL UP TO YOU

You, alone, are responsible for deciding which of life's infinite paths to take. Before you decide, listen with your heart and with your soul to spiritual views from poets long dead. They eloquently describe the author's motivation and the consequences.

Still glides the Stream and shall forever glide;
The Form remains, the Function never dies.
While we, the brave, the mighty and the wise;
We men, who in our morn of youth
Defied the elements, must vanish. Be it so.

Enough, if something from our hands have power
To live, and act, and serve the future hour;
And if, as toward the silent tomb we go, Through love,
through hope, and faith's transcendent dower,
We feel that we are greater then we know.
William Wordsworth *The River Duddon*

For in great wisdom there is much grief.
He that increaseth knowledge, increaseth sorrow.
For who knows what is good for men in this life?
Who can tell a man what shall be after him?
Ecclesiastes 300 BC

Reinforce key principles of winning at office politics and winning at life, read *In Summary*. Then, over the next few weeks or months, learn from other experts by reading every single one of the *Must Books*.

Please write and point out mistakes I've made, offer comments, deliver criticism, suggest improvements for the next edition. I'll answer concise questions by mail if you enclose a SASE.

Goodbye and "good luck." R. Don Steele, Whittier, California, September 1994.

Steel Balls Press
Box 807
Whittier CA 90608

Everything you want to know
is in a book except how to be yourself.
That book, you must write.
ADVICE TO HIS DAUGHTER THE AUTHOR

Must Books

Books explaining how to succeed in a man's world, the corporate world, when written by a woman, are futile or fraudulent. English majors, who never worked for a corporation, produce the futile versions. After interviewing "successful" women and some PR-type males, the authors masquerade as authorities telling you how to succeed in a man's world, a world they never knew. Equally useless are books by psychologists who have never had a real job and books by professors — those who can do, those who can't teach.

The frauds are women who failed in the corporate world. After reading pop psychology self-help books and success books by the English majors and professors mentioned above, they masquerade as Communications Consultant, Management Expert, Management Consultant, Speaker, Lecturer, Executive Consultant, Consulting Firm Owner. They write books that tell you how to succeed in a man's world, a world in which they failed.

In short, all how to succeed-in-business books are ridiculous unless the book is by a person who does or has done what he's telling you how to do.

Read every book listed. The authors will save you countless years of learning the hard way and will explain what you should learn from the mistakes you make.

Many of these books are out of print. I found them in the Whittier Public Library or at used bookstores. Every single one deserves the time, effort and money to locate. Most libraries have inter-library lending and searching services. Attempt that first. Then try used bookstores. Some are hooked up via computer to do cooperative searches. Finally, pay a book finder whatever it takes. These books are worth it.

The Woman's Dress For Success Book, John Molloy, get latest edition. Re-read *The Play's The Thing* after this mandatory book.

Up The Organization, Robert Townsend, circa 1970. This is absolutely the best critique of Fortune 3000s ever written. You'll see exactly what's wrong and why. It didn't change companies one bit, but you'll know and realize the futility of dedicating yourself to "the company."

The Fast Track, John S. Budd, 1982. After your third job, memorize it. Written by someone who has been there. Some leftover Collectivist Guilt and Christian Dogma but easily ignored. Also, ignore that the fool actually thinks white collar workers can unionize and get great benefits from the company including work rules. What a foolish boy. Out of print in 1989.

Games Mother Never Taught You: Corporate Gamesmanship for Women, Betty Lehan Harragan, 1977. The shameful part is that she does not have a clue about the consequences of fundamental differences between males and females hormonally, physically and mentally. Almost as bad, she doesn't understand the actual significance of not playing team sports — confrontation is natural and necessary. Tippee toes instead of saying things bluntly and clearly. Ignore those faults and read it.

Knowing the Score: Play by play directions for women on the job. Betty Lehan Harragan, 1982. Ignore the crap about fighting for the cause. Women are not going to get in no matter what idealists think. Women have to do what Jews did when they were kept out of medical schools, build their own. If women want to run companies they'll have to build their own.

When I Say No, I Feel Guilty, Manuel Smith, 1976. Practice everything he teaches. Get thyself into Assertiveness Training. You'll become a woman who happens to be human first and female second in everyone's eyes and heart at work. You'll be able to handle the most manipulative boyfriend with ease. No one will be able to manipulate you except mother and father. There is no way to stop them, no cure except time and distance.

Mastering Assertiveness Skills At Work, Elaina Zuker. 1983. To be read only after *When I Say No, I Feel Guilty*. Sets up many common office manipulative moves others try and explains how to handle them.

How To Win The Meeting, Frank Snell, 1979. Explains how to control the decision making process in any organization. A meeting is not where discussion or the exchange of ideas takes place. A meeting is where future decisions are most easily influenced by force and persuasion. As I said in *Meeting Hints,* read this once a year while you're still in the corporate world.

How I Found Freedom In An Unfree World, Harry Browne, 1974. It gets your head out of the clouds or out of a hole "where the sun don't shine." He enables you to see clearly what the choices are and who's responsible for your life.

Winning Through Intimidation, Robert Ringer, 1972. Tells it like it is in the business world and the real world. Ringer ignored his own advice and was raped by Hollywood sharks who stole his entire fortune. Don't ignore his advice.

Catch 22, Joseph Heller, 1968. The first 100 pages are deliberately confusing. It's your duty to get through those 100 pages. You are being set up. On page 94 things start to fall into place. You'll see the parallels between the Army and General Cow and realize how unreal it all is so that you keep your sanity and perspective on what's really important.

Getting From 20 To 30, can't remember, circa 1979. Someone stole the library's copy. I had every young woman I knew read it cover to cover. The author makes the chaos of this decade understandable. Extremely hard to find but worth it.

The Caine Mutiny, Herman Wouk, 1952. The endless searches for strawberries at General Cow will make sense only after you read this. You'll understand why "The System" always backs its mediocre, forever. Pulitzer winner.

Welcome To The Monkey House, Kurt Vonnegut, 1968. A powerful collection of stories that teach and entertain. In particular, *Harrison Bergeron* and *Welcome To The Monkey House,* the book's title story. The company and government become understandable, from a big picture perspective.

The Revolt of Gunnar Ashe, can't remember, 1952. Although he's wearing the uniform, he's not in the army. They have your body but they can't have your soul, if you follow his philosophy. You'll learn what one can do even in the darkest moments to maintain a sense of dignity and sense of humor. Drafted into Hitler's Army before WWII started, Ashe was trapped but prevailed. You'll prevail over General Cow.

The Prince, Nick "The Brain" Machiavelli. Start with the Cliffs Notes. Read several analyses and summaries by anybody. Don't bother reading it. His principles are timeless. Practice them if you choose to stay in the corporate world after you have capital and have re-read *Mythical Glass Ceilings*.

Management And Machiavelli, Anthony Jay, 1968. Priceless! Eternal! I wish I had discovered it in 1968 instead of 1978. Damn! How much more money I could have had! If you're staying in the corporate world after you have accumulated your capital, re-read *Mythical Glass Ceilings*. After that dose of reality, if you stay in the corporate world, don't waste another second. Memorize it.

The Headhunter And You, Marge Rossman, circa 1980. A headhunter writing about headhunters, not a writer. How, why, when, and what to do and say when you contact or are contacted by a headhunter. Great!

The Trial, Franz Kafka. Read the Cliffs Notes first, analyses and summaries by anybody, then read it. The insanity of corporate bureaucracy becomes tolerable.

How To Make It In A Man's World, Letty Pogrebin, 1970. Timeless! Written by someone who's not a writer! She knows because she's done it, lived it, mastered it. Weary because she insists on being cute in print.

Parkinson's Law, C. Northecote Parkinson, circa 1962. Timeless! Work expands or contracts to fill the time allotted. Exactly! Quoting from this book at General Cow at the right moment will earn you several promotions. Quoting from it at the wrong moment is the same as saying, "The emperor wears no clothes."

The Peter Principle, Lawrence J. Peter, circa 1970. Timeless! People are promoted until they can't handle the position. They stay there, screwing up everything forever because they obviously can't be promoted. A realistic explanation of why companies are so screwed up. Just like *Parkinson's Law,* quoting from this book at the right moment . . . .

The Virtue Of Selfishness, Ayn Rand, 1970. A collection of essays that puts everything into perspective. It's much easier to read Rand's novels first and more fun: *Anthem, The Fountainhead, Atlas Shrugged, We The Living* and her play, *The Night of January 16th.* Life and work become intertwined realistically. Rand is foolishly mistaken about the virtue of abstinence during absence and dangerously psychotic about ignoring or not expressing one's emotions. Overlook those flaws and have a grand time roaring, on rails of Rearden metal, into an irrefutable understanding of what really makes the world go 'round.

Winning Through Negotiation, don't remember, 1980. Best explanation of how to deal with everyone in your life. Exceptionally clear on getting a raise. Great! Get it anyway possible.

Rites Of Passage At $100,000+ and ***Executive Job-Changing Workbook***, John Lucht, 1994. Beyond mandatory! See note at the end of *Creative Writing–Resumes* for details.

As mentioned many times, buy and read every book on body language you can find. Start with mine. See *Other Books By R. Don Steele* for ordering instructions.

There is no such thing as
a moral book or an immoral book.
Books are well written or badly written.
Preface to *Picture of Dorian Gray* 1891 OSCAR WILDE

In Summary

Business is nothing more than common sense. Ninety percent of most jobs is communicating clearly while getting along with people. Every company does nothing more than I-P-O. Every company does the same things. Every company does those things differently.

Survival drives every decision. Not growth, not profit, not expansion. Survival.

Money, alone, makes it possible for you to be the person who determines your future. General Cows are the only kinds of companies that pay $60k to women under 30.

Everyone who reads your resume discounts it 10 to 40 percent.

Your appearance is the single most important means being taken seriously. That costume doesn't scream, "I am successful, all business, reliable and know exactly what I'm doing." Religiously follow Molloy's *The Woman's Dress For Success Book.* Women with glasses are taken more seriously. Get a pair.

Women who want to make $100k must dress like the *men* who do make $100k. Never look sexy, even at work on weekends. If men don't comment on your appearance, you're doing it right.

People don't change jobs until it hurts too much, so, most people don't give good interview. Learning to get hired is nothing more than practice. Go interviewing.

Shaking hands enables your subconscious to make lightning value judgements. Assert your equality with each and every male, and female, you meet. Put your hand out first.

Pause, gather yourself. Deliver your lines with energy, eye contact and enthusiasm, then shut up. Sell: you're not going to leave for *kirsch, kinder und kusch*. Persuade by the way you dress, talk, walk, sit. Speak of career paths and long range plans.

No one likes change. Job jumpers earn more because they have to be paid more to leave the comfort of Mother Cow.

Getting hired is like getting seduced. If you are easy, the guy thinks you aren't worth much. If you play too hard to get, you don't get seduced.

The only thing that works is asking for more and settling for less. When you have to say "no," cry a lot first. They're not angry, they feel sorry for you! You have a job. You don't need them. They need you. All you have to do is say "no" and wait.

It's easy to get rid of you before probation is over, afterward, nearly impossible. Everyone appreciates being remembered by name. It makes us feel important. New fish in the tank are tested until they prove to be dangerous.

The longer you stay, the softer, lazier you become. We all coast once we get into a routine. Stay hungry.

If you don't understand how lonely, afraid and neurotic your co-workers are, you'll never understand why things are so screwed up. They have changed from aiming at the maximum possible to the minimum excusable. The company-as-community fulfills co-workers. They need the company, not vice versa.

You can only say what you really think behind closed doors, off the record to an ambitious, talented, Machiavellian.

The longer you're unhappy, the more normal it seems. You don't expect to be happy, so you don't try.

Love or respect, emphasis on *or,* is what each and every person wants.

If you can't trash deadwood, deadbeats and the brain dead, you're dead. Being responsible without the authority to accomplish the task is career suicide.

The Good Life is nothing more than getting the best out of the cards you were dealt. "Getting the best out of" means being the happiest you can be.

The fifth card is the most dangerous, *POWERFUL FOR ONLY A FEW YEARS*. Don't let it destroy your long-run happiness because you don't consider the long-run consequences of squandering your powerful years (a) playing in the wrong game (b) playing in the right game without knowing what the rules really are (c) changing games after you've lost nearly all your power.

What do you want to be doing ten years from now? Arguing with your eight year old about picking up his toys or arguing with the Art Director about the layout? It's one or the other. You decide. You must choose, and soon.

When only 1 woman in 20 has only 1 chance in 30, neither a conspiracy or a glass ceiling is necessary. You can have any job you want, as long as it's a "woman's job." *Translation:* not top management. The only reason to work for a Fortune 3000 is because that's where you can make the most money during the next ten years. The only reason to make the most money, is so that you can do what you want, sooner.

Never borrow money unless you can make more money with it. Do not spend money you can save. Do not borrow money, you'll be a wage slave forever. ***Exception:*** Student loans backed by the US Government. Borrow every penny you can.

Money is not an end. Money increases your options. Money increases your independence and autonomy. Money is the power to say, "Screw you!" Money makes it possible to live your life where, how and with whom you want.

The people with the gold make the rules. It always was that way, it is that way, it will always be that way. Those with gold have it because they are smarter, more ruthless, more cunning, more fill-in-the-blank than the rest of us. The rich didn't get that way by accident. The poor aren't that way because we don't give them something.

Damned few in top management care if you, your co-workers, your boss or even his boss are treated unfairly or abused. Most employees, are as expendable as a sheet of paper.

Before any goal can be reached, you must know what the goal is. Before any journey can begin, you must know where you are going. To get to your destination, you must know where you are now. To truly know where you are, you must know how you got here. If you don't know what you want, you can't go after it. If you don't go after it, you'll never get it. If you don't know where you want to go, you can't get anywhere.

To prevent wasting precious short time, you need to know (a) what you like to do (b) what you have the ability to do (c) what you don't have the ability to do.

Men own, men run, men control, men decide. The corporation is a man's world. To be successful, you must understand men.

Decline help as diplomatically as possible. Make statements to ask questions. Some men won't criticize your work. They're afraid you'll cry. Ask for criticism in plain English. Don't let them keep you down by apologizing for language.

You move up the ladder faster when you grasp, and can discuss intelligently, the big picture. Find out everything you can about your company and your industry.

The more inside info you know, the better your chances are of maneuvering into the right place at the right time to get the promotion. The more your know, the better you can position yourself to avoid the layoff. The most valuable information is about change. Change is opportunity.

Secretaries let things slip when jabbering with you. They leave the folder open. Cultivate relationships with secretaries.

To get promoted you have to take many small risks and several major ones every year. Begin by taking risks that you'll probably be successful with. When there's less at stake you're relaxed and function better so you're successful. In Assertiveness Training, you learn how to take risks so that you are successful from the beginning. Get into Assertiveness Training, today.

You'll like two of them simply because of who and what they are. You'll want to slowly strangle two of them simply because of who and what they are. Polite indifference will be your feeling toward the others. They feel the same about you.

Dispassionate, objective relationships are all one can achieve at a corporation. Never, absolutely never, disclose anything personal, particularly to another woman. Never even mention your personal life to anyone.

Good friends prevent you from becoming too lonely. Being too lonely makes us careless about the kind of persons we let get close to us at work and out in the real world.

Never attempt to get your social or sexual needs met by

people at work. You become ripe for use and abuse by everyone because you need them, not vice versa.

After we males have air, water and food, the next priority is sex. Yeah. We'd like to be friends too, but sex is at the top of our list. Everyone, that includes you, gets sex and love all mixed up.

You need friends in high places to get into high places. Bring your friends along. 20 percent of the staff accomplishes 80 percent of the work. Identify the 20 percent by noticing they do what they say they will do. Believe only deeds. Words are cheap.

Create an enemy by causing someone to feel extremely strong, unpleasant emotions: fear, shame, hurt, anger.

Who gets the promotion if you don't? He's your main rival. Anyone who believes he deserves, or has a chance for the promotion, is a rival. After identifying an enemy, keep notes on his weak and strong points. Develop a strategy to exploit his weakness and avoid his strength.

Dealing with women is extremely complex and extremely dangerous. They are devious, two-faced, cold and catty.

The physical, psychological, emotional and hormonal differences between men and women is why women behave differently than men. Women behave differently in the workplace, that's why they are treated differently in the workplace.

To make big bucks you have to stand up for yourself. You have to confront people talking behind your back, starting rumors, sabotaging your work and other ways of fighting. Learn how to confront them and win. Get into Assertiveness Training!

The enemies of *The Other Woman* are all women who want to get ahead. There is little room near the top for women. All women wearing the uniform want that opening. The woman who acts like she's on your side is the most dangerous. Treachery and betrayal can only follow trust. You cannot be stabbed in the back if you don't turn your back. She cannot strike your Achilles heel if she doesn't know where it is.

Not every person will like you, especially when you become a supervisor. It is impossible to be liked when you're in charge. Focus on earning respect — do, or have done, what you're asking your troops to do.

Without alliances, you are powerless. Without power you are

nothing. If you don't ally, no matter which one wins, you're on the outside. Promotions and perks do not reach outsiders. Outsiders don't get protected from layoffs, don't get inside information.

Fighting for what you want is necessary, normal and natural. If something is desirable you must fight. Fighting is necessary to get what you want and to keep what you have.

Strife is a given. In life, things do not go smoothly. Tranquil is abnormal. Conflict occurs when somebody resists aggression. No resistance, no conflict. Surrender to keep the peace or fight for what you want.

Make certain your opponent has something at stake. Pick your enemies carefully. Only fight when winning helps you reach the long run goal you seek. Otherwise, avoid fighting. You can't lose if you don't fight.

Peace is assured only when your rival's greed is controlled by his fear. He must be afraid to attack. You must have a rep before your enemies will control themselves. You get a rep only when you earn it, after you kill some challengers.

When it's necessary to do battle, never let it be known you are going to fight. Smile sweetly, then silently smash his skull, from behind. Do not bluff unless you're willing to fight or if fleeing is too costly.

A rumor of the sexual kind spreads faster and is embellished more grandly than other rumors. She doesn't realize her audience is only one person, the person she denies it to, while his audience will be the entire office. Worst of all, she doesn't realize her denial will not be spread.

Re-read *Be Tough* three times. Promotions come your way only if your boss respects you. Men only respect and reward toughness.

People respect you only if you are hard-nosed about money because of all the psychological and mystical power money carries with it. Pay for your own lunch. Do not back off.

An employee without a degree is unpromotable. After your first job, the only thing that counts is how much your present company pays you and that you have a degree, any degree.

Selling yourself is the most important aspect of office politics. Learn how to get up in front of people and have them believe you, and believe in you. Take Assertiveness Training, Acting and Speech classes. Become more confident about life in general. Running is the best way. It's good for your self-esteem and that's good for your self confidence.

There is no company to sacrifice yourself to, or for. The company is a piece of paper in Delaware. That paper gives those who own it the legal right to pretend the corporation is an individual. The company will survive if it has to sacrifice all of you grunts. If you're not at the company for the money, what in the hell are you there for?

The life cycle of a corporation is the same as yours — birth, growth, maturity, degeneration, death. Fortune 3000 corporations are so big, further growth is impossible. All are either in decline or approaching it. Top Management concerns itself solely with milking every last possible perk and personal dollar out of the corporation.

When males and females are put together in the same building, sooner or later they get together. Round pegs fit into round holes. Sex is the driving force, even at the office.

Fight back instantly with no sweetness. "Get your hand off my leg! NOW!" Storm out. Any delay implies consent. Any politeness implies he's supposed to try harder.

When men are away from home, their rule of engagement is, there are no rules.

Flirting is death. Being friendly is dangerous. All business and no bullshit is mandatory. Men believe any female who is nice wants to get horizontal. Get this: males interpret friendliness as an invitation. Don't be friendly.

A married man is, *getting some on the side, the sly devil.* The young woman is a slut, someone never to be trusted in a position of responsibility.

Don't distract men. Look moderately severe, not like a she-male. Be unapproachable because of your engagement. Avoid situations where a move is possible: after work, overtime, weekends, travel.

Self-deluded CEOs surrounded by yes-men are not why most Fortune 3000s are screwed up. The primary reason is everyone tells his own boss what he wants to hear. Nobody knows what the hell is going on down below.

Those at the very top, by their oblique communication, have made it clear that you must be as indirect as possible but make it seem as if you are being straightforward. Every order has three possible interpretations. Vagueness is the key to flexibility. Even written orders are open to misunderstanding. One misunderstands to his own advantage. The person issuing the order deliberately confounds the wording so he can later deny or claim responsibility.

The CEO doesn't tell his Executive VPs everything. They don't tell their Division Managers everything and of course the Division Managers don't tell their VPs everything and so on all the way down to the grunts who do the actual work. Everybody is in the dark and keeps everybody else in the dark. Straightforward, communications do not exist, it's that simple.

There are no real issues, only who's going to make money if the status quo gets changed? or who keeps making money if the status quo remains? To understand, follow the money. Who keeps his job if the status quo stays? Who loses his job if the status quo changes? Too many people have too much to lose if anything changes. That's why it's so hard to change anything.

People only go to a dentist when it hurts bad enough. People only go to a shrink when it hurts bad enough. Profit from this. If a situation at the office is causing pain, that's when people are open to new ideas. In your own life, don't wait until it hurts so bad you are forced to change. Pain distorts your vision, preventing accurate choices.

You, alone, must choose what your "real purpose" is. If you want children, have job skills to support yourself and your children should Mr. Rite turn into Mr. Hyde.

When a woman tries to fulfill her own expectations and the expectations her husband of what a wife and mother should be, she behaves like a farmer's wife. But she behaves as unlike a farmer's wife when she tries to fulfill her own expectations of what a suburban career woman is.

You can't be a career woman and a mother and do a respectable job at either. If you are not the person who raises your child, she is your offspring, not your daughter.

Everyone hopes that if he doesn't focus on the magnitude of the consequences, doesn't discuss the pros and cons, doesn't allow himself to feel, then evaluate the meaning of the powerful emotions connected with the choice, that somehow the necessity to choose goes away. In reality, most people choose by not preventing the "accident" from happening. Consider the lifelong consequences and lifelong costs and lifelong risks. Be logical, rational and realistic.

None of top management's decisions have anything to do with what makes sense, or makes the most money, or what ensures the prosperity and survival of the company into the middle of the next century. Decisions are not arrived at by considering principles. Decisions are pragmatic. "Works" means: What do we have to do to pay the stockholders a dividend?

The incompetent are afraid of change. They fear being discovered. At age 48, this is all there is, or can ever be. He knows that. But he also knows he's incompetent. A reprimand from higher ups is the worst thing. Terrified they'll realize he's a fraud, he conducts his life to, above all else, avoid criticism.

Middle managers believe that by doing absolutely nothing, no higher ups will notice them. If no higher ups notice them, they can't be criticized. If they aren't criticized, they won't be discovered as incompetent.

Most blatantly stupid decisions are made for high level political reasons. Do not make a scene. Do not ridicule.

Avoid exit-interviews with any excuse. If trapped say nothing bad about anyone. Don't burn bridges.

Happiness: Ayn Rand says it's a man you love and a career you love. Amen. ***Success:*** Being able to do what you want to do, when you want to do it, with whom you want to do it. ***Feedback:*** Ask men what turns them off most about women at work, which ones they respect, which ones they hate and why. Ask anyone who didn't hire you, why he didn't. Don't defend yourself. Shut up and listen.

Don't give anyone from work advice. Don't even listen to someone's problems. Never mention you're on your way to another company as soon as you can get ten percent. Never mention you're working on a ten year plan of independence.

Do not drink alcohol. Booze loosens your tongue and lowers your guard. It makes him brave enough to make a pass.

Would you recruit from the unemployed or the employed?

People with jobs are automatically better than those without. It makes no difference if you got fired, laidoff or quit. Nothing in this book will do you one damn bit of good if you quit.

Make all customers love and cherish you. Charm and win over every customer at every level. Have him, them, gush about you, in writing, to your boss's boss. ***Contradictory Advice:*** Use every single one of your feminine wiles to woo and win your customer's favor.

Nothing important gets done by the book. Everything gets done because of power, influence, negotiation and compromise. And, everything gets done without even referring to unwritten rules. The ultimate rule: The big fish eat the little fish.

Obeying the rules, written and unwritten, makes it impossible to advance quickly. The Big Boys got where they are by bending the rules. *Unwritten Rule VIII:* What thou can get away with is what's allowed. Anyone who wants to be considered a comer in the company must show her shrewdness by taking short cuts.

There are two things to learn about any game (a) what the rules really are (b) how far each rule can be bent, stretched or broken before you're thrown out of the game.

After a few years and a few corporations this tiny piece of play acting won't seem hypocritical, it'll seem insignificant compared to the lies, misrepresentation, broken promises, delays, excuses each and every company pulls on you. Take acting classes. You're going to need them.

Work for a temporary agency. Go from company to company for a year. You'll learn more than women who work five years at the same company.

Since they're trying to hire you they obviously want you. They won't fire you for saying "no." If they stall, do not chase them. The person who says "no" has all the power.

Meetings are about figuring out how JB is thinking and feeling as part of paving the way for an effort that's still a few months away. Emotion drives decisions more powerfully than logic. The idea is to edge everyone toward some eventual consensus.

Your ideas are from a suspect source, from the mind of a female. Men are willing to fight for their ideas. Men enjoy the fight. They are going to attack you because they don't believe you could think of anything useful.

Enlist the troops before the battle. Get them to think it is partially their idea. Explain your idea so that you'll take all the risk and they'll get some credit without saying that.

Express yourself clearly and to the point. Figure out what you're going to say. Edit until you have a concise statement. Go last. Present your thoughts in a single 20-word sentence or even better, two 10-word sentences.

If there is a witch hunt a witch must be burned at the stake. If a Who Shot John meeting is held, blame must be placed.

When a middle manager dies, he is replaced by someone who's not quite as dead. The replacement's been here the longest, never pissed off anyone important.

Crisis is a way of life. Managers don't act, they react. Brushfire after brushfire has to be put out because he's too busy putting out fires to figure out why they start.

Management Club keeps them happy and homogenized and gets them all in one room so Top Management can examine them closely for latent troublemakers and the dangerously incompetent.

Although every boss has been sent to seminars that teach him how to plan, schedule, coordinate, cooperate and communicate, most only react. Their primary concern is to avoid criticism from above after every crisis. Instead of developing a procedure to prevent the crisis from happening again, they fix blame. They never have the right person doing the right job. People who are detail-oriented are in charge of big-picture people doing detail work. Most bosses can't choose the right person for the right job because (a) they, themselves, can't see the big-picture (b) they don't know what the task requires because they've never done it (c) they don't have a clue as to how to judge anyone's strengths and weaknesses. It never occurs to them to ask someone what she likes to do or hates to do, what she's good at or what she considers herself not so good at.

Young women have trouble seeing men-in-authority as merely human. This causes them to doubt their own intelligence, thereby delaying the onset of self-confidence without which they cannot proceed. Cure yourself.

Symbols of power seldom reflect the capability of the man. It takes a woman three years before she finally realizes most bosses are incompetent. Most employees don't want to know that those in authority are not capable, not effective, not in control, not logical, not rational. They want Daddy to be strong. They don't want to know Daddy is a frightened buffoon.

Every boss works a certain way. He has his neurotic, safe, secure rut. Do not create anything new for him. Figure out what his rut is, then feed whatever he wants into the rut.

Nearly every boss makes simple work complicated, tiresome and exasperating. Each does this differently. It depends on his own lack of ability, his own fears, and his own neuroses. It makes no difference what bizarre concerns your boss has, identify his madness and conform. When you conform, he sees you as efficient and mentally healthy like he sees himself.

If he's focused on trivia, your chances to have him authorize big, long range changes are enhanced. He'll only question trivial portions of the plan! When The Pope, visited for a progress review, he immediately noticed the "mistake," ordered it changed, felt smug and important then left without noticing the big picture, Michelangelo's world-changing, work of art.

All he knows is he's gotta change something or he ain't earning his $200k. So I give him somethin' to notice, somethin' easy to change. He's happy. I'm happy.

These guys saw themselves as Big Picture Executives concerned with the bottom line. They never once questioned the cost of a line item. They never once questioned if the line item was necessary. "Cutting" millions at the stroke of a felt tip pen made them feel powerful and important.

Stereotypes are based in fact and on fact. Common nicknames given to female managers: Dragon Lady. Bitch Witch. Dyke of Earl. Women cannot get ahead unless they are TOUGH. Tough on their employees, tough on everybody. Obey her like a man but treat her like a lady.

If you think you may stay in the corporate world, do whatever you must to work for a bright, powerful old-timer. You'll learn more from him in two years than you will from all other bosses combined.

Your boss is responsible to his boss for the work you do. It's not your work, it's your boss's work, he merely delegates it to you. The only job you have is the one he wants done.

The corporation is set up like the military. "Salute the uniform not the man." Sow respect for superiors even if they are inferiors. Respect for the chain of command is a must.

Forthright talk is reserved for specific moments in certain situations, behind closed doors, off the record and only to someone you can trust with your career. Knowing when, and to whom, is the essence and art of Office Politics.

Adaptable, considerate, flexible, smart people get ahead. Stubborn, rude, ignorant people don't. Being flexible doesn't mean selling out, it means adjusting to fit in.

Behave the same with everyone: polite, considerate, respectful. Everyone considers you fair, honest and straight. Confident people don't kowtow. Defer, yes. Kowtow, no.

Give quiet recognition of your boss's extremely modest talents. Pick out something he did right. Acknowledge it. His boss never pats him on the back. Anything beyond polite, simple acknowledgement marks you as a potential sex partner.

Do not disagree with your boss. Do not snipe or back bite your boss or his boss. Share your opinion, exchange views but don't fight.

Play along when stupid decisions are made at or above your boss's level. Exposing the obvious is traitorously disloyal.

Buy and read every book on body language you can find.

See a crisis as the opportunity to shine. Remain calm and rational amidst the chaos. Show concern, thoughtfulness and steadfastness while the project burns. Don't yell or get angry. You'll look like a pillar of strength.

Most members of management don't have a clue as to what's really important. They attained their status by doing as they were ordered. They enforce rules that make no sense. He doesn't care if you do your job at half the cost of your predecessor. He cares if you're in your seat at 7:58 AM and are still there at 5:06 PM.

Work your ass off, put in the long hours, do the grunt work and endure the drudgery. It gets you noticed. The first step to getting promoted is getting noticed.

Smooth sailing is not possible. Disease, death, divorce, abortion, treachery, insanity? You cannot escape life's natural and normal problems. Change is the only law.

Change companies every chance until you are have enough money to survive the eventual rainy days. Continue changing until you have enough money to do what you really want to do.

Stop waiting to be chosen, invited, persuaded, asked to accept. Stop waiting to be told what to do. Take the initiative. Learn new skills. Volunteer for more work. Show you are motivated. Show you'll take risks.

Re-read *52 Random Truths* three times.

Knowing how much you should be paid is the first step to getting paid more. How much your predecessor made is crucial. Key points: Do one helluva a job. Make him look good by doing a helluva job. Credit him as the basis for your good proposals. Make him feel important by acknowledging his limited capabilities. He thinks you may leave him because he suspects others are trying to hire you.

Reach out. Ask directly, once you've shown your boss you're worth the money. Be positive, upbeat and interested in helping him look better. If you don't get a raise by asking for it, you get respect. You never get fired for asking. You get fired for issuing ultimatums or demanding.

Rating everyone excellent is caused by Top Management not wanting to get sued. "On paper, everybody's equal." Do not sign a less than excellent evaluation under any circumstances.

They don't pay you to do your job because it's fun. They pay you because it's not fun.

The quickest way up the hierarchy is to win the favor of a high ranking executive. The only way is to be noticed, work where he works. Finagle a job in front of the biggest boy you can. Make small talk he's interested in. Get informed.

Solve problems. List all the means by which you want to increase your own power while shedding uncongenial work and unwelcome responsibility. Make it appear these are the inevitable steps toward the solution of a pressing problem.

Being able to write it down and have it understood then executed will take you far up the ladder. This skill adds another $10k on top of whatever else you make the first five years.

Working on the Five Year Plan exposes you to the biggest Big Boys. Better, you see the big picture of the entire company and how your division fits in.

Avoid it becoming yes or no. Plan B, a well above average raise. Plan C, transfer to Contracts. Always have ways to save face, his and yours.

You, alone, must decide which of life's infinite paths to take.

And when you finally fly away, I'll be hoping I served you well.
For all the wisdom of a lifetime, no one can ever tell.
But whatever road you choose, I'm right behind you, win or lose.
Forever Young, sung by Rod Stewart BOB DYLAN

Last word: appearance counts, sometimes even in the real world. Nine years ago I sold my Jag E-Type and bought a Volvo. My manic driving style did not change, yet I haven't had a ticket since. After volleyball, over a beer, I talked with an cop about this. He said, "Don't even see Volvos. We're programmed to notice Vettes, Jags, Porsches, you know, go-fast stuff . . . anything jacked up, with stripes or painted red, even Toyotas."

Once again, goodbye and "good luck." R. Don Steele, Whittier, California, September 1994.

Other Books By R. Don Steele

BODY LANGUAGE

A Guide For Men And Women
During Courtship And Dating

The title says it all. Full of photos and clear, easy to understand explanations of the *how-what-when* as well as the thought provoking, controversial *whys*. Approximately 100 pages, 8.5 x 5.5, $18.95 and $3 shipping. Publication date: 2-95.

THE STUPID GAZETTE

As the pope cheers, civilization is being overrun by cretins breeding like lemmings. It's time for a laugh break. Roar as Retards, Porkers, Don Quixotes, Hypocrites, Religious Leaders and stories of the just-plain-stupid unfold. The world's finest stupid people entertain you with authentic newspaper reports of bungled suicides, lost causes, foolish robberies, sexual miscues, bureaucratic ineptness, political thievery. Guaranteed not to contain articles from *The Star, National Enquirer* or *People* magazine. 324 pages 8.5 by 11. $18.95 and $3 shipping.

NOTE: Don is developing Instructional Video Tapes on body language, one for Office Politics and one for Courtship. They are scheduled to be available in late 1995. Price estimated at $49.95 postage paid for a one hour tape of either subject. Please write and inquire about availability before ordering.

Order From:

STEEL BALLS PRESS
Box 807 Whittier CA 90608

GUARANTEED MONEY BACK, NO QUESTIONS ASKED!

INDEX

accumulate capital: 74, 278, 282
acting classes: 32, 93, 191, 193
affair(s): 87, 102, 107, 125, 148, 150, 211
after work: 145, 152, 153, 156, 271-275
ageism: 267
aggression: 121, 126
aggressive: 35, 101, 110, 111, 121, 126, 139, 148, 156, 272, 274, 276, 277
alcohol: 175, 230
alcoholic: 87, 184, 220
all business: 26, 30, 106, 113, 146, 148, 151, 233, 287
annual reports: 83, 252
annual review: 243, 247, 249
anti-semitic: 240
apologize: 41, 68, 71, 106, 130, 153, 214, 223, 270, 291
appearances: 3, 115, 150, 226
arch enemy: 71-73, 105-107, 125, 127, 132, 133
Aristophanes: 80, 108
Armani: 115
ass kisser(ing): 81, 160, 161, 219, 221, 243
assertiveness training: 66, 95, 96, 110-112, 137, 171, 246, 303
attrition: 38, 89, 202
Audrey, Robert: 117
Auschwitz syndrome: 60
autonomous: 267
avoid blame: 166, 297
babies: 13, 94, 108, 114, 151, 164
baby: 14, 38, 47, 67, 147, 152, 176, 224
Bacon, Francis: 1, 75, 77, 87, 100, 105, 158, 168, 187, 246, 252, 283, 293
Baruch, Bernard: 280
benefits: 35, 44, 195, 234, 255, 278, 303
betrayal: 56, 113, 119, 131, 228, 295
big picture: 82-86, 203, 206, 211-215, 253, 254, 258, 259, 304
Big Boys: 31, 82, 84, 85, 157, 167, 239, 252, 259, 279
biological clock: 294
biological nature: 276
biology: 2, 75, 109, 110, 162, 299
Bismarck: 107, 280, 281
Black, Cathleen: 226
blacklisted: 106, 107, 240
blonde: 30
bluff: 70, 126, 246, 248
board of directors: 90, 142, 167, 229, 291
body language: 35, 51, 70, 91, 111, 126, 132, 136, 146, 198, 222, 223, 306
bonding: 272, 274
boss's boss: 92, 170, 173, 184, 185, 225, 230, 261
boss, female: 215, 285
boyfriend: 30, 66, 78, 93, 108, 174, 207, 208, 268, 269, 303
brain wiring: 162, 235, 275
brainwashed(ing): 74, 77, 78, 94, 97, 98, 108, 111, 139, 172, 293, 294
Branden, Nathaniel: 93, 96
breasts: 26, 30, 39, 157, 181, 189
bridges: 171, 186, 263
Brown, Helen Gurley: 149, 174, 268
Browne, Harry: 42, 304
buddy bosses: 207
bureaucratic: 44, 47, 136, 182, 247
bureaucrats: 47, 135, 155, 158, 163, 190, 224, 247, 290
business uniform: 27-32
buzzwords: 18, 22, 36
Byron, Lord: 175
Campbell, Joseph: 270
career plans: 37, 38
careers: 14, 31, 124, 146
Catch 22: 95, 199, 211, 304
catty(iness): 28, 100, 108, 116, 237
chain of command: 218, 219, 248, 262
change jobs: 7, 9, 34, 37, 42, 164, 285
cheerful: 33, 176, 178
Chesterfield, Lord: 14, 48, 64, 194
children: 14-16, 38, 50, 56, 85, 93, 124, 151, 168, 172, 180, 229, 236, 267, 269, 272, 273, 277, 287, 292-297
choices: 2, 6, 13, 76, 128, 164, 275, 297, 304
christmas cards: 176
Cinderella: 270, 293, 294
coffin: 13, 269, 299
Collins, Jackie: 145
communicate: 43, 159, 206, 210, 239
communicating: 4, 161, 162, 202, 212, 220, 224
communication: 88, 161, 162
compete: 94, 109, 118, 144, 151, 175, 189, 233, 276-278, 282, 299, 300
competition: 5, 16, 22, 28, 65, 71, 78, 94, 102, 109, 111, 112, 120, 182, 244, 249, 260, 271, 276-278, 285
competitors: 22, 84, 123, 159, 188, 196, 244, 245
compliment(s): 29, 221
conditioning: 111, 277
confidence: 21-23, 31, 35,

37, 91, 95, 96, 115, 138, 208, 233, 261, 263, 287
confident: 17, 32, 35, 43, 50, 95, 96, 128, 138, 140, 180, 212, 220, 233, 244, 268
conflict(s): 51, 92, 108, 120, 121, 126
confront: 51, 60, 69, 93, 95, 97, 109-112, 152, 179, 218, 272, 289
confrontation: 68, 110-112, 128, 130, 303
Confucius: 116
conscientious: 3, 15, 19, 36, 142, 209
court: 67, 133, 141, 148, 155, 156, 190, 230, 240, 261
courted: 43, 241, 249
courtship: 40, 146, 147, 223, 244, 245
cover letter: 21, 24, 40
criticism: 47, 67, 95, 136, 168, 206, 235, 236, 301
criticize: 67, 218, 247, 256
cry: 34, 40, 41, 66, 67, 95, 112, 131, 179, 200, 234, 247, 286, 287, 291
cry a lot: 34, 40, 41, 247
crying: 66, 95, 111, 131, 155, 235, 237, 285
culture: 2, 3, 65, 93, 96, 208, 235, 267, 294, 295
customer(s): 21, 69, 70, 131, 185, 186, 219, 250, 253, 278, 279
cute: 4, 29, 32, 68, 112, 267, 290, 291, 305
Davis, Al: 97, 128
Dayan, Moshe: 104
defer: 220-222
deferential: 9, 217, 262
degrees: 47, 135, 136, 210, 232
diction: 32
Dirty Harry: 266, 292
divorce rate: 11, 295
divorced women: 57, 124, 145
dress for success: 27, 28, 33, 156, 303
Drucker, Peter: 197
Duke of Wellington: 271
Ecclesiastes: 48, 300
engagement ring: 16, 29, 38, 114, 156, 207, 215
equality: 31, 68, 277, 281
evolution: 109, 272, 274
fair play: 3, 79, 81, 269
fear of success: 237
feminist: 49, 81, 109, 120, 180, 200, 215, 274, 296
feminists: 99, 109, 270, 271, 273, 275, 281
fight or flight: 121, 126
fighting: 5, 65, 103, 105, 109, 112, 119, 120, 122, 125, 126, 133, 154, 155, 180, 222, 283, 303
first impressions: 26, 43, 48, 116
five year plans: 92, 252, 254
flirt(ing): 50, 146, 291
follow the money: 1, 163, 164
Forbes Magazine: 266
Forbes, Malcolm: 266
Ford, Henry: 276
formula behavior: 177
Fortune 500: 64, 276
founder: 141, 182
Friedan, Betty: 150, 181
friendly: 48, 100, 106, 146, 148, 155, 156, 176, 184, 277
friends with men: 101
future boss: 16, 33, 36, 40-42
gender: 4, 152, 172, 189, 270, 277, 281
gender equality: 277, 281
gender neutral: 4, 270
generation x: 56, 296
gestures: 146, 147
getaway car: 119, 171
getting noticed: 226, 260
glass ceilings: 271, 275, 276, 278, 305
glasses: 31, 45, 144, 146, 225, 234
goals: 10-12, 22, 38, 83, 123, 216, 233, 247, 264, 294
gofer: 213
golden rule: 184, 280
gone with the wind: 294
good and evil: 172
good mother: 267, 296
good-old-boy: 2
good old feedback: 177
good worker: 47, 226, 261
gossip: 16, 47, 49, 87, 89, 202, 212, 219, 244, 271
GPA: 135, 268
grammar: 32
gravy train: 107, 229, 231
hair: 26, 30, 80, 113, 146, 189
haircuts: 30
handshake: 36, 68
happiness: 8, 79, 172, 250, 269, 294
hard evidence: 8, 125, 154, 155, 242, 243, 248, 288
hard to get: 39, 40, 114
headhunter: 22, 43, 242, 249, 305
heels: 29, 30, 32
Heraclitus: 228
hierarchy of needs: 28, 145
high school: 4, 5, 20, 47, 108, 115, 120
home run: 114, 115
home wrecker: 125, 150
homosexual(s): 21, 152, 240
honesty: 81, 267, 283
honor: 105, 109, 273
house organ: 58, 60, 260
How I Found Freedom In An Unfree World: 42, 304
hunt: 108, 200, 271, 273
hurts bad enough: 159, 164
hypocrites: 150, 282
hypocritical: 193, 230
hysterical female: 285, 286
I-P-O: 4, 5, 83

illness: 88-90
impression: 27, 43, 89, 138, 174, 252
in touch: 99, 103, 192, 194, 227, 241, 260
independence: 8, 44, 75, 172, 180
independent: 6, 10, 20, 57, 62, 119, 134, 172, 173, 267, 275, 290
inflating yourself: 18
inside information: 102, 119
insubordination: 172
interviewer: 7, 20, 24, 33, 35, 37
intuition: 48, 63, 72, 98, 101, 116, 122, 136, 191, 197, 209, 218, 235
IQ: 173, 240, 247
Jesus Of Nazareth: 232
Jews: 85, 127, 238, 303
job description: 23, 92, 210, 224, 254, 258, 259
job jumpers: 39
journey: 40, 44, 265, 267
Julius Caesar: 119
jungle: 29, 104, 120, 141, 174
justice: 81, 134, 139, 150, 175, 220, 230, 267, 269, 283
kd lang: 265
keep a secret: 180, 246
kid(s): 11, 27, 50, 55-57, 62, 68, 81, 115, 127, 151, 180, 210, 267, 287, 293, 296
kind: 34, 77, 99, 100, 128, 157, 189, 242, 250, 284, 286
KISS: 204, 221, 225, 234, 246, 255, 289
kissing up: 3, 209, 212
kowtow: 220
laid off: 9, 12, 88
laugh: 106, 122, 130, 201, 291, 292
lawyer: 142, 155, 158
layoff: 87-89, 99, 167, 182-186, 207, 239, 246
Lear, Frances: 268
learn from mistakes: 287
lesbians: 125, 152, 178, 181
life cycle: 142, 313
limousine liberals: 282
linebacker: 151, 207
lipstick: 26, 29, 30
long range goal: 4, 10, 298
lose it: 285, 286
lottery: 11, 131, 172
love or respect: 62
lover: 101, 107, 151
Lowell, James Russell: 120
loyalty: 53, 61, 81, 117, 167
Lucas, George: 135
lunch: 25, 29, 30, 43, 49, 74, 75, 102, 152, 175, 179, 219, 225, 291
lust: 77, 78, 153, 233
Lyttelton, Lord: 98
Machiavelli: 1, 57, 256, 276, 305
mafia: 276
magic number: 7, 9, 43, 107, 123, 218
makeup: 26, 30, 147, 288
man's world: 1, 116, 137, 264, 270, 299, 300, 302, 305
management club: 85, 178, 204
manipulativeness: 110
married man: 145, 150, 151
Maslow, Abe: 28, 145
MBA: 4, 5, 135-137, 247, 259
Mead, Margaret: 135
media: 19, 24, 282
men-in-authority: 208
mentor: 40, 216, 247
Michelangelo: 213
mid-life crisis: 8, 105
might makes right: 174, 188
military: 28, 61, 65, 161, 163, 182, 217, 218, 229, 254-256, 276
millionaire: 149, 269
minimum excusable: 56, 57
mistakes: 34, 67, 73, 79, 95, 111, 203, 206, 213, 237, 260, 287, 301, 302
Molloy, John: 27, 33, 303
Monroe, Marilyn: 156
Montana, Joe: 285
mood: 42, 173, 198, 215, 216
most dangerous: 79, 107, 113, 123, 147, 309, 311
most powerful: 54, 144, 164, 187, 209, 226, 257, 281
mother: 16, 39, 56, 63, 78, 109, 135, 153, 184, 267, 270, 293, 295-297, 303
mutiny: 218, 243
mystique: 9
Nazis: 238
negotiate: 23, 35, 40, 42, 126, 195, 250
negotiating: 35, 40, 41, 43, 137, 185, 247, 251
nepotism: 50, 234
Nietzsche, Friedreich: 227
no-man: 236
non-profit: 2, 3, 157
non-verbal: 146
northern european white males: 281
nuclear family: 294
nuclear weapon: 242
obfuscated: 190, 220
oblique communication: 161
obsequiousness: 3, 221
obtuse: 190, 220
off the record: 17, 155, 218, 219, 243, 262, 308
open ended questions: 37
options: 9, 11, 13, 75, 164, 229, 231, 245, 256, 266
organization chart: 92, 118, 210, 278
overtime: 46, 145, 153, 156, 214
palace revolt: 188, 195

paper pushing: 4, 18, 266
parachutes: 62, 160, 183, 239
parents: 2, 56, 60, 62, 114, 144, 145, 153, 174, 179, 188, 295, 296
part-time: 12, 13, 19, 296, 297
passes: 41, 132, 144-146, 152, 153, 156, 157, 222
passion: 233
passive: 77, 89, 139, 189
passively: 139, 233
patriarchal: 65, 109, 208
patronizing: 69, 253
Peace Corps: 20
pecking order: 51, 113, 173, 257
perfume: 30
periods: 215, 288
persistence: 246
personnel geek: 35, 37-40, 45, 250
platitudes: 84, 142, 230
Plato: 132, 139
play fair: 39, 105, 229, 268
ploy: 39, 63, 71, 102, 153, 224
PMS: 125, 288
policy manual: 135, 136, 174, 237
politically brilliant: 164, 185, 221
politically correct: 4, 270
politician: 76, 119, 166, 221, 241, 244, 245
politicians: 2, 80, 159, 166, 179, 188, 269, 277, 282, 284
Pope: 188, 204, 213
popular: 98, 189
popularity: 97
positive thinking: 237
posture: 35, 43, 96, 133, 223, 292
pragmatic: 166, 167, 273
praise: 69, 221
preachers: 2, 172
predecessor: 14, 227, 241
preemptive strike: 132
pregnant: 14, 15, 56, 88, 224, 261, 263, 289, 297
priests: 76, 145, 188
primitive: 274, 294
Prince Charming: 14, 234
priorities: 49, 65, 173, 210, 256, 257
priorities, real: 173
probation: 48, 50, 51, 152, 153
procedure manual: 237, 258
professors: 2, 5, 6, 177, 188, 269, 270, 279, 302
profit: 2-4, 10, 18, 64, 86, 124, 157, 161, 164, 165, 187, 234, 250, 268, 307
promotion: 5, 9, 26, 33, 35, 38, 43, 55, 56, 63, 65, 70, 71, 73, 78, 87-89, 92, 95, 99, 104, 105, 106, 112, 113, 115, 121, 123, 127, 132, 150, 152, 177, 178, 203, 211, 212, 219, 238, 260-263, 277-279, 285-287, 297
propaganda: 120, 215, 274
propositioned: 145, 155, 157, 178, 238
prostitute: 76, 236
Protestant Work Ethic: 226
pushover: 25, 26, 40, 42, 126
racial, racism: 240, 267, 289
racist: 176, 234, 240
radiate: 35, 43, 95, 148
raise: 3, 7, 9, 12, 38, 41-43, 47, 53, 66, 79, 81, 99, 102, 122, 137, 164, 169, 174, 178, 211, 234, 235, 240-247, 249-251, 261, 262, 282, 283, 287-290, 297
react: 27, 56, 98, 110, 169, 203, 206, 257
real politician: 119, 166
real world: 2, 5, 20, 46, 81, 99, 111, 172, 173, 184, 238, 263, 269, 299, 304
realistic romance: 180
rehearse: 30, 37, 219
relaxed: 17, 35, 43, 48, 72, 95, 96, 114, 140, 200, 285
religious: 127, 267, 289
reorganization: 90, 239
rep: 123, 124, 126, 128, 131
reproduce: 294
reputation: 123, 178
resumes: 16-19, 21-24, 36, 43, 85, 94, 119, 155, 171, 236, 244, 246, 260
revolution: 107, 198, 280-282
rich get richer: 74, 77, 282
rights: 133, 141, 152, 155, 174, 281, 290
rights, women's: 174
rigor mortis: 56, 59, 179
Ringer, Robert: 23, 42, 105, 246, 304
risk(s): 18, 19, 72, 92-97, 114, 121, 124, 138, 151, 165, 185, 199, 205, 233, 234, 298
risk taking: 18, 92, 93, 138, 165
rival: 92, 104, 105, 122, 124, 200, 201, 210, 223, 271, 277, 288, 291
rivals: 10, 65, 89, 103-105, 114, 116, 118, 123, 130, 198, 236, 262, 288
romance: 180
romantic: 41, 102, 111, 116, 180, 221
Rousseau, Jean: 74
rules: 4, 17, 41, 63, 76, 77, 79, 105, 120, 125, 131, 136, 146, 168, 181, 184, 186-190, 208, 217, 218, 222, 224, 226, 240, 276, 280, 303
rules of the game: 77, 188, 189
rumor: 88, 112, 127-130,

132
rumor of the sexual kind: 128
rumors: 88, 89, 104, 111, 116, 127, 150, 159, 184
ruthless: 103, 108, 122-124, 280
sacrifice: 117, 124, 141, 143, 236, 277
salute the uniform: 217
Colt, Sam: 233
Goldwyn, Sam: 166, 276
Johnson, Samuel: 191, 236
screw-you money: 8, 78, 172, 216, 221, 231, 299
secret: 4, 6, 7, 15, 30, 64, 105, 159, 180, 183, 187, 208, 246, 253
secretary (ies):8, 26, 45, 48, 49, 78, 91-94, 113, 116, 149, 154, 200, 211, 218, 242, 245, 254, 261
security: 13, 39, 58, 62, 118, 145, 212, 256, 299
seduce: 16, 40, 70, 116
self assurance: 95
self-awareness: 77, 146, 287
self blinded: 205
self confidence: 138, 261
self deception: 76
self doubt: 191
self-esteem: 4, 54, 58, 59, 62, 76, 97, 115, 138, 168, 177, 228, 238, 280, 296
self interest: 172, 198, 236, 244
self-made woman: 115
sense-of-self: 110, 111, 162, 299
sex: 26, 31, 78, 100-102, 106, 134, 143-146, 149, 154, 163, 178, 207, 222, 267, 274, 275, 290, 291, 299
sex partner: 101, 222, 291
sexism: 267
sexual harassment: 70, 132, 133, 154, 155, 242
sexual needs: 99, 208, 310
sexy: 25-27, 30, 149, 151
shake: 36, 48, 67, 68, 93, 146, 260
shake hands: 36, 68, 93, 146, 260
Shakespeare: 25, 108
shaking hands: 36, 49
shark: 145, 157
Shaw, George Bernard: 57, 74, 163, 184, 206, 241, 257
she-male: 26, 28, 30, 156
shit happens: 228, 229
short men: 32
short range goals: 10, 11
Sigmund Freud: 297
single: 5, 11, 15, 24, 28, 29, 42, 62-64, 79, 92, 93, 121, 124, 146, 160, 163, 167, 180, 183, 185, 198, 230, 255, 288, 293, 294, 301, 302
skirt(s): 28, 30
slant(ing): 19, 21, 23
slim and trim: 232
slut: 120, 127, 150
Smith, Manuel: 66, 303
social needs: 58
socialists: 20, 281
socialize(ing):57, 93, 99, 103, 111, 175, 212, 287
society: 75, 76, 109, 137, 240, 260, 294, 295
Socrates: 265
solutions: 78, 126, 211, 254, 256
sports: 20, 109, 111, 271, 277, 303
sportsmanship: 109
spy(ing): 10, 65, 86, 87, 90, 119, 124, 126, 160, 241, 253, 254
Stalin, Josef: 188
stall: 70, 144, 152, 153, 170, 190, 195, 196, 199, 201, 220, 226
status quo: 126, 162-165, 280-282
Steinem, Gloria: 150, 174, 181, 268
stockholders: 3, 83, 84, 90, 141, 142, 156, 166, 167, 182, 183
straight talk: 218, 219
student loans: 74
subconscious learning: 34, 35
subordinates: 199, 209, 236, 267, 287
success: 3, 8, 27, 28, 33, 37, 43, 56, 75, 78, 80, 95, 96, 109, 156, 174, 182, 189, 223, 233, 236, 237, 250, 254, 302, 303
success books: 37, 302
suggestion(s): 9, 19, 212
summer job(s): 9, 135, 212
Sun Tzu: 87, 120
Supreme Court: 67, 133, 141, 230
survival: 64, 88, 124, 143, 144, 162, 166, 170, 199, 230, 272-274, 294
survival of the fittest: 272, 274
suspicious: 33, 102, 168
sweet: 4, 29, 43, 67, 68, 71, 77-79, 93, 100, 147, 200
sweet talkers: 147
tact: 132
taken seriously: 24, 25, 30, 32, 77, 78, 198, 225, 232
talent: 149, 204, 269, 277
team player(s): 9, 20, 219, 222, 226, 261
team sports: 20, 109, 111, 271, 277, 303
Kennedy, Teddy: 282
television: 13, 14, 55, 294
temp: 122, 149, 194, 195, 241, 242, 245, 286
temporary agency: 193
test(s): 32, 51, 52, 73, 87, 227, 266, 267
tested: 49, 51, 52, 123, 125, 182, 200, 285
testosterone: 106, 110, 272, 276, 277
the system: 1, 2, 4, 17, 18, 207, 217, 218, 226, 255, 280, 304

The Author: 96, 232, 246, 269, 302
Caine Mutiny, The: 243, 304
The emperor wears no clothes: 165, 170, 172, 190, 222, 259, 289, 305
Peter Principle, The: 230, 306
Territorial Imperative, The: 117
Hobbes, Thomas: 121
Thoreau, Henry David: 55, 83
Thucydides: 123
token: 107, 176, 177, 190, 235
tokens: 45, 176
Fuller, Tomas: 198
tone of voice: 51, 111, 132, 136, 198, 223, 243, 288
touch(ing): 36, 67, 99, 103, 146, 192, 194, 203, 227, 241, 260, 291
Tower Of Jello: 52, 123, 164, 169, 248, 249, 255
transferrable skills: 18, 21
travel(ing): 3, 19, 69, 146, 153, 156, 178, 278, 313
treachery: 113, 119, 228
trivia: 212, 213
trivial: 3, 44, 173, 213
truce: 123
Truman, Harry S: 232
trust: 4, 19, 40, 52, 61, 63, 91, 97, 98, 100, 103, 113, 116, 208, 209, 235, 255, 263, 267, 268, 282
truth: 17, 37, 77, 81, 105, 159-162, 165, 172, 177, 191, 231, 232, 240, 268, 269, 277, 283, 295, 299
tuition program: 136
turf: 123, 173, 188
TV: 4, 62, 179, 213, 294
two percent: 98-100, 105, 246, 247, 261
ultimate rule: 184, 188
understand men: 264, 270, 272
unemployed: 35, 184
uniform: 9, 15, 27, 28, 32, 38, 112, 113, 124, 147, 172, 208, 217, 252, 262, 305
unwritten rules: 41, 63, 131, 181, 186-188, 190, 218
USMC: 238
values: 10, 58, 65, 80, 105, 114, 146, 264, 268, 271, 273, 293, 294
Frankle, Victor: 217
violence: 110, 272
visibility: 9, 51, 120, 165, 185, 290
vocabulary: 32, 177
voice: 32, 51, 71, 111, 128, 129, 132, 136, 147, 157, 198, 223, 243, 248, 286, 288
volunteer: 93, 137, 178, 234, 249, 252, 258, 260, 261
Von Clauswitz: 288
vulgar: 71, 73, 160
vulgarities: 71-73
vulnerable: 73, 100, 113, 148, 152, 242
Fields, W.C.: 187, 188
wage slave: 6, 7, 11, 74, 275
walk: 25, 29, 31-33, 35, 36, 38, 51, 69, 130, 134, 145, 157, 238, 246, 290, 299
walking: 29, 32, 36, 165, 289
weaknesses and strengths: 116, 132
weekends: 26, 145, 153, 156, 203
Welch, Raquel: 240
When I Say No, I Feel Guilty: 66, 126, 246, 303, 304
whine: 131, 179, 239, 286, 287
whining: 116, 131, 159, 212, 235, 237, 242, 287
Who Shot John: 199, 200, 214, 223, 224
who's who: 84, 85, 92, 118, 180, 197, 221
Wilde, Oscar: 104, 130, 191, 221, 307
win-win: 174, 191
Win The Meeting: 197, 304
Winning Through Intimidation: 23, 105, 246, 304
Winning Through Negotiation: 289, 306
witch hunt: 91, 200
women bosses: 215
women with children: 16, 124, 297
women's jobs: 278
women's liberation: 180, 181, 278
working hard: 15, 59, 226, 227
yes-men: 158
young men: 14, 64, 145, 178, 208, 271, 273, 277
young woman: 3, 11, 15, 74, 80, 81, 115, 127, 149, 150, 172, 178, 180, 181, 208, 209, 234, 293, 296
young women: 4, 14, 28, 77, 79, 93, 109, 111, 114, 145, 146, 149, 157, 172, 208, 228, 266, 280
zero-sum game: 112

Where To Turn For Help

Equal Rights Advocates: Legal advice and representation on sexual harassment and pay discrimination. Judith Kurtz, Director, 1370 Mission Street, San Francisco CA 94103 415-621-0505

NOW: Advocacy, lobbying and counseling on employment issues. President, Patricia Ireland, 1000 16th Street NW, Washington DC 20036 202-331-0066 (Call for local chapter)

National Women's Law Center: Attorneys handle cases on lawsuits relating to women. President, Marcia Greenberger, 1616 P Street NW, Washington DC 20036 202-328-5169

9to5: Membership organization helps women handle job discrimination. Executive Director, Karen Nussbaum, 614 Superior Avenue NW, Cleveland OH 44113 216-566-9308

Complaint Hotline: 800-522-0925

Women Employed: Advocacy, research and training. Offers legal advice. Executive Director, Anne Ladky, 22 W. Monroe Street, Chicago IL 60603 312-782-3902

Women's Legal Defense Fund: Represents women in court. Director, Judith Lichtman, 1875 Connecticut Avenue NW, Washington DC 20009 202-986-2600

Daughters should be trained with higher and holier motives than that of being fashionable and securing wealthy husbands. There are other missions for women than that of wife and mother. I believe all good men should be married. Yet I don't believe in women being married. Somehow they all sink into nonentities after this epoch in their existence. That is the fault of female education. They are taught from their cradles to look upon marriage as the one event of their lives. That accomplished, nothing remains.

Exotic Dancer 1835-1868 ADAH ISAACS MENKEN
The Madonna of her time, except Adah had a three-digit IQ

I am sick of women's career vs marriage complaints. I have no quarrel with the woman who works because she must. It's the overeducated, under-learned, bitching, whelping career woman who is giving all women a bad name.

Satirist and Spinster 1982 FLORENCE KING